THE RAIDERS OF
WALL STREET

Also by Eric Allison

Managing Up, Managing Down (with Mary Ann Allison)

THE RAIDERS OF WALL STREET

Eric W. Allison

STEIN AND DAY/*Publishers*/New York

First published in 1986
Copyright © 1986 by Eric Wm. Allison and Ethan Ellenberg
Produced by Ethan Ellenberg
All rights reserved, Stein and Day, Incorporated
Designed by Terese Bulinkis Platten
Printed in the United States of America
STEIN AND DAY/*Publishers*
Scarborough House
Briarcliff Manor, N.Y. 10510

Library of Congress Cataloging-in-Publication Data

Allison, Eric W. (Eric William)
    The raiders of Wall Street.

    Includes index.
    1. Capitalists and financiers—United States.
2. Consolidation and merger of corporations—United
States.   I. Title.
HG172.A2A45   1986   338.8′3′0973   85-40962
ISBN 0-8128-3092-X

To Mary Ann

CONTENTS

Introduction

THE RAIDERS

The SEC advisory committee concluded that take-overs are a valid method of capital allocation, that the regulatory scheme should neither promote nor deter such activity nor favor bidder or target companies, and that competitive markets should be the ultimate regulator. A similar approach was endorsed by Congress in the Williams Act. The SEC concurs in this approach.
—John S. R. Shad, Chairman, Securities and Exchange Commission, testifying before a House subcommittee, March 28, 1984.

We recognize that sometimes tender offers may be economically useful and beneficial to shareholders in the Nation. However, we do not believe that is always the case. What may begin as an effort with a justifiable business purpose too often degenerates into a contest of raw power. Company executives, investment bankers, public relations professionals, and lawyers battle one another in a contest of wills that inevitably pays little concern to public needs. The impact on investors and markets and the broad economic and social effects of such battles are frequently ignored.

—Michael Unger, President, North American Securities Administrators Association, testifying immediately after Mr. Shad.

CORPORATE TAKEOVERS ARE a fact of life today. Names like Icahn, Pickens, Steinberg, and Jacobs are known to people who only occasionally read the financial papers. The debate about the benefits or harm of the current wave of corporate takeovers rages in Congressional hearing rooms and state legislatures, in state and federal courts, in corporate boardrooms—and on the evening news. An entire vocabulary—words like golden parachutes, white knights, poison pills, and junk bonds—has grown up to describe the tactics and maneuvers of the contestants in takeover battles.

And sometimes, the staid financial pages of the nation's newspapers read as if they were describing the latest episodes of "Dallas" or "Falcon Crest."

But corporate takeovers are nothing new. Companies have taken over and been taken over by each other for years. What is it that distinguishes the current crop of raids so that it generates so much press and so much official attention?

The answer is simple: the raiders themselves. Corporations tend, with few exceptions, to be faceless monoliths to the average observer. The men who run them are merely names in the paper, attached to identifications such as chairman, president, or CEO. When Megacorp takes over Gigantic Industries, there is no *human* involvement that the outsider can easily see. The merger or takeover, hostile or friendly, is between faceless corporations run by equally faceless boards.

Occasionally, a figure looms out of the crowd and attracts attention. Howard Hughes was one such, distinguished first by his playboy life-style, then by his reclusiveness. Charles Bluhdorn of Gulf + Western and Harold Geneen of ITT became well known as corporate empire builders in the sixties. And once they *did* become known, they became not only the subject of press attention but also of interest to the "man on the street." In the sixties, investors who couldn't tell you who ran AT&T could tell you who ran the much smaller ITT.

But even the Geneens and the Bluhdorns were operating within the more or less standard corporate environment. They were not making takeovers as individuals but as corporations. Charles Bluhdorn did not take over Paramount Pictures; Gulf + Western did.

Today's raiders are different. While they work through corporations, these are frequently paper companies set up only for a particular takeover. Even in the cases where they do represent a large company—Steinberg's Reliance Group, for example—there is usually little doubt in the mind of an observer that the company is merely a vehicle for the takeover; it is a means, rather than an end.

Today's raiders are individuals. They are the opposite of the faceless corporations that dominated takeovers only a few years ago. They are, instead, entrepreneurs building empires through proxy fights and leveraged buyouts rather than through breakthrough inventions and skillful marketing. They are modern buccaneers, sailing the waters of the international stock markets seeking prey. And that prey, undervalued corporations, is today's equivalent of the fat, slow merchant ships of yesteryear. And like their predecessors, they, too, scurry for sheltered harbors, building complex defenses designed by high-paid lawyers.

In the process, the raiders have become as famous as those buccaneer forebears. And like the Spanish and English of old, when the determination of whether a buccaneer was good or bad depended on which side you were on, today's raiders have both their detractors and their admirers. Some think they are agents of destruction, a pernicious influence that should be outlawed. Others think the raiders are forces for good, sweeping away the deadwood of hidebound corporate managements and bringing profits to the small investor.

Whichever side you favor, one thing is clear. The raiders are a force in the market that must be taken into account by every corporate board and senior manager, by institutional investors, by anyone with money invested in the market, and by anyone who works for or does business with a publicly owned corporation.

Which includes just about everyone.

THERE ARE MANY corporate raiders, some big, some small. To write about all of them would take something the size of an encyclopedia. This book covers seven raiders, ranging from such long-time corporate nemeses as Victor Posner and Saul Steinberg to comparative newcomers like Asher Edelman. They were selected for a variety of reasons.

Some, such as Icahn, Pickens, and Jacobs, would find their way onto anyone's list of major corporate raiders. Some deserve attention for special reasons: Saul Steinberg is almost the prototype of the modern raider; Sir James Goldsmith, if he had done nothing else in his career (and he's done much), attracts a spotlight as the man who found a way to beat the poison pill.

Some illustrious names have been left out. The Bass Brothers and the Belzbergs have greatly enlarged their fortunes through corporate takeovers. Charles Hurwitz, David Murdock, and William Farley are all worthy of study. Rather than treat them all lightly, I chose to focus in more depth on seven extraordinary men—each with a unique style, but each a good representative of the modern corporate raider.

I found the seven men portrayed here—Saul Steinberg, Carl Icahn, Victor Posner, T. Boone Pickens, Asher Edelman, Irwin Jacobs, Sir James Goldsmith—fascinating. All are fabulously wealthy, with personal fortunes ranging from $50 million to nearly $1 billion. The oldest is in his sixties, the youngest in his early forties. Few started with any real inherited wealth. They have followed the American dream and found fortune—and fame—and generated profits and controversy with an even hand.

They are Raiders.

1

The Bad Boy Grows Up

SAUL STEINBERG

SAUL STEINBERG WANTED to become a millionaire before he was thirty. At the age of twenty-nine, his wealth was estimated at $50 million.

He was just beginning.

LIKE MANY ANOTHER young man starting out on a career, Steinberg began with a timely loan from a relative: $25,000 from his father, Julius, the owner of a Brooklyn plastics factory. His father was not a rich man—the $25,000 was borrowed from Chase Manhattan Bank—but he was able to provide not only the money but a home for Steinberg's first company. Leasco Data Processing started operations in an empty room in the elder Steinberg's factory. In its first year in business, Leasco earned $56,000. In its second year, it made $110,000.

But to really understand Steinberg's rise, you have to go back further. Steinberg has the distinction among all the raiders that

15

he pulled off his first raid—and collected his first greenmail—before he graduated from college.

STEINBERG WAS BORN in 1939. He says he started reading the *Wall Street Journal* when he was thirteen—cover to cover. Finance dominated his thinking from then on. When it came time for college, he went to the Wharton School of Management at the University of Pennsylvania. He was only a C-average student, but in his senior year he accomplished far more than those students who spent their time studying for grades.

He acquired 3 percent of a small company called O'Sullivan Rubber—a large enough block to make them take notice. Steinberg demanded that the company diversify into automotive parts. When the company refused, Steinberg threatened a proxy fight. O'Sullivan bought Steinberg out for three times what he had paid for his stock.

The O'Sullivan Rubber Company had just helped Saul Steinberg invent greenmail.

STEINBERG—STILL A senior in college—did not rest on his laurels. He still had a thesis to do in order to graduate. With the help of a faculty advisor, he chose as his topic "The Decline and Fall of IBM." But before his thesis was completed, Steinberg had come to a rather different conclusion: IBM was not about to decline. He decided that, instead, IBM was on its way to becoming one of the twentieth century's dominant corporations.

He also discovered an interesting fact. IBM had always leased, rather than sold, its computers—a way of maintaining strict control of availability and pricing. But in 1956 the company signed an antitrust consent decree forcing it to begin selling the machines outright to those who wanted to purchase them. Steinberg saw an opportunity. He could buy a computer from IBM and then lease it himself. By pricing his leases lower than IBM's, he could guarantee himself a market.

"The potential of data processing amazed me," Steinberg says. "I had previously been interested in leasing. I thought, Put these two together and there is money to be made."

The thesis on the decline and fall of IBM was junked. Instead,

Steinberg wrote a study on computer leasing. It was to be the basis of his own rise to riches. In 1961, after spending the two years since graduation working for his father and lending money to operators of leased newstands in the New York City subways, he founded Leasco Data Processing Equipment Corp. He was twenty-two years old.

Leasco was to be in the business of buying IBM computers and leasing them to companies who wanted a computer but didn't want to buy one. In order for Leasco to make money, the trick was to make the computer pay for itself. The computer could be depreciated for tax purposes—increasing cash flow—and could be bought with borrowed money. By figuring in all tax and cash flow considerations, Steinberg realized he could lease the computer out for less than IBM was charging and still have the proceeds of a five-year lease cover the cost of the machine. Then he could lease out the machine for another five years and everything it earned would be pure profit.

Best of all, he had no inventory to contend with. Leasco never even saw the machines. When a customer wanted a machine, Leasco bought one from IBM and had it shipped to the customer in whatever configuration the customer wanted. Leasco merely processed the paper.

It was a gold mine. Today, the idea that one could lease out a piece of computer equipment for ten years seems absurd—most machines would be obsolete long before that—but the pace in the computer industry was much slower in the early sixties than it is today, and companies were much more conservative about changing computer equipment. Steinberg found a ready market for his machines. Leasco prospered. When it went public four years after its founding, it had assets of $5.4 million.

In the supercharged stock market of the early sixties, technology was hot and so were "concept" stocks. Leasco was both. No one seemed to notice that anyone could do what Leasco was doing, or that the company was extremely vulnerable to technological change (if IBM came out with a new machine, making the old ones obsolete, Leasco might have trouble renewing its leases—and the profits came on the second lease, not the first), and to interest rate changes (a rise in interest rates could erase

the profit margin since the machines were heavily leveraged).
Wall Street was still a technological innocent. No one realized
that computers were not like tractors (used until they wore out).
Fluctuations in interest rates were still relatively minor; the
inflation of the seventies was still in the future. Leasco, a go-go
stock in a go-go market, sold for as high as fifty times earnings.

A lot of companies used their high-priced stock as takeover
vehicles in the sixties and Leasco was no exception. What raised a
few eyebrows on Wall Street was the size of its target. Steinberg
went after Reliance Insurance, a company nearly ten times the
size of Leasco.

In retrospect, the deal is not surprising. The 1980s have been a
time of megadeals, when takeovers and raids involving staggering sums are commonplace. In a recent article on Steinberg,
Manhattan, inc. described Leasco's takeover of Reliance as having caused "a moderate amount of controversy."

Even that is an exaggeration. The takeover of Reliance created
barely a stir in the headlines.

THE YEAR 1968 is a long time ago in both the social and business
history of the United States. On June 24, Leasco's bid for Reliance
was announced in the newspapers—newspapers that elsewhere
were reporting on the Gaullist victory in the French elections.
Other items of interest were two new films opening that weekend: *The Thomas Crown Affair* with Faye Dunaway and Steve
McQueen and *The Bride Wore Black* with Jeanne Moreau. Nolan
Ryan had just won his sixth game of the season for the Mets,
against the Dodgers at Shea Stadium. The Mets were still a year
away from the season that would finally make them respectable.

There is an air of innocence about the Reliance takeover when
viewed with eyes accustomed to the routine acrimony of the
modern raid. The Leasco bid for Reliance was marked by a
subdued headline in *The New York Times*: "Insurer's Shares
Sought by Leasco." Underneath, in smaller type, the *Times*
announced: "Deal is Similar to Proposed Merger of Control Data
and Commercial Credit."

The general feeling on the street was that Leasco wanted

Reliance because of the "almost insatiable demand for fresh capital" of the computer business. It would not be the first takeover by Steinberg. Leasco had already absorbed ten smaller companies (mostly in leasing or related fields, such as Container Leasing Corp., acquired in 1968), using cash and stock for the transaction. But this was a hostile takeover bid.

Reliance did not seem unduly alarmed. A. Addison Roberts, the president and CEO of Reliance, announced that there had been no serious negotiations yet and that Reliance hadn't yet had a chance to study the offer. He added, "We have had other proposals and will ask the stockholders in a letter to take no hasty actions until we can evaluate all the offers."

No threats of lawsuits, no full-page ads in the *Wall Street Journal,* no hastily called press conferences, just "we will ask the stockholders in a letter to take no hasty actions . . ."

The deal was estimated at about $400 million. Steinberg was offering to trade convertible debentures and warrants in Leasco for Reliance's stock, trading on the inflated price of thirty times earnings at which Leasco was trading.

Nearly a month then went by without much happening. On July 20, Reliance announced it was exploring a merger with another company, Data Processing Financial and General Corporation—not exactly a white knight, but at least the right idea. But there still was no sense of urgency. Roberts announced that Reliance and Data Processing Financial had been talking on the telephone, and the president of Data Processing said, "I think they would like us to make them an offer." Roberts said that the Reliance directors would meet "maybe in a few days."

Meanwhile, Leasco hadn't gotten around to making a formal offer, though it had filed a registration statement with the SEC for the debentures and warrants needed for the tender offer.

Finally, Reliance's directors met, and the company announced it would "fight with all the resources at our command" against Leasco's bid. Leasco countered with the announcement that it had purchased a block of convertible stock in a private deal.

A bare week later, Leasco sweetened the deal, and Reliance capitulated. The *Times* article about the capitulation began:

"The Reliance Insurance Company has dropped its vigorous opposition to a takeover bid by the Leasco Data Processing Equipment Corporation."

Vigorous by the standards of 1968, perhaps. In retrospect it all looks rather civilized.

Saul Steinberg's Leasco, all of seven years old, had gained control of a one-hundred-fifty-year-old insurance company. Now he had the assets to really go to town.

In 1969, he went after Chemical Bank.

IN 1969, CHEMICAL Bank was the sixth-largest commercial bank in the United States. It was a major force in the money markets and a big dealer in government securities. It had assets of $9 billion. Leasco's assets were estimated at about $400 million, although in press reports Steinberg claimed they were closer to $1 billion.

The attempt on Chemical created shock waves in financial circles across the country, but from beginning to end the actual raid lasted only fifteen days: February 6 to February 20, 1969.

Compared to the Reliance takeover, there was little that was civilized about it. In fact, just as Steinberg may have—with the O'Sullivan Rubber deal—been one of the originators of greenmail, the Chemical takeover attempt presaged the kind of savage, no-holds-barred fight that was to become a characteristic of later raiding.

Steinberg was still new at the takeover game despite his success with Reliance. Everyone was new at the game in 1969. The Pickens and Icahns of the future would be able to look at Steinberg's successes and failures and plan accordingly. Steinberg was the pioneer.

Sometimes pioneers get shot full of arrows.

By the late sixties, Leasco was more than a data processing outfit. With the takeover of Reliance and other companies, as well as internal expansion, Leasco was now into management consulting, computer software, was moving into computer time-sharing, and, of course, had inherited all of Reliance's insurance and financial business. But Steinberg had a vision.

Steinberg foresaw the benefits of an integrated financial service company long before American Express or Sears Roebuck did. And he also saw the way to build one. As he said at the time, "It would take a bank twenty years to have what we have now and they need it. They have the easy thing, deposits. We have the hard things—technology, brainpower. Leasco is a one-bank holding company without a bank."

Steinberg decided to acquire a bank. Leasco had already held talks with a medium-size New York bank a few years before the Chemical takeover attempt, but the discussions had come to nothing. In 1968, Steinberg tried again. Leasco began buying stock in most of the big banks, including Chemical and Manufacturers Hanover Trust. Steinberg said, "We felt we would buy stock in those banks we thought would have good, long-term interest for Leasco."

Chemical was the most interesting of the bunch although rumors about Manufacturers Hanover were also flying about. Chemical, though large and with a good piece of institutional and money-market business, was a lackluster performer on the stock market. It thus presented what was to become the classic target profile for a raider: asset rich and underpriced.

By early 1969, Leasco had acquired some 300,000 shares of Chemical. What might have happened then is conjecture. What actually happened is that Steinberg's hand was forced.

On February 6, Robert Metz broke the story in *The New York Times* that Steinberg was after Chemical. The story mentioned Chemical chairman William S. Renchard's intention to fight Steinberg's plans.

Suspicion abounds to this day that Metz was fed the story by Chemical. Metz would only say the story came to him "from a valued news source." Whatever the origin of the story, Steinberg would now have to deal with Chemical amid a blaze of publicity.

Leasco officials, including Steinberg, had not yet even contacted Chemical. Unofficially, though, they now said a tender offer for Chemical would be made.

Then the pressure began. Chemical, a blue-blood among blue-bloods, began calling in its markers. White, Weld, Leasco's principal investment banker, notified Steinberg that it would not participate in a takeover attempt on Chemical. Other investment bankers backed away quickly (one, Lehman Bros., later admitted it had been pressured by the commercial banks it borrowed from not to help Leasco). Nelson Rockefeller, the governor of New York (and brother of Chase Manhattan's David Rockefeller), called for legislation to prevent bank takeovers. The call was echoed in Washington. (On February 28, after Steinberg had already backed down, the chairman of the Senate Banking Committee, John Sparkman—a Democrat—introduced a bill to prevent national banks from being taken over.)

A lot of the pressure was not initiated by Chemical. Chemical didn't have to. The banking establishment perceived the threat to Chemical as a threat to them all and acted immediately. In the cozy world of banking then—before hyper-inflation, before third-world loan defaults, before the competition from American Express and Merrill Lynch—Steinberg was regarded as the ultimate outsider. As *Business Week* described it, he was "young, sometimes brash, a johnny-come-lately, and Jewish to boot. . . ."

The bank also felt threatened by the idea of a takeover by a non-bank. There was a question of confidentiality; if Leasco owned Chemical, wouldn't Leasco know too much about the financial affairs of Chemical's customers? The question was real enough to cause concern in a lot of corporate boardrooms. Major customers of Leasco threatened to cancel their contracts if Leasco went ahead with a tender.

Leasco was selling for 140 on February 5, the day before Metz's column. On the day after the column, February 7, the stock was down to 133. In another week it was down to 127. No one knows for sure, but it appears that bank trust departments began selling Leasco shares as soon as the news got out. By the end of two weeks, Leasco was down to 106.

Chemical also threatened Leasco directly. A hand-delivered letter to Steinberg on February 7 informed him that Chemical intended to go into many of the same businesses as Leasco—which would make a takeover illegal on antitrust grounds.

Several very civilized meetings took place between Steinberg and Chemical's management, but despite the outward show of cordiality, the pressure continued. On February 11, Leasco held it's annual shareholders' meeting. It had been widely expected that Steinberg would announce a tender offer for Chemical.

Instead, he announced vague plans for Leasco to become a "comprehensive financial services organization."

"We have concluded," he said, "that our corporate plans and purposes would be enhanced by bringing Leasco's capabilities and assets together with those of a large bank." He added, however, "at the present time we have not made a decision as to a particular bank."

Meanwhile, the emphasis had shifted. Chemical and Leasco were exploring the possibility of Leasco becoming a part of Chemical. It was an attractive idea. Many banks were already considering the possibility of expanding beyond traditional banking fields (it was about this time that Citicorp—then First National City Bank—embarked on the aggressive course that was to take it into such fields as credit cards and make it the largest bank in the world), and acquiring Leasco, including Reliance, would save Chemical years of work. The deal failed however, over Steinberg's insistence that Leasco shareholders hold half the stock in the merged company. Chemical did not want Saul Steinberg to be its largest shareholder.

On February 20, Steinberg made his public capitulation. Leasco, he announced, "has no plans to acquire control of the Chemical New York Corporation. . . . Without the support and enthusiasm of management, Leasco has no interest whatsoever in pressing for an affiliation with Chemical."

He added piously, "Hostile takeovers of money center banks are against the best interest of the economy because of the danger of upsetting the stability and prestige of the banking system and diminishing public confidence in it." Later, he made the rueful comment: "I always knew there was an establishment. I just used to think I was part of it."

Saul Steinberg had tucked his tail between his legs and gone home. Leasco never did take over a bank.

But it is rare for a raider to come off even an unsuccessful raid with nothing. Leasco still owned all those shares of Chemical. When they were finally sold, Leasco made a profit of $36 million.

THERE IS NO question that Steinberg was hurt and shocked by the response to his attempt on Chemical. "I'm no takeover artist," he told *Forbes* magazine in 1969, shortly after the debacle. "I only did one and that turned friendly in the end. My wife and I, we're decent people. We like tennis, art, music. We have three children. We're not really bad at all."

He wasn't ready to retire, though. Later that year, he went after Pergamon Press, a British publishing house. Hostile takeovers were simply not done in England in 1969, not by adventurous Americans. The British establishment reacted with much the same horror as the American banking industry did. But this time it wasn't pressure that caused Steinberg to back down. Instead, he discovered that Pergamon Press wasn't quite the money-maker he had thought it was. He abandoned his takeover attempt, much to the relief of the London financial world. Steinberg is still not a welcome name in many London circles.

For the next few years, Steinberg was relatively quiet, devoting himself to Leasco. In 1969, however, he sowed the seeds that would lead to more adverse press coverage and a series of lawsuits.

It started quite harmlessly. Steinberg pledged $375,000 to the Woodmere Academy, a private school on the south shore of Long Island that his children attended. The money was to go to the building of the Barbara Steinberg Library and Computer Center, named for his wife. The money was due in 1972. The year 1972 rolled around, construction was completed, and Steinberg came up with $175,000. He claimed he didn't have the cash at the moment (although he *had* managed to find $250,000 to give to Richard Nixon's reelection campaign) and promised to pay the remainder in 1973. The next year, he claimed that he had donated so much money to Israel during the Yom Kippur War that he was short again. The Woodmere Academy sued for the money. The case got to the New York State Court of Appeals—the state's highest court—before he paid the money in 1977.

It kept his name in the papers.

Meanwhile, things had not gone so well at Reliance Group (the new name of the Leasco-Reliance companies). The recession of 1974-75 was particularly hard on property and casualty companies. In 1973, Reliance had a net worth of $205 million. By 1974, that figure had dropped to $65 million. Steinberg was forced to pay attention to the company. He shook up the management and began to participate actively in the day-to-day workings of the business. Despite a $20 million loss in 1975, Steinberg, helped by an improving economy, turned the company around. Three years later, earnings were $55 million and growing. By 1980, the figure had reached $103 million. In addition, the company recorded a one-time gain of $114 million through the sale of CTI International, a container-leasing subsidiary Steinberg had built from scratch.

HIS PREOCCUPATION WITH Reliance, however, did not keep him out of controversies. In 1975 and 1976, a messy controversy erupted in New York around the building of bus-stop shelters. A Frenchman, William Bouchara, approached the city with the idea of building glass and steel shelters at bus stops, like those in Paris. Advertising space would be sold on the shelters and the company that built them and the city would share the proceeds.

Bouchara's company, Bus Top Shelters, was granted an experimental three-year franchise. It was a success, but Bus Top ran short of cash. Steinberg was approached as a potential investor, but he turned Bus Top down. Instead, he formed a similar company, called Convenience & Safety, Inc., with, among others, Jay Pritzker, the chairman of Hyatt Corp, obstensibly to seek franchises in other cities. A couple of months later, though, the company put in a bid for the New York City franchise, now coming up for renewal.

Things get murky here and several city and state investigations, as well as those of the city's newspapers, have failed to agree on just who did what to whom. What is known is that a Steinberg friend, State Senator Jack Bronston—who was, at one point, listed as secretary of Convenience & Safety—wrote a letter to City Controller Harrison J. Goldin. The letter urged that Bus Top not be given a renewal on their franchise. A month later, Goldin's office issued a report—an audit—critical of Bus Top. The city's Board of Estimate, acting in part on the controller's report, agreed to open the franchise to public bidding. Bus Top called foul.

Meanwhile, Goldin was running for state controller. Allegations were made that at a lunch at the "21" Club—the original
"power lunch" spot—Steinberg was asked to contribute or raise
$25,000 for Goldin's campaign. No proof has ever surfaced that
Steinberg actually raised any money, but he did later write a
check for $12,500 to Bronston who then contributed $3,500 to
Goldin's campaign. The chain of circumstances made rich headlines without proving anything, but they raised such a stink that
after Convenience & Safety won the bidding—with what was by
a good margin the best bid—New York Mayor Koch felt compelled
to set aside the bids and ask for a new bidding process.

It might seem that there was little smoke, let alone any fire,
except that during a city investigation Steinberg invoked the
Fifth Amendment (against self-incrimination) when asked about
his involvement. Later, during a lurid divorce suit, Laura Steinberg, his second wife, charged that her husband had contributed
$100,000 to Goldin's campaign in order to influence the award of
the contract. Later still, she retracted the charge.

In 1976, he made headlines again. *Barron's* ran an article accusing Steinberg of "questionable accounting practices in the
computer-leasing business." Steinberg sued the investment
weekly. He lost.

Steinberg also had an unhappy flirtation with the law in 1978.
The SEC charged that Steinberg had touted a stock called Pulte
Home Corp.—which built houses in Michigan—to his friends,
encouraging them to buy it at the same time he was preparing to
unload the stock. As is customary in such cases, Steinberg signed
a consent degree barring future violations without admitting
guilt. This is a process that has been described as saying, "I didn't
do it, but I won't do it again."

LOMAS & NETTLETON FINANCIAL Corp. was Steinberg's biggest
target after Reliance became healthy again. Lomas was the biggest mortgage-banking house in the United States. In 1978, it had
assets of about $350 million—and, in the lackluster market of the
late seventies, Steinberg thought it was undervalued. Lomas
used four Texas banks to house most of its cash. Steinberg
announced, publicly, that he felt by spreading the cash over more

banks the competition for Lomas's funds would increase, more services would be provided the company for free, and Lomas's costs would drop, increasing earnings. Reliance purchased 1.7 million shares of Lomas, almost 25 percent of the stock, and started making suggestions to management. The stock cost Reliance $22 million.

Lomas got very restive. Finally, in October 1978, the company bought back its stock for $38 million in cash and notes. Reliance made a 70-percent profit.

When asked if he had practiced a little *black*mail on Lomas, Steinberg replied, "Absolutely not." The term greenmail had not yet been invented.

OVER THE NEXT few years Steinberg picked up chunks of many different companies. Some were simply investments, held for a time then sold. Some of these investments spooked the investee so badly that, like Lomas, they paid to get rid of him.

One of the more bizarre takeover fights involved UV Industries. UV Industries was one of the first American corporations in modern times to decide that it could make more for its shareholders by liquidating itself than by staying in business. Steinberg, operating through Reliance Group, made a bid for UV's assets in early November of 1979. UV accepted. Within a week, Victor Posner, a raider with a less than sterling reputation, was in the market buying shares in Reliance. "Obviously, he's trying to get my attention," Steinberg said, "but he could have picked up the telephone." There was little chance that Posner would actually try to take over Reliance—for one thing, Steinberg owned 15.8 percent of Reliance outright, enough to give him effective control—but in the world of raiding, a little muscle goes a long way.

Next, another party stuck its head into the ring: Penn Central Corp., which was worried about a Steinberg takeover attempt. Reliance had, among other things, taken a controlling interest in the bankrupt New Haven Railroad, a major Penn Central creditor. Under the terms of the New Haven's bankruptcy reorganization, Reliance would eventually end up with 13 percent of Penn Central's voting stock. Now, Penn Central sued Reliance and UV, charging that Reliance wanted UV so it could use UV's assets to finance a takeover of Penn Central.

If all this seems convoluted, that's because it is.

The upshot of it all was that Sharon Steel (Posner's company) upped its bid for UV above that of Reliance (Steinberg's company). Meanwhile, Steinberg had decided that UV's assets weren't worth as much as he had thought. Reliance's original offer of $449 million (plus assumption of UV's $131 million of liabilities) had included a profit; Steinberg reportedly thought the assets were actually worth as much as $67 million more than he was offering. By the time Posner was on the scene, Steinberg had discovered that UV had, while liquidating, allowed some of its unused coal mines to fill with water. Now it looked as if it would cost, a company source told the *Wall Street Journal,* "between $18 million and $60 million to put the coal-mining properties back where they were."

As a result, Steinberg was disinclined to enter a bidding war with Posner. He may in fact have felt some relief that Sharon Steel entered the bidding and got him off the hook.

And what happened to Penn Central? After struggling for a bit and filing unsuccessful lawsuits, it finally bought back Steinberg's stock in February of 1980, for $48 million. By the time Reliance had disposed of the New Haven securities, the total profit on the Penn Central deal was $20 million before taxes, $11 million after taxes.

Greenmail had proved lucrative once again.

PERHAPS NOTHING SHOWS Steinberg at his best than the Leasco spinoff. By 1978, Steinberg controlled 12 percent of Reliance Group. That year the directors of Reliance voted to spin off Leasco—Steinberg's original company—which had taken over Reliance ten years before. So Leasco was spun off; for every six shares of Reliance, a shareholder received one share of Leasco. In May of 1979, Leasco became a separate, publicly traded company.

Of which Saul Steinberg owned 12 percent.

Leasco's shares began to move soon afterward. By August, the price per share was double what it had been at the time trading began in the spring. The reason was simple. Steinberg was buying Leasco stock. By the end of July, Steinberg had bought over half a million shares of Leasco. By August, he and the other members of his family owned over 50 percent of Leasco.

His cost was about $9 million.

A lot of people were puzzled by this. Since Steinberg dominated Reliance, he didn't need to spin Leasco off in order to control it. People asked, why spend the $9 million?

Then Leasco began to buy stock in Reliance, eventually selling some $100 million in debentures to finance the purchases.

Saul Steinberg was buying up Reliance using Leasco's money.

In retrospect, it seems brilliantly simple. Steinberg couldn't afford to buy up Reliance by himself. But he could afford to buy outright control of Leasco, a much smaller company, once it was spun off. Then Leasco used its borrowing power to get the money to buy Reliance stock—without Steinberg having to put up more than the $9 million he had already used to buy control of Leasco. He didn't even have to buy all of Leasco, merely enough to insure complete control.

Meanwhile, Reliance began to buy back its own shares on the market, reducing the number of shares outstanding—a common ploy of cash-rich companies that serves to raise earnings per share. The buyback also had the effect of increasing Steinberg's percentage share of Reliance (he held the same number of shares, but there were less shares in total). Leasco's percent ownership also jumped with each share repurchased.

By the middle of 1981, Steinberg had a lock on Reliance. He had dominated the company before, now he had virtually complete control. He and his family, because of the reduced number of outstanding shares, now owned about 15 percent of Reliance, and Leasco, which he controlled, owned a further 25 percent.

Ironically, Leasco purchased so much of Reliance's stock that at one point it had to get an exemption from the Investment Company Act of 1940. Simply put, the act defines investment companies and mutual funds as corporations whose assets are primarily the stock of other companies. Under SEC rules, Leasco was in danger of being subjected to regulation as a mutual fund.

Leasco got the exemption and Steinberg ended up, effectively, with 40 percent of Reliance.

The next step was even more audacious. Reliance went private as the result of a $550 million leveraged buyout, one of the biggest LBOs ever at that time.

A leveraged buyout is a neat trick. First you find a friendly bank who is willing to lend you a lot of money. Then you make an offer for the company with the money your bank has promised to lend you. If the company says no, too bad. If they say yes, you borrow the money and own the company.

If you can't find a bank who's willing, you find a good investment banker, one who knows how to *raise* a lot of money. You put up a small amount of capital, and your friendly investment banker gets commitments from customers to buy your bonds when they are issued. In the case of Reliance group, you get commitments for $550 million. Then you offer to buy the company for that amount of money. If the company says no, you're out expenses. If the company says yes, you sell the bonds, take over the company, and everyone is happy.

But what backs up the bonds or the loans? Very simple: the assets of the company you've taken over.

Reliance Holdings Group, the company Saul Steinberg and his family own, was the issuer of the $550 million worth of bonds. The major asset of Reliance Holdings Group now is Reliance Group, the company Reliance Holdings Group bought with the $550 million.

Reliance Holdings bought up Leasco as part of the deal.

Saul Steinberg would no longer have to worry that some disgruntled shareholder might sue over something he had done. He and his family owned the whole company.

Unless, of course, the disgruntled shareholder happened to *be* a member of his family.

It sounds unlikely, but it had already happened before Reliance went private.

IT IS UNUSUAL, to say the least, for a wife to institute a shareholder suit as part of divorcing her husband but that's exactly what Laura Steinberg did in 1980. (Laura was Saul Steinberg's second wife; the first, Barbara, a high-school sweetheart, was the one the Woodmere Academy center was named after.) Laura Steinberg held stock in Reliance Group.

Divorce proceedings had already begun when the stockholder suit was filed. The allegations made tabloid headlines.

Laura charged that Steinberg had taken $100,000 in company funds to give to the Goldin campaign as part of the bus shelter "conspiracy." She said that he had used corporate funds to pay for the furnishings of the Park Avenue apartment (which Laura had decorated, according to one friend, in "elephant tusks and leopard skins") and to pay for private security guards. She also claimed he was using the corporate jet strictly for private flights.

Most sensational was her charge that Steinberg was a "heavy user" of cocaine, with the result that he had "failed to attend many corporate meetings and to perform certain corporate duties." The suit claimed he had spent over $190,000 of Reliance's money on cocaine and other drugs.

The result was predictable. Headlines such as "Wife Pins Coke Rap on Top Exec" appeared. Steinberg reacted with outrage. "Everything she has said so far is a goddamn lie. I'm dealing with an outraged and vengeful woman." The publicity went on long enough that Reliance's directors felt it necessary to conduct an investigation into the charges. The investigation, according to the directors, "satisfied us that there was nothing to it."

The divorce and the attendant charges dragged on for three years. Finally, the Steinbergs settled. Laura Steinberg dropped the shareholder suit, stating, "I was hurt, upset, and confused. All of the charges and lawsuits that I instituted were untrue." Her alimony is $10,000 a month.

The publicity about his alleged misdoings reportedly helped Steinberg's decision to take Reliance private. "As a private company," he said, "I don't have to have a G2 for a company plane. I can have a 727. . . . I can invest in whatever company I want to. I don't have to stick to financial services."

According to Reliance's Form 10-K (Reliance must file the annual report with the SEC since it still has preferred stock and debentures in public hands), all Reliance's common stock is held by "Saul P. Steinberg, members of his family, an affiliated estate, and affiliated trusts." Perhaps because he felt freer without other shareholders looking over his shoulder, Steinberg has become a more active raider in the eighties that he ever was before.

ONE STORY THAT is always told about Steinberg concerns his negotiations with *The New York Times.* In 1980, while still engaged in the maneuvering that eventually ended with Reliance becoming his own private firm, he began buying stock in The New York Times Co. Shortly after he announced that he had acquired over 5 percent of the company's stock, he and his advisors had lunch with Times Co. executives to discuss his investment. Reportedly, at the luncheon a Times Co. lawyer confused Steinberg with someone else and called him "Mr. Silverman." Steinberg, the legend says, left the luncheon in a huff and, the next day, purchased another large block of Times Co. stock.

Whatever the truth of the matter, its hard to see just what Steinberg was trying to accomplish with the Times Co. It is possible he was trying a little greenmail, or perhaps he might have figured that if he bought stock it might cause the price to rise and he could sell out at a profit. Other raiders have done that. There seems to have been little chance he could have tried a tender offer; besides the fact that Steinberg had announced that his Times Co. purchases were "just an investment," the voting stock of the Times Co. is closely held and controlled by members of the Ochs and Sulzberger families and the trusts they control.

In any case, Steinberg sold the Times Co. stock during the summer of 1981 for a small profit—reportedly less than a million dollars. At the same time, he sold a block of Chris-Craft stock back to Chris-Craft for a profit of $15 million. The two sales ended a lot of speculation. Chris-Craft owns television stations and, at the time, also owned 21 percent of Twentieth Century-Fox; among other things, Fox is a major producer of television programs. The Times Co. owns other publishing properties besides *The New York Times.* Wall Street had spent the last part of 1980 and the early part of 1981 crystal-ball gazing and opining that Steinberg was trying to get into broadcasting or publishing.

Most likely, he was just trying to get into money.

THE LIST OF companies we know Steinberg went after from 1980 on is long and probably not conclusive. It isn't necessary to announce holdings that comprise less than 5 percent of the stock in a company; many raids have taken place where the greenmail was paid before the stock holdings got beyond 4.9 percent. Reliance always has positions in many companies; some may be genuine investments, some may be takeover candidates—and some may be greenmail targets. Only Saul Steinberg and his intimates know for sure.

Frank B. Hall (marine, aviation, property, and casualty insurance), Tiger International (air cargo and trucking), Wickes Companies (retail lumber, building materials, food and drugs, and apparel stores), Zenith National Insurance (workman's compensation insurance)—the list goes on. Tiger International fought Steinberg tooth and nail but eventually yielded seats on the Board of Directors to his nominees. Steinberg relatives and business associates sit on the boards of Frank B. Hall, Wickes, Zenith National, Crump Companies, and others, all once targets of Reliance stock buying.

Then there are the ones that got away—by paying a price. Republic Financial Services fought Steinberg for three years before finally, in 1982, fleeing into the arms of a white knight, Winterthur Swiss Insurance Co. of Switzerland. Quaker State Oil Refining paid greenmail. Steinberg bought into Quaker State early in 1984—for $36 million. Quaker bought him out soon after—for $47 million. They were not the only ones.

Later in 1984 came another of Steinberg's real headline makers. Steinberg formed a syndicate called MM Acquisition Corp. What the initials "MM" stood for was highly secret. They stood for "Mickey Mouse," a dead giveaway of the target. Drexel, Burham, Lambert, Inc.—an investment banking house that has pioneered junk-bond financing and has bankrolled many of the major raiders—raised a "fighting fund" of $1.3 billion for MM Acquisitions. Of course, little of this was in cash, but the commitments were in place so that the cash would be available if needed. MM Acquisitions then went after Walt Disney Productions Corp.

(Junk-bond financing uses low-grade bonds rather than bank

loans to raise money. The classic leveraged buyout used bank loans. The use of the junk bond was Drexel's contribution to the takeover game.)

MM Acquisitions gathered together an 11.1-percent stake in Disney, then made a tender offer for 37.9 percent of the outstanding shares. Had the tender offer succeeded, Steinberg would have controlled Disney.

Disney was a ripe target for a raider. It was (and is) asset rich, with real estate holdings in Florida, the theme parks, and its movie library, and its stock was relatively low in price because of years of earnings that had fallen below the rest of the entertainment industry. In addition, management was making a real effort to bring back to life its moribund film studio. (*Splash* was Disney's first success in years.)

Steinberg seems to have been sincere in his desire to take over Disney. At one point, he tried to enlist Roy E. Disney's support. As Roy E. Disney is the son of Roy O. Disney, brother of Walt Disney and cofounder of the company, it seems unlikely Steinberg would have tried to get his aid if he simply intended greenmail—or if he wanted to liquidate the company after taking it over.

Disney wanted no part of Steinberg. After the now-usual acrimony, Disney agreed to a $325.3 million buyout if Steinberg would discontinue his tender offer. Steinberg walked away with between $30 million and $60 million in profit plus $28 million in "out-of-pocket" expenses. Disney was in the position of paying Steinberg not just a profit but also paying for the costs of the raid.

Steinberg claimed later that the reason he allowed himself to be bought off was that Disney was threatening to do "dangerous and stupid things" if he succeeded in his offer. In a sworn deposition taken for one of the numerous lawsuits the raid spawned, Steinberg claimed Disney had plans to offer $80 a share for all the shares he didn't take in his tender offer. The result would have been, Steinberg said, to leave his group the sole owner of Disney—all other shares having been bought back by the company—but saddled with "well over $2 billion in debt." He continued, "It would have been a very serious problem."

If Disney really did plan the tender offer—Steinberg said he was told of the plan by Laurence Tisch, a friend of Roy Disney, rather than officially by the company—it would have been a new wrinkle on the "scorched earth defense," in which a company guarantees that a raider will find little of value after a takeover. In any case, he accepted the $325 million offer.

The deal, however, was not over yet. Some Disney shareholders were so outraged about the settlement that they brought suit in California state court, seeking to overturn the greenmail. First a local court, then an appeals court, ruled that there was a "reasonable probability" that a trial might force Steinberg to give back his profits, and an injunction was granted limiting Steinberg's investment of the funds. The suit alleges that Disney's directors failed to act properly because, by paying off Steinberg, they preserved their own positions at the expense of shareholders.

What will happen if the case goes to trial is anybody's guess. In the meantime, Reliance has said they have no problems with the restriction on investing—which holds them to California's "prudent trustee" rule, similar to the standard "prudent man" rule of pension fund management—as the subsidiary that holds the funds has "always invested under a prudent man standard."

Besides having its board and executives involved in the shareholder lawsuit against Steinberg, Disney found that paying greenmail to Steinberg brought on other troubles. No sooner had Steinberg left the field than Disney found itself the target of another raider, Irwin Jacobs. Unfortunately for a target company, buying off one raider does not necessarily make the company unattractive to takeovers.

Sometimes, like blood in the water attracting sharks, a fought-off raid merely attracts more unwanted attention.

THE DISNEY SUIT did not stop Steinberg from other raids—or from expanding his area of attack. In 1985, he returned to the site of his 1969 raid on Pergamon Press: England. First he went after Vickers PLC, the owner of Rolls Royce. He picked up 6 percent of Vickers, announcing an idea to introduce a "mini-Rolls" to compete with Mercedes-Benz. Three months later, he sold his Vickers stock. His cost had been $16 million. His profit was $10 million— 62.5 percent in three months. Annualized, that works out to 250 percent per year.

Also in 1985, and still in England, he became embroiled in an attempt to take over Mercury Securities PLC. Mercury had already agreed to merge with several other firms—a well-known British merchant bank, S. G. Warburg, as well as a stock brokerage house, a British government bond specialist, and a market maker in stocks and bonds—and Steinberg's intrusion was not welcomed. Steinberg, though Reliance, bought up nearly 11 percent of Mercury and announced he was looking for more. Late in November of 1985, though, Reliance and Mercury announced a standstill agreement under which Reliance wouldn't buy more than 15 percent of the company. After the projected merger of Mercury with Warburg and the other financial firms, Reliance's stake in the combined company will be just under 10 percent. Steinberg appears, for the moment, to have accepted this, saying, "We . . . are pleased with this understanding and reaffirm our previously stated recognition of the business desirability of Mercury and the combined group remaining independent with no dominant shareholder."

The only people who appeared disappointed were the speculators who had been buying up Mercury stock in anticipation of a bidding war. Mercury's stock price dropped immediately after the announcement.

One other interesting development of 1985 involved another lawsuit, but this time not against Steinberg. Steinberg was, however, a prime cause of the suit.

A company called Green Tree Acceptance Inc., a Minneapolis-St. Paul area buyer and seller of loan contracts for mobile homes and recreational vehicles, contracted with investment banker Drexel Burnham Lambert Inc. to underwrite a $250 million offer of stock and debentures. To Green Tree's horror, it discovered that, when the offering was successfully completed, Reliance Financial Services Corp.—a subsidiary of Reliance Holdings Group—now owned 9.3 percent of its stock. Soon thereafter, Reliance boosted its holdings to 15.1 percent. A business associate of Steinberg's picked up an additional 9.7 percent of Green Tree. Green Tree looked around and realized that almost a quarter of their stock was exactly where they didn't want it to be and filed suit, charging that Drexel manipulated the price of the company's stock in bringing it to market and that it allowed the stock to end up in the hands of "known corporate raiders." Green Tree claims Drexel assured it that the stock would be distributed so as to "minimize the risk of a hostile takeover raid."

A month later, Steinberg notified Green Tree that he was interested in picking up more stock in the company. Green Tree countered by adopting a "poison-pill" defense. The poison-pill defense sets up a trigger mechanism in which any attempt at a hostile takeover results in the issuance of securities that would be unpalatable to the acquiring company. In Green Tree's case, this involves rights to a preferred stock that would only be exercisable in the event of a takeover.

It remains to be seen whether Steinberg can find a way around the poison pill.

Or if he wants to.

WHEN FELLOW RAIDER Carl Icahn started a raid on TWA in the spring of 1985, an investment banker reportedly called Steinberg to see if he would help TWA fight Icahn off. Not very long ago, the idea of going to Steinberg for help in beating off a raider would have seemed as absurd as asking Blackbeard to help defend against Captain Kidd. Saul Steinberg is, after all, the prototype of the modern corporate raider, the man who made a fortune from greenmail before the term had even been coined.

By some reports, Steinberg has mellowed, no longer sailing out to do battle and reap profits from every target in sight. The directors of Disney might disagree, but it is true that he makes the headlines less often than he did a few years ago. Partly it's because he is no longer the only one playing the game, and partly it's because his tactics no longer shock. It's also that Steinberg is no longer perceived as cocky or brash. He's been around too long. Though as active a raider as ever, Saul Steinberg has become respectable.

Compared to 1969, when Steinberg launched his takeover attempt on Chemical Bank, his press coverage today seems almost friendly. And the call from the investment banker about TWA had to have been sweet revenge.

Steinberg turned him down.

UNLIKE MOST RAIDERS, Steinberg has admitted to greenmailing companies and doesn't shy away from the word. But he also says—and here he begins to sound like others in the raiding game—"I never invest in a company I am not prepared to own" and claims, "I am an investor, not a raider. I do deals. I finance deals. I'm not out for a fast buck."

Fast? That, of course, depends on your definition. The raid on Disney took about two months. That's pretty quick for a profit of over $30 million.

Looking over Steinberg's career, though, one thing stands out. By the early seventies, Steinberg had sufficient reputation as a raider to scare companies into greenmail just because he had taken a position in their stocks. Yet, when compared to other raiders such as Icahn, Pickens, or Jacobs, until the late seventies Steinberg had actually done very little raiding. He *had* made hostile takeover attempts on Reliance and Chemical, but it is evident that these were not attempts at greenmail; Steinberg really wanted the companies. In fact, until the Lomas & Nettleton settlement in 1978, Steinberg had spent most of the 1970s quietly running Reliance Group. Yet as soon as he acquired a large stake in Lomas, people reacted with fear. "A number of institutions had liquidated their positions in our company," said Lomas president Ted Enloe, "and there was uncertainty among the financial community as to what Reliance was going to do." So Lomas bought Steinberg out.

There are some probable reasons for Steinberg's gaining so fearsome a reputation (*Fortune* entitled an article about him "Fear and Loathing in the Boardroom") with very little cause by 1980s standards. The takeover attempt (if that's what it was) on Chemical Bank explains a lot. The reaction was so hysterical that Steinberg, whose takeover of Reliance had not raised too many eyebrows, suddenly assumed ogrelike dimensions. Also, while hostile takeovers were not new, Steinberg was brash—and he was young—and he was an outsider.

The pace of takeovers was slower in the sixties when Steinberg made his reputation. He went after Reliance, Chemical, and Pergamon one right after the other. Readers of the financial press saw his name over and over again at a time when no one else was doing what he was doing.

And what Steinberg was doing was inventing the means, methods, and legends of raiding.

THE DEBATE OVER the rights and wrongs of raiding continues. The raiders insist that what they are doing is not only undeniably legal but also salutory. The former is rarely argued with. The latter is where the controversy lies.

The raiders say that the only losers in a raid are corporate managements trying to hang onto their jobs. They maintain that the ideal target of a raid—an asset-rich company whose stock price doesn't reflect the company's real worth—is a company whose management is faulty. Otherwise, the argument goes, the stock would be priced higher.

The raiders say that by bidding for companies in such a position, they force management to be accountable for its actions. By driving up the price of the stock, they benefit all shareholders. Thus, they say, the current attempts of corporate management to persuade legislatures to enact protective legislation is in no one's interest except entrenched managements. Steinberg says, "Almost all existing antitakeover legislation begins with the premise that management in place should be protected. Who, you might ask, are they protected from? The answer, unfortunately, is their shareholders. What an absurd notion."

It is true, of course, that many asset-rich companies have low stock prices because management has failed to capitalize on the companies' strengths, thus bringing about lower earnings than a stronger management could. If this were the only case where a raid took place, the raiders' brief would be less controversial.

But critics point out that raids often seek out targets other than inefficiently managed companies. "Such takeovers can be beneficial if they result in the replacement of an ineffective management," says Peter Rodino, the chairman of the Judiciary Committee of the House of Representatives. "But there is reason to doubt that the ineffectively managed company is the most frequent target of corporate raiders. Moreover, such takeovers distract corporate executives from their primary task of long-term, productive management."

One complaint often heard in financial circles is that today's corporate manager, whose compensation often includes stock and bonuses, is too fixed on producing short-term profits—which raise stock prices—and not concerned enough about the long-term health of the company, which might mean deferring current profits in order to build for the future. The raiders, by penalizing managements who don't maximize immediate earnings, only contribute to that shortsightedness.

Once again, the raiders reject the accusation. From their point of view, healthy companies don't become the victims of raids. To charges that, all too often, a raider dismembers all or part of a company afterward, they answer that such pruning is necessary and it is only sentimentalism—out of place in a business environment—that wishes to preserve the status quo.

But liquidation or divestiture does not always come about through choice. The payment of greenmail, as well as such "shark repellent" (anti-raider measures) as the scorched-earth defense or a white squire (unlike a white knight, who stages a friendly takeover of the target company to prevent a hostile one, the white squire is a company that buys a large block of stock in the target company to prevent the raider acquiring control), can weaken a company. The cost of a takeover defense can saddle a company with so much debt that it is a mere ghost of its pretake-over self, forced to sell divisions and assets to stay alive. All too often, it is the best, most profitable divisions that must be sold because they bring the best price. "The substantial costs of excessive takeover activity," Rodino says, "go well beyond nostalgia."

The raiders' answer might be that none of this would happen if the management didn't fight the takeover. Sometimes, of course, this is true. But it should be remembered that the leveraged buyout is the standard raider tactic, especially the junk-bond variant. When such a takeover happens, the successful acquirer also has a company saddled with debt—and may have to sell assets to cover the cost.

And all the shareholders can suffer. Even the raider.

SAUL STEINBERG WAS twenty-two when he founded Leasco. Twenty-five years later, it's fair to ask the question: how much is Steinberg worth?

His life-style has been compared to that of the nineteenth-century nobility. He has a triplex on New York's Park Avenue that once belonged to John D. Rockefeller, Jr.—thirty-four rooms, twenty-eight thousand square feet, fifteen fireplaces, gym, screening room, and two dining rooms. He has a house with a thousand feet of beachfront in Quogue, one of the quieter parts of the Hamptons. He has a cottage in Key Largo and is proprietor of a hotel in the south of France. He uses a Boeing 727 to travel between them.

He is married for the third time, to a stunning brunette, Gayfryd Johnson, who, before she met Steinberg, was the owner of a company that distributed tubular steel products to the oil industry. Friends say she has helped to calm him down. They have one child in addition to five children from his two previous marriages.

His art collection includes Dutch, Flemish, and Italian old-master paintings and Rodin bronzes, as well as German expressionists and modern art. He is a substantial supporter of institutions such as the Metropolitan Museum of Art (he paid for the recently installed Frank Lloyd Wright Room), the Wharton School, and Long Island Jewish Hospital. He gives heavily to charity and sits on the board of Cornell Medical School. Certainly, he is one of the ultra-rich. *Manhattan, inc.,* a publication focusing on the New York business scene, estimates his fortune at $400 million.

But there may be trouble in paradise. When *Forbes* published its list of the four hundred wealthiest people in America, Steinberg's name was not among them. He showed up, instead, on a separate list: "Dropouts." Said *Forbes,* which last year had also listed Steinberg as worth $400 million, "High debt load from leveraged buyout of outside Reliance Insurance stockholders, negative cash flow, goodwill item exceeding shareholders' equity make true worth of fortune uncertain." Translated into English, it means that the Reliance buyout may have used up a lot of Steinberg's capital.

Ironically, Steinberg may be suffering from the kind of adverse aftereffects of an LBO that have afflicted many targets of raiders like himself. The man who may have done more than anyone else to put the LBO on the map may now have his own case of LBO indigestion.

Even so, Saul Steinberg shows no signs of losing his touch. He is a shrewd judge of opportunity. And no matter how much his fortune has been eaten away, he is still a very rich man and a force to be reckoned with.

"After a certain point," Steinberg says, "you're not in business to make money. You do what interests you. What excites you. The money is incidental. It just comes. It isn't any longer something you think about for itself."

He's come a long way with that borrowed $25,000.

2

The Wall Street Privateer

CARL C. ICAHN

IN THE FORTIES and fifties, Far Rockaway, New York, was a low-to moderate-income area of small houses on tree-lined streets. A central business district of small stores bisected this peninsula of land separating the Atlantic Ocean from Jamaica Bay. Only the street signs and the subway stops told a casual visitor that this was New York City.

It was not an area that sends a lot of its high-school graduates to Princeton.

Even fewer ended up owning TWA.

Carl C. Icahn, Far Rockaway High School, class of '53, has done both.

ICAHN LIKES TO say that as soon as he acquires a significant stake in a company, he invites the top man to lunch to discuss his investment. "The next day," he adds, "they sue me."

He has been sued many times. "You get threatened to hell," Icahn says.

He also causes panic in boardrooms. "TWA Put Up For Sale by Board" read the headline on the first page of the business section of *The New York Times* on May 29, 1985. Why had the directors of the company suddenly decided they wanted to be bought? The next line told the tale: "Airline seeking offer 'superior' to Icahn's bid."

Carl Icahn was offering to take over the airline; the directors wanted almost anyone else but him. The man who had raided Tappan, Marshall Field, American Can, Chesebrough Pond's and Dan River—among others—had once again become the cat among the pigeons.

And, as usual, the pigeons were screaming bloody murder.

EVERY SUCCESSFUL ENTREPRENEUR has to start somewhere. Icahn began his career as a raider in 1979. He put together a syndicate that acquired a stake in Tappan Co., the appliance manufacturer. Icahn demanded a seat on the board of directors. Tappan fought back. After a bitter proxy contest, Carl Icahn was elected to the board. Six months later, Electrolux made a cash tender offer for Tappan, offering $18 a share (Icahn had paid approximately $8). Electrolux took over Tappan. Icahn made nearly $3 million in profit, after expenses, on an investment of less than $1.5 million. He had held the stock for twelve months. On an annualized basis, that's a return on his investment of 192 percent.

Tappan was only the beginning. Before 1979 was over, Icahn went after Saxon Industries, Inc., buying stock at 7. Four months later, Saxon bought it back at 10½. In 1980 it was Hammermill Paper Co.'s turn.

Hammermill fought back hard—harder even than Tappan. After extensive litigation, the company won a proxy contest, decreasing the number of seats on the board of directors to prevent Icahn from gaining a seat. Icahn got a $750,000 consolation prize for agreeing to the new board structure. Later, Hammermill bought back Icahn's shares (acquired at 20) for $36 a share, almost $10 million in profit.

That profit number, though, is not complete. Like many

another deal involving a raider, the announced settlement figure doesn't cover everything. To discover the rest of the profit, you have to look elsewhere.

In 1979, in addition to the Tappan and Saxon raids, Icahn had gained control of Baird & Warner REIT. REIT stands for Real Estate Investment Trust. The REIT was a product of the seventies, a new form of investment vehicle that sold shares similar to stock certificates and then invested the money in real estate. The real estate crunch of the late seventies bankrupted many of them and to a large extent discredited REITs in the eyes of the investing public—especially as they had been publicized as conservative, safe investments. But many of the REITs, though selling for low prices per trust share, owned potentially very valuable real estate. Baird & Warner owned, among other things, large tracts of land in Westchester County, one of the wealthier suburban areas north of New York City—an area that was not only a bedroom community for the city but also a growing headquarters area for companies wishing to escape high city real-estate prices and taxes yet staying near the communication and financial hub New York City provides.

Baird & Warner REIT went down fighting, but they went down nonetheless. Icahn won the proxy fight. The name of Baird & Warner was changed to Bayswater Realty & Capital Corp., named for the section of New York City where Icahn grew up. Later, he took the company private, buying out the remaining shareholders.

The former REIT was put to new uses immediately. Bayswater also acquired shares in Hammermill (some 82,000 shares as a matter of fact) and likewise made a profit on the deal.

Bayswater was to fill an even bigger role in the next Icahn raid. In 1981, the Icahn group went after Simplicity Pattern Co. Bayswater made a tender offer for Simplicity. Graham Ferguson Lacey, a large controlling shareholder of Simplicity, opposed the bid. Surprisingly, considering the amount of acrimony these deals seem to generate, there was no litigation. Lacey found a white knight, the Australian entrepreneur Alan Bond (who, among other things, was to head up the *Australia II* syndicate that won the America's Cup away from the United States in 1983), to purchase the Icahn stake of 1,826,100 shares. The price was 13½. Icahn had purchased the stock four months earlier at 10. On an annualized basis, that's a return on investment of 235 percent.

In terms of major investment activity, Simplicity was it for 1981; 1982, however, was to generate enough headlines to make sure that anyone on Wall Street who hadn't already known Carl Icahn's name would have no excuse not to in the future. It is fair to say that before 1982, Icahn was one of many investors making takeovers. Afterward, he was one of the select group at the top of the raiding game.

In 1982, Icahn's group (most raiders bring in others as part of their consortium on a deal; one of the most interesting in Icahn's groups has been Richard Tappan, the former chairman of Tappan, once Icahn's adversary) went after Marshall Field, American Can, Anchor Hocking, Owens-Illinois, and Dan River. At the end of the year, the combined profit on these deals was over $45 million.

American Can, Anchor Hocking, and Owens-Illinois were relatively simple deals. Icahn bought a stake. The companies pulled up their skirts in horror, shrieking loudly, and Icahn allowed himself to be bought off to go away. Standard greenmail. He held American Can for two months, Owens-Illinois and Anchor Hocking for one month each.

Marshall Field and Dan River were not so easy. The Marshall Field takeover attempt was reported in business headlines for six months. Charges and countercharges flew back and forth. Lawyers and investment bankers earned hefty fees. Icahn and his allies built their stake in Marshall Field to a total of 3.5 million shares of stock, 32 percent of the company. The purchase price averaged out at $15 per share, over $50 million worth of stock.

Marshall Field realized it couldn't win and sought out a white knight. One appeared in the form of BATUS, a U.S. subsidiary of BAT (British American Tobacco), a giant British company with extensive U.S. retailing interests. BAT bought out Marshall Field for $30 a share. Icahn's group, which by itself owned almost a million and a half shares, made a profit of over $17 million.

Shareholders who owned Marshall Field before Icahn's maneuvers—and held to the end—made out very well.

IT IS THE profit earned by all shareholders, not just the raider, that muddies the waters when analysts try to decide if raiders are bad or good. "We have defined raiders as real bad guys and corporate management as good guys," Icahn says. In articles and speeches, however, he contends that this is not always true.

His brief is simple. Since most corporate boards are composed of heads of other corporations or the bankers they work with, the board is really an ally of management rather than an advocate of the shareholder. As a result, he said (in an article in *The New York Times*), "The CEOs of publicly held American companies are for the most part *answerable to no one.*" (His italics.) His tender offers, he maintains, force corporate management to try to wring the most from company assets by selling out to a white knight or by offering to buy back stock from the raider *and other shareholders* at a higher price than the market was offering. This, Icahn feels, corrects the poor market price that is a reflection of management's failure to fully realize corporate profitability.

As examples, he cites Tappan and Marshall Field. Tappan was selling for $8 a share when he became interested in it, despite a book value (the theoretical value of the company's assets) of $22 a share. As a result of his raid, Tappan was sold to Electrolux for $18 a share. Icahn made a profit, of course, but *all* Tappan shareholders received 225 percent more for their stock than it was selling for before he got involved.

It is Icahn's contention that the only people harmed by a raid such as the one on Tappan—or Marshall Field, where shareholders received double the market price when the raid started—is corporate management. Management becomes a part of another corporation instead of running its own shop and loses not only freedom but job security. From Icahn's point of view, though, the management of a company that fails to maximize the corporation's return on its assets doesn't deserve protection.

Still, Icahn admits he is no Robin Hood. He is after a profit and is willing to put up with a lot of verbal abuse and legal harassment to get it. But—and this is the key not only to Icahn's argument but to the justifications put forth by other raiders as well—the only reason he can make these profits is because, in his view, corporate management is not doing the job the shareholders pay them to do. If he makes a profit as a raider, so does everyone else.

It is a compelling argument. But what about the cases where all stockholders are *not* offered the same price as the raider? In all too many cases, greenmail is paid. The only people who receive the premium price (sometimes twice or more the going price per share on the open market) is the raider's group. Icahn's answer is that the raider doesn't initiate the buyback, the corporation does. If other stockholders don't like it, they can support the raider. If a raider loses a proxy fight—a vote by shareholders—and takes money to go away, he can legitimately ask whose fault it is.

In fact, Icahn has a point. In the Phillips Petroleum multiparty raid (Pickens, Icahn, Jacobs, and Goldsmith were involved at one time or another), after management tried to buy off T. Boone Pickens and others at a price not available to all shareholders, lack of shareholder support *did* force management to make a better offer to everyone. Icahn helped to make that happen.

Unfortunately, there is a dark side to all this. In several cases where raiders have been bought off and other shareholders have profited as well, there have been accusations that the raider *still* got a better deal. One way critics suggest this is done is when the raider sells a property to the greenmailed company, possibly for an inflated price. Icahn has been accused of this.

In his 1984 raid on Chesebrough Pond's, Icahn made what was for him a small profit. The buyback price was available to all stockholders. But soon afterward, Chesebrough, a consumer products company active in such areas as food and cosmetics, bought the Polymer Corp. from ACF Industries. Polymer makes plastic parts for automobiles, an odd fit for Chesebrough (the company said the purchase was "an experiment"). It just happens that ACF, Polymer's parent, is controlled by Icahn. The price paid was also twice the book value of Polymer.

The question is, was the price paid for Polymer a part of the price paid to make Icahn go away, at a profit *not* available to other shareholders? If so, then this is greenmail pure and simple and not defensible by any claims of shareholders' rights.

Nevertheless, greenmail is not illegal, whatever an observer's opinions may be. And, as Icahn says, it is always within the at least theoretical power of shareholders to throw out the management that pays it.

THE OTHER PROBLEM with raiders is what happens to a company after a raider has tried and succeeded—or tried and failed. Few syndicates trying to take over a company actually have the cash to buy the target outright. This is as true of corporate managements taking a company private or white knights as it is of raiders. Instead, the money is raised by an investment banking house essentially as a short-term loan that is backed *by the assets of the company being acquired.*

If the acquisition doesn't take place, the money is paid back with interest—and the interest is paid from the raider's profits. The raider's risk, therefore, is that he won't earn enough profit on the deal to pay the interest.

If the deal does go through, though, the raider issues new securities in the company and repays the loan with the profits. Most of the securities are debt instruments—bonds or debentures—of the type known on the street as junk bonds.

Junk bonds are subordinated debt, coming after all other debt in a company and, generally, backed by no specific assets. Because of the huge amounts of money involved in buying a Tappan or a Uniroyal—or TWA—the debt issued can actually equal or exceed all the previous debt on a company's books. Interest payments, because of the subordinated status of the bonds, are very high. A corporation can be nearly crippled with the new debt. Often it is forced to sell valuable assets—entire chunks of the company—in order to bring the debt down to safe levels. Even corporations who fight off a raid can end up in the same boat. In order to pay the settlement to raiders and stockholders that ended the various takeover attempts on Phillips Petroleum, the company had to sell debt. Phillips ended up with an $8 billion debt, 80 percent of its total capital. It was faced with selling between $2 billion and $4 billion in assets—a substantial part of the company—in order to bring the debt down to a manageable level.

Many people question whether forcing a healthy company to break itself up and load itself with debt really helps anyone—the company, the markets, or the economy.

Icahn doesn't see it that way, of course. Like T. Boone Pickens, he likes to present himself as a champion of the investor against entrenched management. And he sees corporate America as full of marginally competent, entrenched managements.

"American management today is what I call a pernicious type of nepotism, where you have a CEO that gets there sort of like the fraternity brother in college. The fellow you elected to be president of the fraternity in college was certainly not necessarily the best and the brightest or the guy that you would have run your company or your funds or your money or even advise your son or your brother. He was the good guy, the guy you liked to go drinking with. And that is the guy who gets into the corporation and again, I am talking generally because there are good CEOs, but that is the guy that gets into the corporation today, works his way up, likable guy. He gets football tickets for the guys on the board and goes drinking with them when they come in for a board meeting. And what happens is, the CEO likes him and as the CEO decides to retire or become chairman emeritus, he makes this fellow, who has been there twenty or thirty years, the CEO, and this is what evolves. What happens is that as a result, we have, I believe, poor management today."

Sometimes Icahn has been even stronger in his contempt. "It's what I call the anti-Darwinian theory, the survival of the unfittest. In a lot of corporations, a guy gets to the top by kowtowing, and then picks somebody to succeed him who has done the same."

It is Icahn's contention that managements like that are the ones who suffer from his raids. His critics disagree, but Icahn doesn't seem too concerned by their complaints.

"There are plenty of companies that need rocking," he says.

Icahn is not alone when he enters a fight. All of his takeover deals have been made with syndicates, often bearing such innocent sounding names as Unicorn, Pelican, or Crane that won't tip off corporate management when the names appear on stockholder lists. Participants in the syndicates range from a member of the Rothschild banking family to friends Icahn made in medical school. At one time, Icahn had to look for investors. No longer. Now the task is turning people away. And even having the $5 million (old friends get in for less: half or three-quarters of a million dollars) needed to make a minimum investment in one of his partnerships doesn't guarantee entry. Icahn can afford to be selective; he sticks with old friends and long-time business associates for the most part. (Interestingly enough, one of his partners in the Phillips deal was Saul Steinberg, who had pledged to buy $60 million worth of bonds.)

On the other hand, Icahn is occasionally capricious. David Mahoney, the former head of Norton Simon, once met Icahn at a party. They hit it off, and Mahoney was subsequently invited to join in on a raid—for a $1 million investment.

But keep your eyes open. Icahn does say that someone with a good tip on a hot prospect might be allowed in on the raid—for half a million.

ONE OF CARL Icahn's most famous—or infamous—deals capped his activities in 1982: Dan River. The Dan River raid was as acrimonious and bitter as any Icahn has been involved in.

That Icahn made a handsome profit on the deal allows him, perhaps, to look back on it with some detachment, even humor. At the height of the furor, the Greenville, South Carolina, *News* (Dan River, like many textile companies, is a major employer in the South) published a cartoon showing a thuggish Icahn waylaying a surprised Dan River. Instead of demanding, "Your money or your life," the cartoon Icahn is asking, "Wanna sell me some stock?" Icahn's attitude toward the affair is displayed by the fact that the cartoon hangs on the wall of the Icahn & Co. offices in New York.

It shares wall space with framed copies of the annual reports of the targets of each of his major raids. The other major wall decoration is old prints of pirates.

Once, when asked if he was "the premier corporate raider," Icahn replied, "Well, someone might have described me that way." Dan River had another name for Carl Icahn: racketeer.

The Dan River deal began in typical fashion for a raid—without anyone, including the target company, knowing anything was happening. On June 4, 1982, a small announcement in

The New York Times created no stir: Dan River was moving its corporate headquarters from Greenville, South Carolina, to Danville, Virginia, as part of a restructuring and consolidation of the company.

In fact, Dan River, like other textile companies (it is one of the ten largest in the United States), was suffering from the recession. It had also just beaten back two raids. The first, by a group led by Unitex Ltd., a Hong Kong-based textile company, had ended with a truce in 1981. In a standstill agreement, Unitex, which ended up with 8 percent of Dan River, agreed not to acquire more than 12 percent of the company until after December 1, 1984. Shortly thereafter, David H. Murdock, a San Francisco financier, also made a run at the company. Dan River fought him off as well, eventually buying back 327,400 shares that Murdock had accumulated. Murdock gave up on Dan River and acquired Cannon Mills Co. instead.

Dan River was that ideal target of a raider—a company with valuable assets whose stock was way down. And if Icahn hadn't paid any attention to it before, the Unitex and Murdock attempts at acquisition would certainly have drawn his notice.

On August 18, 1982, Dan River announced it was cutting its dividend in half, from $.28 to $.14 a share. What better way to upset stockholders—perhaps enough that they would be interested in selling out?

Dan River had yet another strike against it. With the exception of the Unitex block, there were few large holdings. Management and the board of directors owned only 3 percent; institutions owned about 15 percent. If stock is concentrated in a few hands, management has only a few people to convince not to sell. It is much harder to sway the loyalties of hundreds of thousands of small stockholders.

On September 16, 1982, Icahn announced that a group he headed owned 6.9 percent of Dan River and was interested in "gaining control" or, possibly, splitting up the company. Soon after, he bought the block owned by Unitex and its partners. Icahn now controlled over 15 percent of Dan River. The raid was on.

Dan River fought back. On October 6, it filed suit in the U.S.

District Court for the Western District of Virginia, charging the Icahn group with violations of security laws. This is a common first move of the defense.

In addition—and more threatening to Icahn—Dan River announced it was issuing a new series of preferred shares: 1.7 million to be exact. They were earmarked "to reward salaried employees for their service to the company." They would also dilute Icahn's block to 11 percent of the voting shares.

The next day, Icahn filed suit in federal court in New York (not just the lawyers but also the airlines must do well out of these raids), asking that the stock issue be rescinded. He also filed with the Securities and Exchange Commission, charging the stock issue violated exchange rules and might lead to "the delisting of the issuer's common stock."

The New York Stock Exchange then announced it was investigating the new issue.

Five days later, Dan River went for the jugular. In *its* federal court (the Virginia one), it charged Icahn with racketeering.

This was a mean thrust, intended to embarrass Icahn even if it did nothing else. It also was a new use of a law never intended to be used in a takeover defense.

The federal Racketeer Influenced and Corrupt Organization Act of 1970, commonly called RICO, was aimed at organized crime. But the law is loosely worded. A "pattern of racketeering"—the only determination needed to cause a conviction—is defined as any two violations of any of a number of different laws within a ten-year period. Dan River charged that Icahn acquired his stock with "proceeds derived through prior acts of extortion, mail fraud, and securities fraud," adding that "Dan River is only the latest victim of Icahn's tactics. . . . Icahn and his group have already successfully dislodged $83 million from various American corporations in the last two months alone."

Dan River was trying to make greenmail a federal offense.

Icahn was, not surprisingly, furious. "I consider it an abomination that company's management should resort to these gutter and smear tactics," he said in a statement. "These allegations are completely unfounded and are simply designed to dissuade me from continuing my interest in the company."

It didn't take a man of Icahn's intelligence and street smarts to figure out that last part.

Icahn countered with a new tactic. He made a double tender offer for the company; each offer had different prices and provisions. The higher offered $16.50 for each Dan River share, but was contingent upon management stopping its harassment. Should management continue the hostilities, the other offer would come into play. It offered only $15 a share. Icahn was trying to separate the stockholders from management, hoping the shareholders would put pressure on management to roll over and play dead.

It didn't work. Dan River management played for time, saying they would think about it for a while. Once they were sure that stockholders were still largely behind them, they rejected the $16.50 offer.

The financial community was not surprised. It had already become obvious that this fight would continue until one side or the other was beaten.

Icahn vowed to continue. In November, he upped his bid to $18.

Dan River promptly sold 475,000 shares of stock to McDonough Company, a subsidiary of Hanson Trust. Hanson Trust is a British company involved with textiles.

The street began talking about white knights.

Issuing the new stock had also diluted Icahn's percentage of holdings again.

Icahn responded by increasing his offer to $21 and expanding the tender to include all the shares of Dan River. Before this, he had only been looking for a controlling interest: just over 50 percent.

On December 29, while half of Wall Street was off on winter vacations, Dan River dropped a bombshell. It offered to pay $22.50 a share for all shares of Dan River. The stock was to be bought for a new company, owned by Dan River's employees. Translation: corporate management would not only run the new company but own a big block of stock in it—probably a controlling interest. Dan River had decided to "go private."

Icahn still wouldn't give up. He extended his tender offer for the second time. He now owned 29 percent of the company.

On January 21, 1983, a truce was finally declared. Icahn and Dan River signed a standstill agreement. In it, both sides agreed to call off the war until September 15, 1983, after which "the parties will be free to resume the pending litigation."

However, as anyone reading between the lines would know, the truce was actually the end of the war. By September, Dan River would have long since completed its internal buyout. In fact, by May, Dan River had borrowed $149 million to pay for its own stock and, as a private company, can now do what it pleases without having to worry about raiders.

Icahn was involved with Dan River for six months. His investment was less than $15 million. He made a profit of $8.5 million, after expenses.

AFTER DAN RIVER, the mere rumor of Icahn's presence was enough to send stock prices sailing. In 1983, Icahn acquired 3,088,700 shares of Gulf + Western. There was no need to approach the company. After three months, the stock had risen from an average price of 16 to the point where Icahn was content to sell on the open market. His average sale price: 29⅛. Profit: over $19 million.

1983 also saw one of Icahn's rare successful attempts to take over the target company. He went after ACF Industries. ACF's principal business is manufacturing and leasing railroad cars, though they own other businesses (Polymer Corp., mentioned above, being one of them). Icahn paid about $32 a share for his stake in ACF. His tender offer was successful at 54½ and the Icahn group acquired the company.

It was a classic leveraged buyout and points up the dangers critics see in LBOs. Soon after the acquisition, ACF sold $460 million in debentures. Half of the proceeds went to repay what ACF calls "bank indebtedness." Translation: the cost of the leveraged buyout. ACF also says that "Cuts in overhead necessary for ACF to remain an industry leader in railcars were implemented without affecting the quality of our product or service to our customers." Icahn claims he is restructuring the company to make it more profitable. Critics, including disgruntled former ACF employees whose jobs were lost as part of those "cuts in overhead," claim Icahn is gutting the company, turning as much of it as possible into cash. ACF does admit that the other half of the proceeds from the debenture sale "will be used to acquire companies in businesses related or unrelated to that of ACF." Translation: to help the Icahn group in its raids.

Icahn has never been accused of looting companies (a charge that has been leveled against other raiders), but then ACF was his first big acquisition—his only one of consequence until TWA came along. Time will tell whether the restructuring is in the interest of corporate profitability or simply making more money for the acquirers at the expense of the company. What happens to ACF—and TWA—in the future will, perhaps, settle the question as to whether Carl Icahn is a hero or a villain.

After ACF in 1983 came another busy year. First came J.P. Stevens (textiles), then Chesebrough Ponds (cosmetics, foods, hospital supplies), and finally Pioneer Corp. (a natural gas exploration and production company). All the stock acquired was sold back to the companies at a profit; on the last, Pioneer Corp., the Icahn group made $12.6 million in profit on a $21.6 million investment in *one month*.

Icahn & Co.'s own publicity handouts show an approximate gain on investments between 1979 and 1984 of $111.2 million. The figure is almost certainly too low. It doesn't count the value of ACF corporation, which Icahn still holds. It doesn't count the proceeds from the sale of Polymer Corp. to Chesebrough Pond's.

That $111 million figure also doesn't count the profits from Phillips Petroleum. In early 1985, Icahn bought 4.8 percent of Phillips just when Phillips thought it had stopped a takeover attempt from T. Boone Pickens (*Business Week* used the headline "Just When Phillips Thought It Was Safe to Go Back in the Water"). When the dust cleared, Phillips had remained independent at horrendous cost to itself. The group headed by Icahn got about $75 million plus expenses. A lot of that, if not most of it, had to be profit.

And it doesn't count the likely profits from Uniroyal, the tire and chemical company. Icahn acquired 9 percent of Uniroyal in April of 1985, while the dust was still settling from Phillips. Uniroyal fended him off by agreeing to be bought by a white knight, a Wall Street investment firm (which usually means that, in reality, the executives of the company are going to end up owning it; the investment firm is simply the conduit in most of these cases). Uniroyal offered $22 a share, far more than Icahn paid for his stock. His profit is estimated at $16 million.

The *Wall Street Journal* estimates the total profit of all Icahn syndicates through 1985 as $190 million. Icahn himself shares in the profits twice—as an investor and as general manager of the investment partnerships. His share should have been about 80 percent—$152 million. And even that doesn't count Trans World Airlines. The results of that deal are still to come.

Icahn waited all of three days after settling with Uniroyal before he announced that he and his partners owned 20.5 percent of TWA.

It's likely to be a long time before the word "final" can *really* be written in front of a profit number for Carl Icahn.

BUT WHAT ABOUT Icahn the man? Listening to his targets, Carl Icahn sounds like a modern cross between Ghengis Khan and Captain Kidd. Icahn himself seems unlikely casting for the role. He is a tall (six foot three), good-looking man who could easily be younger than his forty-nine years. He is married (his wife, Liba, was born in Czechoslovakia) and has two children. He contributes to major charities such as the United Jewish Appeal. He sits on the Advisory Board of New York Hospital-Cornell Medical Center. He is chairman of the New York State Committee on Human Services.

And, to complete the picture of a most un-ogrelike man, he is founder of the Carl C. Icahn Program for the Prevention of Child Abuse, at New York Hospital. It is hard to picture Ghengis Khan founding a program to prevent child abuse.

Carl Icahn grew up in a modest, red brick house in Bayswater, Queens. It is doubtful if any observer of the young Icahn would have forecast that one day he would have a multimillion-dollar life-style—and terrorize corporate boardrooms.

Queens is one of the so-called "outer boroughs" of New York City. Like Brooklyn, Queens is on Long Island, the 110-mile-long island with part of New York City at one end and the Hamptons at the other (but don't try to tell people in Queens or Brooklyn they live on Long Island—to New Yorkers, Long Island is the suburban counties of Nassau and Suffolk, whatever the geography books say; in fact, road signs on the Long Island Expressway in Queens say "Long Island" with arrows pointing east, as if the drivers weren't already *on* Long Island).

Bayswater itself is about as far away from Manhattan—and Icahn's future stalking ground, Wall Street—as it is possible to get and still be within the city limits. New Yorkers have a peculiar mind-set about their city. Though anyone living in any of the five boroughs—Manhattan, Brooklyn, the Bronx, Queens, and Staten Island—officially lives in New York City, only Manhattan is called "The City" by New Yorkers. The "outer boroughs," which actually comprise most of the population and land area, are always referred to by their names. This sense of distance from what most people think of as New York City (for to most of the rest of the world, the skyscrapers of Manhattan are also "New York City") is important. For a child growing up in eastern Queens or Staten Island, "The City" can be as far away in time and space as for a child growing up half a continent away. New York is a city of neighborhoods, small towns really, with cultures and attitudes in some cases as different from those of "The City" as if they were in different states. Carl Icahn, though brought up within the city limits, did not grow up a "City" boy.

Bayswater is on the Rockaway Peninsula, south of the "mainland" of Queens, with the Atlantic Ocean to the south and Jamaica Bay to the north. If other parts of New York City seem removed from "The City," the Rockaways, as the area is called, may be the most remote. Certainly it is one of the farthest away from Manhattan geographically. Two bridges link the peninsula to the rest of Queens; the only way to get out of the Rockaways without crossing a bridge is to leave the city, cross into Nassau County, and circle back into Queens near John F. Kennedy International Airport. Far Rockaway, which includes Bayswater, is at the eastern end of the peninsula, where it joins the rest of Long Island. Visitors, used to the canyons of Manhattan or the blocks of apartment houses in Brooklyn or Queens, have difficulty remembering that they are still in New York. Whole blocks of

Belle Harbor or Neponsit or other Rockaway Peninsula areas could be dropped whole on the New Jersey shore or Cape Cod without seeming out of place. Bayswater itself is a pleasant suburb of modest brick homes and modern ranches side by side with enormous Victorian frame houses of the sort that once dominated the turn-of-the-century seaside resorts—one of which bulks large across the street from Carl Icahn's childhood home. Bayswater seems to have escaped most of the deterioration that the rest of Far Rockaway has suffered in the years since Carl Icahn grew up there; nevertheless, it is a far cry from Michael Icahn's brick house to the world of corporate jets and large estates that his son Carl lives in today.

His parents were not rich. His father was a lawyer, forced to retire due to ill health while Carl was still a boy. He was also a cantor, singing the prayers beside the rabbi in the synagogue—a responsible and honored position. His mother was a schoolteacher. Carl went to Far Rockaway High School and became an expert chess player. He did well enough in his studies to be accepted to Princeton University in 1953. Reportedly, he was the first graduate of Far Rockaway High to go to Princeton.

His father's retirement left the family without a lot of extra money, and Icahn worked on his vacations to help pay for school. Still, except for his skill at chess, there was nothing to indicate that someday Carl Icahn would be one of the movers and shakers of Wall Street. When Saul Steinberg was in college, his thesis led him directly to the founding of Leasco. Icahn, on the other hand, was a philosophy major; his bachelor's thesis was entitled "An Explication of the Empiricist Criterion of Meaning." It was hardly something to build a career on, but it did win the John Guthrie McCosh Award in Philosophy. Icahn says today he doesn't remember much of his thesis, but he is still proud of the award. It is one of the few things mentioned on the sketchy fact sheet handed out by the firm that handles his public relations.

Nevertheless, it is hardly the training one would expect for a man who would later be compared to Jim Fisk, Jay Gould, and Commodore Vanderbilt.

Icahn graduated from Princeton in 1957. His future in the world of business was still not clear to him. He entered the New

York University School of Medicine and stuck with it for three years but he quit when he realized he wasn't really interested in medicine. He also says he was becoming something of a hypochondriac.

A stint in the army followed. At Fort Sam Houston on the east side of San Antonio, Texas, Icahn played poker as he had earlier played chess—successfully. It was poker that was to lead him to Wall Street.

The stock market was booming in 1961, and like thousands of others Carl Icahn decided to join the fun. With a few thousand dollars in poker winnings, he invested in the market. He made $50,000. He then lost it as quickly as he made it. But the bug had bitten. Though he says today that his quick profit and equally quick loss cured him of trying to guess how stocks would go, the adventure turned him irrevocably toward Wall Street. When he got out of the army, he went to work for Dreyfus & Company as a stockbroker.

Options were still in their infancy in the early sixties. They were regarded as an esoteric form of investing. Few brokers, and even fewer customers, understood them. Carl Icahn was an exception. He mastered options as he had earlier mastered chess and poker. By 1963, he was the manager of the Option Department at Tessel, Paturick & Co., shifting over to the same position at the larger Guntal & Co. in 1964. Carl Icahn was not only making a lot of money for his clients, he was making a good income for himself.

But he was still an employee, and he was now ready for bigger things. In 1968 he took all his cash and borrowed $400,000 from an uncle who had made far more than that by following Icahn's investment recommendations. Icahn bought a seat on the New York Stock Exchange. Icahn & Co., Inc., with Carl C. Icahn as president and chairman, was born.

The rest, as they say, is history. *Fortune* magazine estimated that $20,000 invested in Icahn & Co. at its birth was worth $1 million ten years later.

ICAHN & CO. reached that tenth year in 1978, the year before the raid on Tappan. Carl Icahn, at forty-two, was a very successful man. Largely through his own efforts, he had gone from a medical school dropout to the owner of a Wall Street investment firm. True, he had borrowed much of the money he needed to open that firm from a well-to-do relative but he had earned the right by his handling of his uncle's investments. At one point, Icahn was sending some $100,000 a year in profits to his uncle. The profits came from option trading. When *Fortune* interviewed Elliot Schnall, the uncle, he said, "To be honest, I still don't know the difference between a put and a call." Icahn had earned that loan. (Schnall still claims to know little about his nephew's doings. Though an investor in many of Icahn's takeover syndicates, Schnall says, "I didn't understand what he was doing. But he was right.")

One hundred thousand dollars of the investment was Icahn's own money, money he had earned in commissions or made trading for his own account. There are few thirty-two-year-olds (Icahn's age in 1968) who have managed to amass $100,000. Fewer of them would be willing to invest it in a new business venture.

And, perhaps, this is the essence of Carl Icahn and others like him. They are risk-takers, willing to bet everything they have on their own ideas and talents. Icahn was successful. His talent for getting clients sustained him while he was building his company. His investment acumen was good; he held on to the clients he got. Most importantly, he turned out to be a good businessman. Lots of people with ideas, talent, and money have foundered at running a business at a profit.

Books are written about the men who succeed. Little is heard about the ones who fail.

Carl Icahn took a gamble and won. He rejected the safe course. He could have remained a successful salary, commission, and bonus man, earning good money at a brokerage house. He could have ended up with a nice house in the suburbs, a summer place in the mountains—all the trappings of success in our society. Eventually, he might have risen high in the corporate structure at his firm, and by the time he retired he might have been modestly wealthy. Most people would be satisfied with that kind of life.

Icahn wasn't. He bet on himself and he won. He moved from successful to rich. He has an apartment on Park Avenue, an estate north of the city, and a house in Florida. In 1978, his $100,000 investment in himself was worth $5 million.

Yet the next year he became a raider. Why?

Certainly it was not to get his name in the papers. Icahn is a private person. He gives few interviews. He bought the estate next to his own in order to give himself more privacy (one version of the story is that he bought the houses on *both* sides of his own). Yet by becoming a raider, he has subjected himself to a constant stream of publicity—and more than one summons to testify before congressional committees. Why would anyone not in government, especially a private person, voluntarily put himself in the position of having to answer importunate questions from congressmen and senators under threat of contempt of Congress?

Part of the fascination with the raiders is this question about their motives. Why do they do what they do when they already have more money than they could possibly need?

Simplifying greatly, there are three major categories of self-made men. There are those who take their idea or product or invention and build a fortune with it. Then they retire on their earnings and live the good life. Gioacchino Rossini wrote more than twenty operas before he was forty, his last being *William Tell*. Then he retired. He lived for nearly forty years after his last compositions, rich and respected—and with no apparent desire to compose again. Edwin Land invented the Polaroid camera and built the company of that name into a technological giant. When he decided he could no longer contribute to the company, he retired.

But not all men—and women—are content to fade away. Many spend their lives building and running their companies. Ray Kroc died in harness, having built MacDonald's from one store to a giant fast-food empire. Some overstay their talents, hurting their own creations, as did Eddie Rickenbacker at Eastern Air Lines and Henry Ford at Ford Motor Co. Others seem to find the scope of one company too small and become empire builders, making their creations ever larger and more powerful. John D. Rockefeller was one of these; so was Alexander Graham Bell. The Bass

Brothers, the Belzberg Brothers, and Mesulam Riklis of Rapid-American are empire builders today, as was the late Howard Hughes.

Why do these men and women continue once they have everything they could ever want? Building a company, guiding its progress, even building an empire are things the ordinary person can understand. Like bringing up a child, there is a fascination in watching a creation grow and change and mature. Perhaps that is enough of a reason.

But what about Carl Icahn and the other raiders? In some sixteen forays, Icahn took over only two companies: the relatively small Baird & Warner REIT, and ACF. If this is empire building, then Carl Icahn was a failure at it. A profitable failure, but a failure nevertheless.

But even in his own public statements, he gives no indication of wanting to build an empire. True, he has said he truly wanted to take over the company in each raid, but in his articles and statements he talks more about poor management and shareholder democracy. Is it possible that Icahn puts up with all that abuse in order to force American corporate managements to do a better job? It seems unlikely.

Besides, altruism of that kind is seldom practiced at the risk of losing everything. There are substantial risks in what the raiders do. Icahn could lose more than his privacy. He has seen firsthand what can happen when things go wrong.

Icahn made a big profit on the Simplicity Pattern deal in 1981, but the other big stockholder in Simplicity, Graham Ferguson Lacey, lost everything keeping Icahn out. Simplicity had some $90 million in cash in its treasury. Lacey needed the money because NCC Energy—38 percent owned by Lacey's Birmingham and Midland Counties Trust (Lacey is British)—had commitments in Australia that required big investments. Those commitments were in deals owned by Alan Bond. Bond bought out Icahn in return for a $5 million guarantee from Lacey. BMCT owned 20 percent of Simplicity, bought on credit. With Icahn out of the picture, Lacey tried to use the $90 million to cover NCC's commitments in Australia. The other Simplicity shareholders took him to court. Without the $90 million, the Australian deals fell through. BMCT had overextended its borrowing to buy Simplicity. BMCT went into receivership and was sold at fire-sale prices to Cook International, leaving Lacey high and dry.

The risks are real. It could happen to Icahn too. In February of 1985, while waiting for the results of an important vote by Phillips's shareholders, he remarked, "Sometimes I wonder why I keep doing it. I've got enough goddamn money."

Perhaps the answer lies in the fascination with the game itself? Icahn was obsessive about chess. He approached poker the same way. The challenge of the games was important to him. Significantly, after beating TWA, he said, "We played a very tough game of chess."

Icahn may have answered his own question. "What turns me on," he says, "is the excitement of it all. I really believe in what I'm doing. Don't get me wrong—I like to win. But I love to rock boats that should be rocked."

Someone once asked H. L. Hunt why he continued to scheme and plot for more. He answered that the money wasn't important—it was merely the way he kept score. Saul Steinberg said much the same thing.

Carl Icahn's scorecard is currently up over $100 million. And the game isn't over yet. "We all have to have a little greed to progress," he told a Chicago business group. "That's a virtue in business."

"I don't care who wins," he says, "as long as I do."

AS 1985 DREW to a close, Carl Icahn seemed to achieve what his press releases claimed he wanted all along—control of a major corporation. The raid on TWA appeared to be, until near the end, a classic raid. Icahn's syndicate bought stock in the airline and offered to buy more. The airline refused. Icahn persisted. TWA sought—and found—a white knight.

Then the scenario went completely off the rails.

It's worth examining the TWA takeover battle because it contains so many of the elements found in all modern raids: public relations, court challenges, appeals for government intervention, and high-priced lawyers, among others. It is also instructive because TWA became a loser almost from the moment Icahn

bought his first share of TWA stock. Whether Icahn had won or
lost, TWA couldn't win.

TWA was only fifteen months old when the raid began in April
1985. Trans World Corporation had spun the airline off, as it had
been a continuing drag on Trans World's earnings—an ironic act
when you remember that Trans World Corporation began life as
the airline company. By spinning off TWA it was divorcing itself
from its origins. However, sentiment is not a good guide in making business decisions, and Trans World could no longer justify
running an airline.

TWA had a lot of strikes against it. It had some of the highest
labor costs in the industry. Its international competition was
mostly subsidized government carriers or domestic airlines taking advantage of deregulation to expand selectively into profitable markets. At home, all of the older carriers were being buf-
feted by upstart airlines with low labor costs and new, fuel-efficient aircraft. TWA hardly looked like a takeover target.

Of course, that is what makes the takeover game such a wonderful spectator sport: a fat takeover target exists only in the
mind of the raider. It is the company no one wants—and whose
stock price is thus low—that the raider looks for. In TWA's case,
Carl Icahn saw potential where the stock market did not. He
began to buy.

TWA was a sitting duck. It had taken no antitakeover measures; it didn't see itself as endangered. The most simple forms of
shark repellent—staggered directorships, for instance (which
make it more difficult for a raider to gain control of the board of
directors all at once because the members of the board are elected
in different years)—had not been considered, let alone such complex defenses as the poison pill or scorched earth.

Icahn, like other successful raiders, keeps track of the changing
rules of the game. In the year or two prior to the TWA raid,
several corporations had garnered enough shareholder support to
institute antitakeover measures after a raid had already begun.
Icahn largely forestalled this by picking up a large block to begin
with. Rather than the usual 5 percent to 15 percent, he had 25
percent of TWA's stock before TWA was really aware that anything was happening. With such a large block in hand, Icahn had

a fair likelihood of winning a proxy fight should TWA have started one. Thus TWA started its defense with one hand tied behind its back.

Still, they did their best. They hired Skadden, Arps, Slate, Meagher & Flom, one of the two or three top law firms in the takeover game. Skadden, Arps has worked both sides of the street—attack and defense—and knows the ins and outs well. They are specialists in the area.

But even Skadden, Arps needs something to work with. TWA, with no shark repellent in place, with a board and management that hadn't even considered what to do in case of a takeover (having spent most of the time since spin-off getting the company organized and trying to negotiate wage concessions with its unions), with so much debt that a management-initiated leveraged buyout seemed infeasible, and with the proxy fight option ruled out, was in trouble.

In fact, it was Icahn who threatened a proxy fight. Early on, after bidding $18 a share for the corporation, he announced that if the board did not submit his offer to shareholders immediately (the board wanted to wait sixty days, a stalling tactic), he would move to unseat the board of directors. Since he already had 25 percent of the stock and would need only a little more than one-third of the remaining outstanding shares to get the 51 percent he needed, the threat had to be taken seriously.

Almost from the beginning, TWA's lawyers and investment bankers realized there was little chance TWA could win on its own. Once the board was convinced of that, half the battle was over. Although TWA began to fight Icahn, the moves were aimed at delay rather than victory. TWA went looking for help.

Meanwhile, it did fight. Despite Icahn's assurances that he didn't plan to break up the airline, the TWA board was determined to keep him out. The board was comprised of people who were not about to be pushed around by a corporate raider. When Trans World Corporation had spun off the airline, it had at least given it a potent group of directors. Fifteen of the nineteen directors were "outside directors"—not employees of the company—and they included people like Peter Uebberoth, Jack Valenti, Brock Adams, Lester Crown, Andrall Pearson, and Robert Mac-

Namara. Peter Uebberoth is the commissioner of baseball, the self-made millionaire who ran the Los Angeles Olympic Games so profitably. Jack Valenti is president of the Motion Picture Association. Brock Adams is a former transportation secretary. Lester Crown is the largest shareholder in General Dynamics, a major defense contractor. Andrall Pearson is a former president of Pepsico. Robert MacNamara is the former secretary of defense and president of the World Bank. The rest of the board was made up of equally heavy hitters.

An ad went into the major financial newspapers, warning Icahn: "If you thought we'd just stand by and do nothing while you try to take over our company, think again!"

TWA began court proceedings seeking to prevent Icahn from acquiring more stock. Icahn filed suit to counter this, and the United States District Court in New York ruled against the airline. The TWA directors learned of the decision against them on May 28, while they were in the middle of a board meeting. TWA petitioned the Department of Transportation, asking that Icahn be declared "unfit" to run an airline. The Department of Transportation said it wasn't in the business of ruling on the fitness of airline owners. TWA tried to interest Congress in antitakeover legislation—a lost cause, given the recent deregulation of the industry and the many mergers that have already resulted.

The airline also hired Michael Deaver—recently resigned personal advisor to President Reagan—to help with lobbying efforts. And it went on a public relations offensive, enlisting the help of its unions. Flight attendants wore "Stop Carl Icahn" buttons. Press releases were issued targeted at Missouri newspapers and radio and TV stations, pointing out that TWA's domestic hub was in St. Louis and its service center was in Kansas City. Together, the St. Louis and Kansas City centers employed eleven thousand out of TWA's twenty-six thousand employees. The releases implied that those eleven thousand Missouri residents might find their livelihoods in danger if Icahn took over.

All these were delaying tactics. Convinced it couldn't win a fight, TWA's board was looking for a white knight, but they needed time. They got it—finally—when a Missouri judge pre-

vented Icahn from buying any more shares until June 17. Icahn
had, by then, bought up nearly 33 percent of the airline's stock. If
he hadn't been stopped, he might have acquired a controlling
interest before a white knight could be found. With the court
decision, the airline had some breathing room.

On June 14, the board of TWA triumphantly announced an
impending takeover of TWA by another airline. They were sure
Icahn wouldn't fight the takeover, for the buyout price was not
only higher than Icahn was offering but higher than the price he
had paid for his stock. He was guaranteed a profit of at least $50
million.

Actually, TWA had found two suitors. The first was Resorts
International, which offered $22 a share, $4 higher than Icahn's
$18-a-share bid. But TWA wasn't sure Resorts was the white
knight it was seeking. Then the real white knight arrived, offering $23 a share.

The white knight TWA had found was Texas Air. It seemed a
good fit. Texas Air was one of the new airlines spawned by
deregulation, with a good route structure and low costs. By
rescheduling some flights of Continental Airlines, Texas Air's
major subsidiary, and setting up combined reservations and new
hubs, it was felt that passenger traffic could be increased on both
airlines.

It was a pretty good deal for TWA; better, perhaps, than they
had begun to expect. Salomon Brothers, TWA's investment
banker, had approached nearly a hundred companies with the
idea of taking over the airline. All but Resorts and Texas Air had
declined, frightened by the combination of heavy debt, low profitability, and impending union negotiations that TWA represented.

But Texas Air was not daunted by the possibilities and made
the top offer. TWA agreed. To prevent the possibility of an Icahn
counteroffer, it presented Texas Air with a specific poison pill. It
gave Texas Air options to purchase 18 percent of TWA's stock at
$19.25 a share if anyone topped the Texas Air offer. It would put
Texas Air on a nearly equal footing with Icahn in the event of a
proxy fight, making it far more difficult to get a majority.

Then things began to unravel. Texas Air is run by Frank
Lorenzo. Lorenzo is anathema to airline unions. Lorenzo is the

man who, after acquiring Continental Airlines, put it into bankruptcy and then used the bankruptcy laws to abrogate all the union contracts with the airline. Continental endured a long strike, then rehired many of its former employees at lower salaries. The airline is now profitable, but Lorenzo's name conjures fear and loathing in the hearts of union leaders.

TWA's unions reacted quickly to the possibility that Lorenzo would end up running TWA. Union leaders, who only days before had been enthusiastically supporting management's fight against Icahn (the unions, too, feared Icahn would break up the airline, with inevitable job losses), now saw him as the lesser of two evils. "We're united against Lorenzo," said Vickie Frankovich, president of the flight attendants union. The union leaders approached Icahn and pledged to support him in his takeover bid, offering wage concessions on their part in return for stock ownership and profit participation. The deal was a precarious one—at one point Icahn walked out of a late-night meeting with union leaders prepared to accept the Texas Air-TWA plan (and the $50 million profit it offered his syndicate), but the union leaders enticed him back to the bargaining table. In the end, an agreement was reached that Icahn felt would lower TWA's high labor costs to a point where TWA could be competitive.

TWA's management reeled. Suddenly, just as they thought the merger was a done deal, Icahn was back offering to take over the entire airline, this time with union backing. Texas Air had planned to use a leveraged buyout to take over TWA—ironically, the very tactic TWA's board had decided was not feasible when it rejected the idea of a management buyout. But to carry off an LBO, Texas Air needed not only the $200 million in cash TWA was prepared to contribute but also TWA's cash flow to cover the carrying cost on the new debt. Faced with the threat of a long, bitter strike cutting into both cash flow and reserves if it took the airline over, Texas Air pulled out. With the unions backing Icahn, even the poison pill granted to Texas Air was neutralized. The board had no choice. A deal was made with Icahn.

Carl Icahn had finally won a big one. Not just money—he'd made lots of that—not a small REIT, not ACF, which was a relatively unknown company, but TWA.

Or so it seemed.

IN THE JANUARY 20, 1986, issue of *Newsweek,* a headline read: "How to Lose by Winning." Beneath it was the subhead: "Carl Icahn may be stuck with TWA for the long run."

The gist of the article was that TWA was in such poor shape that Icahn would be unable to sell off enough parts to get his money back. Like most Wall Street observers, the *Newsweek* writers seem to look on Icahn only as a greenmailer or liquidator out for the money and nothing else. If true, their conclusion is understandable. A greenmailer doesn't want to own a company, he wants to be bought off. A liquidator wants to get his money out as fast as possible and damn the consequences.

Therefore, if Icahn *is* a greenmailer and liquidator and he now owns TWA, a company in such bad shape it can't be sold quickly, he must be stuck.

But consider another scenerio. It's possible that Icahn may have misread the situation so completely that he is now trapped in TWA, but it's unlikely. Throughout the takeover he had many opportunities to walk away. He didn't take them.

The reality is somewhere in between. It looks as if Icahn's original plan was to use junk bonds to leverage as much of TWA as he could, which would allow him to get all or most of his money out. He would still have wound up owning the airline, but at little or no cost. That's a typical raider scenario.

Where the plan seems to have gone awry is that, due to TWA's poor financial condition, investors were unwilling to buy enough junk bonds to take Icahn out. He was forced instead to leave the money in the airline, where it could be used to save the company.

UP UNTIL THE beginning of December 1985, everything looked rosy. Icahn had beaten back Lorenzo, gotten concessions from the union, and his tender offer had been successful. He owned 52 percent of the airline, and the board had already approved his plan to buy the rest for $24 a share—$19.50 in cash and the rest in securities. An interim board had been appointed—with half its members Icahn nominees—and all that remained was for the money to be raised to buy out the remaining stock.

Then things began to fall apart. TWA reported that in its third quarter it lost $13.5 million. The third quarter was usually TWA's strongest—the year before had seen a *gain* of $91.2 million in the third quarter—so a loss in 1985 was bad news indeed. All told, the airline had lost $69.7 million (on revenues of $2.89 billion) in the first nine months of the year.

In addition, Icahn was unable to get the flight attendants to agree to the wage concessions that the machinists and pilots had already agreed to. Vicki Frankovich, head of the union—and one of those who had welcomed Icahn as an alternative to Lorenzo—felt that as her union members were paid less than the members of the other two unions, they shouldn't have to take as big a cut. A strike by the flight attendants began to appear as a real possibility (in the spring of 1986, the attendants *did* go on strike).

The combination of lower than anticipated earnings and a possible strike made it difficult for Paine Webber, Icahn's investment banker, to raise the $770 million needed to finance the rest of the takeover. After they were able to raise only $660 million, Icahn turned to Drexel Burnham—the company that had practically invented junk-bond financing—to raise the rest. But even they were having difficulties.

Icahn went back to the board and asked them to let him change his offer. He would pay $15 a share in cash and the rest in preferred stock. This would leave him with more cash after the takeover, enabling him to start buying new, more fuel-efficient planes and giving him a war chest to help in case of a strike. It was hoped that the provision for additional cash would make investors less nervous.

Over the course of the next month, as the bad news continued to flow in, the offer was revised downward several times. TWA seemed to have an almost unbroken string of bad luck. Besides having the highest labor costs in the industry (the wage concessions negotiated by Icahn would take effect only after he took over the airline), the terrorist attacks in Vienna and Rome killed passengers waiting at TWA counters and caused cancellations and reduced bookings to all southern European destinations.

TWA is the major American carrier to southern Europe.

The board approved the offer of $19.50 in cash and the rest in securities only to have Icahn come back with a different offer: $11 in cash and $13 in preferred stock. Again, the idea was to prepare more cash for immediate reshaping of the airline.

Finally, Icahn presented the board with his last proposal: no cash, $24 in preferred stock, and only half the minority owners would be bought out, leaving 12 million shares still trading. This would leave $750 million in cash at the company's disposal as a war chest for the threatened strike by flight attendants and for buying aircraft.

On his side, Icahn agreed not to sell his shares before September 30, 1987, unless all remaining TWA shareholders got the same deal he did.

Reluctantly, the board agreed. On January 3, 1986, Carl Icahn became chairman of the board of TWA.

THE THING THAT most militates against an interpretation that Icahn got stuck in TWA is that he had an escape clause all along. In fact, it was this escape clause that forced the outside members of the board to accept the less favorable terms of the final takeover.

Icahn's original merger agreement with TWA gave him the right to end it.

Of course, he would have been left holding 52 percent of TWA's stock—but he had an out there too. When it looked as if Icahn's financing was in trouble, Frank Lorenzo came back into the picture, offering $22 a share for TWA.

The airline's board rejected this offer for the same reason they rejected Lorenzo's first one—the unions were totally in opposition and were prepared to fight tooth and nail to prevent it. But Icahn was not so constrained. He could have sold his stock at $22 a share to Lorenzo. Much of Icahn's stock had been bought while TWA was much lower; at $22, Icahn would have almost certainly gotten out whole, perhaps even with a profit after expenses. If he had decided to sell out for the $22, the threats of union opposition would have been of no account to Icahn—unlike the board of directors, he simply wouldn't have anything to do with them anymore.

But Icahn didn't sell out. He and his investment bankers fiddled with the deal until they had what seemed to them to be enough money to give TWA a chance.

This looks a lot more like the action of someone who really wants to run the airline than of someone who is "stuck."

Where Icahn *is* stuck is in the steadily decreasing short-term return to him. The restructuring that eventually came through is good for the airline—which will eventually be good for Icahn if TWA can be made profitable again—but leaves him holding a lot of stock on margin over the short term.

Interestingly enough, many of the participants in the deal—union leaders especially—feel that one of the reasons Icahn stayed with TWA even when things began to go sour is that he felt a moral obligation to do so. He had made commitments to the unions not to sell to Lorenzo and Texas Air.

Now, to paraphrase Sam Goldwyn, a moral commitment isn't worth the paper its written on. There was nothing to stop Icahn from selling to Lorenzo except his own sense of obligation and ethics—and he hasn't sold.

It is hardly the behavior expected of the quick-profit-oriented, corporate pirate Icahn is alleged to be.

ONLY CARL ICAHN knows what will happen in the future. Even more than his future stewardship of ACF, what happens at TWA will undoubtedly prove, once and for all, whether Icahn was simply raiding for the money, going after greenmail (as his critics charge), or whether, as his press releases and public statements have maintained, he really wanted these companies because he felt he could run them better than their current managements.

It seems unlikely that TWA, as it stands now, could be broken up for maximum profit. The first actions the post-Icahn management of the airline took seemed to point in exactly the opposite direction. New top executives were appointed in crucial areas such as capacity management—the crucial trick for an airline of filling the maximum seats at the highest fares (deciding, for example, how many full-fare seats to reserve and how many to sell at advance discount fares). Moreover, the airline announced that it was *adding* flights from its hub in St. Louis, which most analysts felt was underutilized compared to the way other airlines use their hubs.

And, in line with an oft-repeated Icahn complaint that most corporate managements are too fat, a major reorganization was launched to trim the airlines administrative staff from six hundred to one hundred fifty people—with most of the cuts coming in management and white-collar jobs. The goal: to cut down the time needed to make a decision.

It remains to be seen whether Icahn can pull this one off. Many industry observers feel that even if he isn't "stuck" with TWA, he may have underestimated the difficulty of the job ahead of him.

Nevertheless, if Icahn does hold on to TWA and runs it success-fully, he will silence a lot of doubters.

T. BOONE PICKENS once said that it was cheaper to prospect for oil on the floor of the New York Stock Exchange than in the ground. Carl Icahn has come up with his own version of that. One of TWA's chief needs is newer, fuel-efficient aircraft. "The cheapest place to buy planes," Icahn said in February of 1986, "is on the floor of the New York Stock Exchange."

On February 27, 1986, TWA announced that it was buying Ozark Air Lines in a friendly merger. Ozark, a small regional carrier, operates out of St. Louis, using the city as a hub. So does TWA. Ozark was profitable but, facing increasing competition in the deregulated airline environment, was not growing as it had in the past.

The fit looks good for both carriers. Ozark gets taken over at a good price and becomes part of a major airline system. And TWA? One analyst made the remark that Ozark was costing TWA—and Icahn—$250 million, the cost of four new 747s. "Instead of four new 747s, he has bought fifty used DC-9s, nearly four thousand employees, twenty or so gates, and his most direct competitor in St. Louis." The figure about gates is more important than it might seem. When airlines use a single airport as a hub, the number of gates they have available determines how many flights can be scheduled into the airport at the same time, facili-tating transfers of passengers. The combined airlines after the Ozark-TWA merger have fifty-six of St. Louis's seventy-four gates. Passengers don't like to sit around airports and will often take the carrier that gets them from one place to another in the shortest time with the least number of changes. More gates means more planes with which to transfer without waiting.

Ozark services twenty-five states. While there will necessarily be some overlapping, the net result will be more passengers feeding into TWA's national and international routes. If TWA can get its costs down, very small changes in the number of passengers carried could mean the difference between profits and losses.

Icahn, as might have been expected, has begun aggressively. And he still has some $600 million or $700 million left to buy more.

Those who thought that with Icahn "stuck" in TWA they could relax and breathe easy for a while have once again learned that Carl Icahn is not a man to be counted out.

3

From Bags to Riches

IRWIN JACOBS

"I THINK GREENMAIL is terrible," Irwin Jacobs says. Then he continues, "But if it's not stopped, I'm going to do it. My objective is to make money."

Irwin Jacobs has made a lot of money.

JACOBS FIRST CAME to the attention of Wall Street in 1976, when he embarked on a joint venture with the wealthy Pohlad family, who, like Jacobs, were based in Minneapolis. The Pohlads controlled F & M Marquette National Bank and 45 percent of MEI, the Minneapolis area Pepsi-Cola distributor.

What sparked the venture was an article Jacobs had seen in the *Wall Street Journal* that related how two well-known liquidators, Alvin and Jerome Schottenstein, were about to pay $35 million for $276 million in receivables owed to the bankrupt W. T. Grant & Co. chain of department stores. Salvage was something Jacobs knew about, and he was familiar with the Ohio based Schottensteins. "Knowing the individuals involved," he says, "I realized that the receivables had to be worth a considerable multiple of $35 million." He took a plane to New York and persuaded the bankruptcy trustee to give him two weeks to come up with a counteroffer.

Now he had to find enough money to outbid the Schottensteins. Jacobs put up $1 million. The three Pohlad brothers put in $500,000. Carl Pohlad, their father, couldn't lend Jacobs the money from his bank since his sons were equity investors, but he used his influence with another local bank. The First National Bank of St. Paul gave Jacobs a $21 million line of credit—its legal limit to one borrower—and helped Jacobs persuade another bank to lend him more.

Jacobs returned to New York, where the bankruptcy trustee held a courtroom auction. Jacobs won, agreeing to pay $44 million plus 5 percent of the first year's pretax profits.

The receivables were not considered a good investment by most of Wall Street. In fact, it was partly the inability of W. T. Grant to collect on its receivables that put it into bankruptcy in the first place. The price paid—less than 16 percent of the face value even after an auction—indicates just how bad an investment it was considered to be.

But Jacobs thought he was smarter than the conventional wisdom. The bankruptcy trustee had already collected some $22 million on the receivables. That went to reduce the out-of-pocket expense of Jacobs's syndicate. Jacobs had to put up only $22 million. Then he went to work collecting more.

The first year, Jacobs and the Pohlads turned a $9 million profit. So much for the wisdom of Wall Street.

In the process, Jacobs picked up the nickname he has been stuck with ever since: Irv the Liquidator.

He may not like the nickname, but he freely admits that the W. T. Grant deal gave him his start. "That was the mother lode that got it all going," he says.

All told, the profits on the Grant deal have been estimated to be as high as $100 million.

UNLIKE STEINBERG OR Icahn, Jacobs never wrote a thesis—on business or philosophy or anything else. He didn't care for school.

He was bored in high school and disliked Hebrew school (where one of his teachers was Meshulam Riklis, then a stockbroker but later to found Rapid-American). He had no interest in college. From the time he was a small boy he had accompanied his father on buying trips; at seventeen, he wanted to join the family business. But, at his father's urging, he went to the University of Minnesota. His father told him, "You don't have to stay if you don't like it," and Irwin Jacobs took Samuel Jacobs at his word. A few days later, he went to work full-time for his father.

As Jacobs says today, "I *did* go to college—for three days, and then I went back into business."

The business that Jacobs senior, a Russian immigrant, had founded in 1941 was an unusual one. He sold used bags. Used burlap bags. And cotton bags. And other bags. He did quite well at it.

Minneapolis is a center of the grain business. Samuel Jacobs picked up used grain bags from the area's grain elevators, which had no use for them once the grain was in the elevators. He took them back to his shop and reconditioned them, sewing up or patching holes, then sold them to feed-grain dealers and farmers. He became, in a way, the ultimate middleman. The grain elevators bought grain that often came in sacks and took it out of the sacks to put in the elevators. The feed-grain dealers bought grain in bulk but had to put it into sacks when they sold it. Samuel Jacobs's used bags were perfectly adequate but considerably cheaper than new ones. He wasn't getting rich, but he made out all right. Irwin joined his father in the business.

"Dad was a good provider," he says, "but more important than that, he was a fabulous teacher. One of the things I learned in the family business was you don't throw anything away. There's a place in life for everything." In the bag business, he adds, "nothing was thrown away—nothing." Even a bag too tattered to hold anything could be resold. Nursery owners bought them to wrap tree roots. "I learned to look for value where other people didn't see it."

The experience has served him well. His first foray beyond the bag business came within a year after he joined up with his father. Still only eighteen, he went to a U.S. Customs auction where impounded or uncalled-for goods were sold. One lot was three hundred Italian skis that had been confiscated for tariff violations.

Most of the people interested in the skis wanted one or two pairs. Jacobs saw an opportunity. He bid for the whole lot, getting it for $13 a pair. "I wrote a check for $3,900. I didn't have the money in the bank, so I had to move fast." He moved the crates outside. "People started coming up to me and asking how much I wanted for them. I said $39 a pair. I sold a bunch of them on the spot and the rest within a few weeks. I made $10,000 on the deal." That's basically what he did on a larger scale with W. T. Grant.

That same year, a chance occurrence pointed him on the way to fame and fortune. While driving, Jacobs saw a burning building. It set him to wondering what happened to the damaged merchandise left in the building after the fire was put out. Over the next few years, he moved into the insurance salvage business—buying up damaged goods that insurance companies had taken custody of after paying out a claim, and then finding buyers for the goods at a profit. He had a knack for value; he did well.

At the same time, he continued working in his father's business. Northwestern Bag was also flourishing. In 1965, the company sold sandbags used to dam the severe floods that swept the Mississippi valley. The next year, Northwestern Bag was selling sandbags to Winnipeg, which was also threatened by floods. Between bags and damaged goods, Jacobs made his first million.

By 1972, he was ready to reap some of the rewards of his wealth. He spent $360,000 for a thirty-room, southern-plantation-style house on forty-five acres of land in Wayzata, a suburb of Minneapolis. The house, located on the shores of Lake Minnetonka, was featured in the movie *The Heartbreak Kid*. The kitchen, pantry, and greenhouse are paved with two-inch-thick marble floors Jacobs picked up when the old Federal Reserve Bank in downtown Minneapolis was torn down.

Like many other things Jacobs has purchased, the house today is worth a lot more than he paid for it.

Jacobs and his wife, Alexandra (known as Alex, she and Irwin were married when he was twenty-one and she was twenty), have raised five children there. Jacobs is close to all his children, particularly to a daughter who is retarded. He has been known to leave business discussions and negotiations to talk with his children on the phone or to pick up one who is flying back from college. A tall man with curly black hair, Jacobs enjoys it all. "Life's been good to me," he says.

There have been ups and downs. Jacobs seems, however, to have the knack of turning even his downs into ups. His first foray into the beer business is a good example.

HOWEVER PROFITABLE, USED bags and insurance salvage were not big business, and by 1974, Irwin Jacobs was ready for bigger things. "There was something about big business that had a mystique in it," he says.

Using a bank loan of $4 million (the loan was from Carl Pohlad's bank; the Pohlad connection grew out of this loan), he bought Grain Belt Breweries. Grain Belt was a regional brewing company with three brands of beer: Grain Belt, Hauenstein, and Storz. He thought the company was undervalued and that he could make it more profitable. He was wrong. "I found out that I didn't have the abilities and didn't know as much about it as I thought," he says with refreshing candor. Grain Belt made a profit only part of the year. Jacobs thought that good management and shrewd marketing would make Grain Belt profitable in all four quarters. Unfortunately, the problem wasn't amenable to either management or marketing. The problem was geographical and meteorological. Minneapolis is in the upper Midwest. It gets awfully cold up there.

Beer just isn't very popular in Minnesota in the winter.

Jacobs tried everything. He even made a commercial, exhorting people to buy Grain Belt brands with the tag line: "It may be my brewery, but it's your beer." It didn't help. At the end of a year, he had spent $1 million and the company hadn't turned around. "I got murdered," Jacobs says. "I never worked so hard in my life." He was depressed and ready to throw in the towel. "I said to myself, 'What do I need any more money for? I've had enough of big business.'"

So he looked around for someone to buy the company. No one offered what he wanted, so he decided to liquidate it. His old skills hadn't left him. He auctioned off the plant and the machinery, then sold the rights to the three beer brand names to G. Heileman Brewing for $3.9 million. He discovered that selling off the parts can be a lot more profitable than selling off the whole company. He made enough on the pieces of Grain Belt to pay off his $4 million loan and walk away with a $5 million profit.

Jacobs didn't need to be told twice that he had just discovered a gold mine. The $5 million was the source of his contribution to the purchase of the W. T. Grant assets.

That deal was still bringing in money in 1985.

JACOBS LEARNED ONE other thing from his experiences at Grain Belt. "I decided that what I wanted to do was make investments in other peoples' businesses. I didn't want to buy the business."

His actions, however, give a slightly different picture. In quick succession, he picked up large stock positions in several companies, made takeover bids, was rebuffed, then sold out at a profit. In 1977, it was Sonesta International Hotels ($700,000 profit). In 1978, it was Holly Sugar ($4 million profit) and Gamble-Skogmo, a manufacturer and retailer of women's apparel ($500,000). He lost on only one deal, Republic Airlines. He dropped $1 million on that one.

If, as Jacobs says, he didn't want to buy the businesses, then his takeover bids were classic examples of greenmail. But Jacobs disagrees. "I never sold any stock back to Holly. I sold my stock on the open market, as everybody else did. The Sonesta offer was made to all shareholders. I didn't get any more than anybody else. . . . I have never sold my stock back to a company under the greenmail theory and stuck all the other shareholders doing it." He adds, "I have never bought stock in a company with the intention of muscling them to buy my stock back."

And in fact, there were some companies he did take over. In 1979, he bought Watkins Co. Watkins, which sold spices door-to-door and through parties (like Tupperware), was in bankruptcy. Jacobs paid $2 million for Watkins and brought in new management. The new management doubled sales to $50 million a year. Watkins became profitable.

In 1980, he got in trouble with the Federal Reserve over one of the companies he acquired. He bought a small bank holding company, Mid America, and almost immediately sold off the banks. The Fed charged that he had acted in bad faith, liquidating the company so soon after he bought it. Jacobs, in turn, sued the Fed for "gross abuse of power." Eventually, he paid a $100,000 fine to settle the enforcement proceedings.

He also made a $12 million profit on the deal.

Besides Republic Airlines, there was another case where he didn't pick the right company. This story had a different ending than the Republic deal. This time, Jacobs made use of his seeming ability to come out on top anyway.

In 1978, he bought into Arctic Enterprises, eventually accumulating a 25-percent interest in the company for $5 million. Though a large stockholder, he disclaimed any interest in running the company. He was simply looking for a good investment, he said.

And Arctic appeared to be just that. Already successful when Jacobs bought in, for the next two years the company's profits soared, with sales of over $100 million. Arctic Enterprises had profitable divisions in boat-building and other things, but primarily it was riding the crest of a new boom, snowmobiling. The Arctic Cat snowmobile was a major force in a fast-growing market. Arctic expanded dramatically, and the future looked rosy.

Then the bottom fell out.

Despite the good earnings, there had been a few storm clouds on the horizon. In the late seventies, Arctic, trying to maximize earnings, had bought up its previously independent dealer network. This meant that Arctic made more money on each machine sold, but at the same time, Arctic didn't get any money *until* the machine sold. Where the dealers had paid Arctic immediately upon shipment, Arctic now had to wait for individual sales. Earnings were better than ever, but cash flow became erratic. Seasonal businesses always have erratic cash flows—Jacobs should have been very familiar with that after Grain Belt Brewing—and snowmobiles are certainly seasonal. The boat-building divisions helped balance out the seasonality, but snowmobiles were the booming part of the business.

Snowmobiles were also a very competitive business. By some estimates, as many as two hundred manufacturers were produc-

ing snowmobiles in the late seventies. Many of them were distributed only in the region where they were made. While the
Arctic Cat snowmobiles were distributed nationally, the majority
of sales were in the Midwest and upper Midwest. This made them
vulnerable to changes in the local market. A company with a
balanced distribution of sales can carry a weak market; a local-
ized company is more severely affected.

Despite erratic cash flow and a concentrated market base,
though, everything was just fine at Arctic Enterprises through
1979. Then came the 1980 model.

In 1980, Arctic brought out new models. Immediately, they had
problems. One model had a tendency to catch fire because of
sticking brakes. A second had a rash of piston and crankshaft
failures. It was nothing that couldn't be handled. The bugs could
be cleared up and the machines' reputations restored. Warranty
repair costs soared and sales went down, making cash flow worse
than ever, but setbacks occur in every industry. The combination
of poor cash flow and expensive warranty repairs should have
been survivable. All Arctic required was a little luck, a bit of
breathing room to recover and get their house in order.

"The third year of my investment," Jacobs says, "there was no
snow."

The lack of snow was the straw that broke the camel's back. A
very large, very heavy straw. Actually, there were two years in a
row of poor snow, the same snowless period that nearly destroyed
the western ski resorts. Snowmobiling continued, but the boom
was over.

At the same time, interest rates skyrocketed, reaching 20 percent. Arctic Enterprises was not alone in going under; among
other firms that pulled out of snowmobiles were such giants as
Kawasaki and John Deere. (By 1985, there were only four manufacturers of snowmobiles left.) But being in good company is a
poor consolation prize. Arctic filed for a Chapter 11 (voluntary)
bankruptcy.

Jacobs had been here before. It must have seemed like Grain
Belt Brewing all over again. He was the largest shareholder, the
man identified in Wall Street's mind with the company. "I was
confident I was going to be branded for the rest of my life with this

failure. Maybe that's what motivated me more than anything else."

Jacobs decided it was time to forsake his role of large but passive stockholder. Using his block as leverage, he took an active managing role in Arctic and began to do what he did best—look for value where no one else could find it. He sold off the snowmobile division that had done so much for the company, first positively then negatively. He concentrated the company's assets in the boat divisions. Whereas everything the company did the year before it went into bankruptcy seemed to turn to ashes, the road back was a different experience. "Everything we did was right," he says. "No matter what I do in my life, there is nothing that will duplicate it."

Nine months after Arctic filed bankruptcy, Jacobs had successfully rehabilitated the company. Renamed Minstar, the former Arctic Enterprises emerged from bankruptcy with $6.3 million in cash and three profitable boat divisions. By 1984 it had earnings of $23 million on sales of over $1 billion.

Minstar is the vehicle Jacob often uses for his raids, just as Steinberg uses Reliance. But in the early days, at least, he was acquiring, not raiding. The distinction is sometimes hard to see, for every raider at least *says* he is out to acquire the target company. The difference is that Jacobs did acquire a lot of companies. He also continued to add to his reputation as Irv the Liquidator.

Jacobs's strategy has been to follow the formula that worked so well at Arctic Enterprises. He buys up a badly run company and ruthlessly prunes away the divisions he doesn't want. The remainder becomes a part of Minstar. "It really is common sense. If you're looking at the long term in something, you must look at the highest and best use, at redeployment." And he contends, "We have never bought a business with the intention of closing it down and liquidating it."

But he has liquidated a lot of parts.

JACOBS NEXT MADE headlines in a big way in connection with Pabst Brewing Co. It all began in 1980 when Jacobs and four other Minneapolis businessmen bought an 8.3-percent stake in Pabst, then the third largest brewer in the country. Pabst management showed no alarm. Despite his dealings with Holly Sugar, Mid America, and other companies, in 1980 Jacobs was not known as a raider, though he was still stuck with the Irv the Liquidator label. A few days after Jacobs's purchase became public knowledge, Pabst chairman and CEO Frank C. DeGuire announced that Jacobs's group was simply interested in Pabst as "an investment."

Jacobs's investment in Pabst was to establish his reputation as a raider.

THE FIGHT FOR Pabst was one of the more complicated in the history of modern takeovers. By the time it was over, Pabst had fought off seven different takeover attempts; it seemed as if everyone had sued every possible combination of everyone else at least once, and three years had gone by. The plot is Byzantine in its complexity.

In February of 1981, Pabst president Anthony Amendola resigned. A marketing man who had taken the job in 1979, he left, citing differences with chairman and CEO DeGuire, who took over the presidency. Analysts were quick to point the finger in a different direction—slumping sales. Five months later, DeGuire also quit the presidency and resigned from the job of CEO as well, though he stayed on as chairman. An "interim" president, Thomas N. McGowan, an attorney and Pabst director, took up the reins.

Jacobs was surprised by DeGuire's resignation. "I view the situation with alarm. I'm going to monitor the company very closely," he said. A week later, he announced that his group now held 9.5 percent of Pabst stock and that he wanted five seats on Pabst's board. He also announced that he wanted to be chairman of the board.

Pabst promised to think about it. Two weeks later, they elected Jacobs a director. He didn't get the other four seats or the chairmanship, as he had demanded, but, in public at least, he expressed no disappointment. "I feel very good," he said. "I'm confident about the future." As a director, he felt he was now in a position to do something about what he called the "lack of leadership and direction at Pabst."

One of the things he wanted to do something about was Thomas McGowan. Jacobs did not think McGowan was the right man for the presidency of Pabst. Jacobs had announced when he first sought the directorships that he would press the search for a new president. (McGowan's appointment had, after all, been on an "interim" basis until a new president could be found.) Jacobs disclaimed any interest in the job for himself. (He was, remember, also involved in rescuing Arctic Enterprises at the time.)

Meanwhile, things were looking bleaker for Pabst. In addition to the slumping sales that had caused first Amendola and then DeGuire to resign, the competitive situation was getting worse. One of Pabst's competitors, G. Heileman Brewing Co., had just announced its intention of taking over another Pabst competitor, Jos. Schlitz Brewing Co. The combined firms would be stronger than either on its own and would only make competition more difficult for Pabst.

But Jacobs was now on the board and Pabst became more aggressive. A week after Jacobs was elected, on August 4, 1981, Pabst tendered for Schlitz, offering $588 million to top Heileman's $494 million bid. This was the kind of dynamic action Jacobs felt Pabst needed to stay alive.

It didn't last. One month later, Pabst had lost the fight for Schlitz, and Jacobs resigned as a director. Jacobs was not happy. He charged that he had presented Pabst with a program of action designed to help the company and that, after the board had approved the action, "an executive officer of the company subverted and failed to carry out the directions of the board." Most observers felt he was talking about McGowan. Jacobs asked the board to remove the "officer" and the members of the board who had supported his activities. When the board refused, he resigned, saying it was impossible for him "as a director to make any meaningful contribution to the progress of the company." He added, darkly, that "interested parties will act in due course to provide Pabst with an effective board of directors."

He asked for a copy of the shareholders list and, when it was refused, filed suit to get it. In December, the list in hand, he announced his intention of waging a proxy fight to unseat the board. He promised he had no intention of selling or liquidating the company. His nickname was still haunting him.

In January 1982, Pabst began its defense. The company filed suit against Jacobs, charging illegal stock purchases and attempted greenmail.

At the same time, though, it was forced to announce its first loss year since 1958, which didn't add to management's popularity with stockholders—a dangerous position to be in at the start of a takeover defense. Dissatisfied shareholders are more easily persuaded to sell their stock.

But Pabst's management was still prepared to fight hard. It also announced that three of its directors, all over seventy-two years old, had resigned to make way for younger men who would strengthen the company. They certainly strengthened the board. One was an American Stock Exchange governor and a former partner in Lazard Frere, one was the president and CEO of Briggs & Stratton, and one was the chairman and president of Federal Signal. Heavy hitters all—just the kind of people you want on your side in a fight.

Then a new factor entered the game. William Smith, Pabst's new chief executive, had mentioned in an interview that Pabst might be interested in acquiring C. Schmidt & Sons, a closely held, profitable Philadelphia brewing company. Schmidt quickly told Pabst it wasn't interested. Shortly thereafter, on February 22, Schmidt turned around and made an offer for Pabst. Since Schmidt was about one-quarter Pabst's size and the $16-a-share offer was only slightly higher than Pabst's stock price (and less than half Pabst's book value) it looked like Schmidt was practicing the Pac-Man defense (the company about to be acquired strikes back by trying to acquire the acquiring company; this can result in a stand-off where both sides give in, or it can end with the second company controlling the first after the first has acquired the second).

Most Pac-Man defenses are meant to be scare tactics. Nonetheless, Pabst couldn't simply ignore it. The Schmidt tender offer diverted management attention just as Jacobs's more serious threat came to fruition.

Jacobs had not been idle. In February, he sent out his proxy solicitation, seeking control of the board of directors. In the solicitation, he announced that if he got control of the company, he would have the company buy back 25 percent of its shares for $20 a share—an inducement for shareholders to vote for him, as they would know that if he got control he would be bidding in the market for stock at a higher price than it was currently selling for. Earnings per share would also increase—which would help the stock price of the unacquired stock—after the buyback because there would be less stock outstanding. The solicitation papers also revealed that his group now owned 13.1 percent of Pabst's stock.

Then Jacobs had his first setback. A Wisconsin court ruled that the Jacobs group had used false and misleading statements to pick up its 13.1 percent interest in Pabst and that a hearing "to determine sanctions" would take place in April. By casting doubt on the legitimacy of Jacobs's actions, this gave Pabst an advantage in the proxy fight.

Meanwhile, in another maneuver, Pabst asked Schmidt to increase its offer to $25 a share, implying they would be willing to be taken over at that price. Schmidt refused. Some observers felt Pabst had expected the refusal and was simply trying to persuade shareholders that if they stuck with management, management would get a better deal for them than Jacobs could offer.

Pabst also got another shot in the arm for its fight. It was able to announce that its first quarter had been profitable.

Schmidt reacted to the Pabst request for a raise in the tender by accusing Pabst of bad faith. Schmidt charged that Pabst had attempted to "influence and compromise one of Schmidt's major sources of financing immediately after Schmidt had disclosed the lender's identity to Pabst." Pabst was certainly playing hardball —which is, of course, the name of the game in takeovers.

Pabst's annual meeting was held in April. The results of the proxy vote would take two weeks to be counted, but immediately after the meeting, Jacobs charged that Pabst had used "unfair and illegal" methods to seek proxies. Jacobs's group, which now owned 16 percent of Pabst, obviously thought they had lost.

Two weeks later, Pabst announced that 54 percent of the proxies had voted for management and against Jacobs.

The first round was over. The second round was about to begin.

THE SECOND ROUND began when Pabst announced it had reached agreement for a friendly takeover of Olympia Brewing Co. Pabst planned to acquire 49 percent of Olympia. The extra debt issued to finance the buyout of Olympia would, of course, make Pabst itself less attractive—a standard form of shark repellent.

Jacobs was not deterred. On June 18, 1982, he attacked again. He announced that JMSL Acquisitions, a company formed by a group of investors that included himself, would offer $22 a share—cash—for Pabst. The deal had a catch to it designed to persuade Pabst—and its shareholders—not to let the Olympia merger go through. If Pabst called off the takeover of Olympia, Jacobs said he would pay $24 a share for Pabst instead of $22.

To finance the deal, JMSL said it had an agreement to sell some of Pabst's assets to Heileman after the takeover. Heileman was the company that Pabst had fought over Schlitz.

The Justice Department, which has the option of intervening if it feels antitrust regulations are being violated, immediately said it would review the proposed deal and rule on whether there was a potential for antitrust action if Heileman took over any part of Pabst.

The Justice Department rulings in a case like this are simple. If it finds no basis for antitrust action, it says so. If it does find a basis, it threatens a civil antitrust suit if the deal is consummated. In that case, a company is free to ignore the ruling and fight Justice in court or to try to strike a deal with Justice that will allow the deal to go through in a modified form that meets Justice's objections.

In a proxy fight, the threat of an antitrust suit can make investors nervous. Once in court, a deal can be stalled for years while litigation continues. Jacobs could only hope that Justice would find nothing it objected to.

Other people were being made nervous by all the maneuvering. On June 23, Pittsburgh Brewing Co., a small regional brewer, announced it was calling off the previously announced Pabst takeover of Pittsburgh "because the growing number of uncertainties and changing conditions—including the recent offer of Irwin L. Jacobs, a dissident Pabst stockholder, to acquire Pabst—has had a substantial effect on the proposed merger."

On July 6, Pabst came up with a modified white-squire defense. Pabst made a new pact with Olympia Brewing Co. Taking advantage of the fact that the Justice Department review of Jacobs's proposed takeover would keep Jacobs from acting for a time, Pabst announced that Olympia would make a two-tier tender for Pabst's shares. Shareholders who tendered immediately—before learning whether Jacobs would get permission to continue—would receive $25 a share. Shareholders who waited would get only $18 of a convertible preferred stock.

It was a slick move. Anyone who waited for Jacobs would be taking a chance. If the Justice Department turned him down, their only option would be the $18-a-share offer. If they accepted right away, they would get $25 a share. The idea was to preempt Jacobs while he was hampered by the Justice Department review.

Olympia would end up owning a large chunk of Pabst—and Pabst, which would go ahead with the previously announced takeover, would end up controlling Olympia. Pabst's management would, of course, then control the stock that Olympia had bought.

Pabst also announced it was suing Jacobs and Heileman. Two days later, Jacobs countersued Pabst and Olympia, charging that the Olympia purchase of Pabst stock was a thinly disguised "illegal self-tender offer made by Pabst for the benefit of its management and at the expense of Pabst stockholders."

The Justice Department soon undercut Jacobs's whole case. On July 22, it said it would challenge Jacobs's purchase of Pabst because of his agreement with Heileman.

On July 23, Jacobs halted his tender offer. He hadn't given up wanting control of Pabst, though. He told the press that he and his associates would explore "various alternative means to accomplish that end."

Pabst president William Smith had a sign up on his office wall that summed things up very well: Show me a good loser and I'll show you a loser.

Round two was over.

ROUND THREE EXPLODED into the open on September 16. Pabst sued Jacobs (again), this time to prevent the solicitation of written consents.

Consents were a new wrinkle in the takeover game. Most companies had provisions for written consents in their charters, but they were rarely used except by closely held corporation directors who wished to do something without convening a directors' meeting. Until, that is, Jacobs decided to use them as a shortcut in a takeover battle.

Basically, a written consent is a signed statement from a shareholder authorizing an action. If anyone accumulates enough written consents, whatever the consents authorize takes place—even the overthrow of the board of directors. Consents are like proxies, authorizing a specific action, but the requirement that a stockholders' meeting take place is eliminated, as are some of the other costly and time-consuming procedures involved in a proxy fight. It is a very quick maneuver—that's what it was designed for—and leaves directors little time to take counter action. (As a result of Jacobs's surprise use of the consent and its subsequent use in other raids—Steinberg, for example, used consents in the Disney raid—most companies have restricted consents as part of standard shark repellent.)

By bringing suit, Pabst was seeking to prevent a *fait accompli.* If Jacobs accumulated written consents from more than 50 percent of the voting stock, he would accomplish an end run around the board. He was asking consent for the replacement of the board of directors.

On September 20, Jacobs announced his group had written consent from 50.7 percent of the stockholders to oust the board of directors. It looked as if he had won.

Less than four weeks later, though, the Federal District Court in Delaware (Pabst's state of incorporation) ruled on technical grounds that the consents were invalid. End of round three.

ROUND FOUR BEGAN thirteen days after the court decision. On October 26, 1982, Jacobs offered $24 a share for Pabst's shares.

The next day, a new bidder entered the picture. Heileman Brewing topped Jacobs's offer with one at $25 a share.

Now there were two competing bids for Pabst. A bidding war is a wonderful thing—if you're a stockholder. It can be very expensive if you're a bidder.

Pabst said it would support the Heileman offer. Pabst was now willing to settle for almost anyone except Jacobs.

Heileman's offer—and Pabst's acceptance—was not as strange as it seems. Heileman had figured out a way around the antitrust rules. It would take over Pabst and Olympia—the original Pabst-Olympia pact was still in place—and keep only those assets that would not put it in jeopardy with the Justice Department. It would then spin off to the remaining Pabst and Olympia stockholders—those who hadn't tendered—the remaining parts as a separate company that would continue to use the Pabst name. Some might wonder why Pabst continued to fight Jacobs—who Pabst feared would sell off divisions if he took over the company—while welcoming Heileman, which planned to do the same. The difference was simple and had little to do with which deal would be better for Pabst and its shareholders. Jacobs had plainly indicated his intention to shake up Pabst's management. On the other hand, Pabst's current management expected to run the spun-off company if Heileman's bid succeeded.

As is frequently the case in takeover battles, the executives at Pabst were looking out for their own jobs. This quite understandable tendency has given raiders their most potent argument in opposing antitakeover legislation.

On November 9, before Heileman's announced but not yet begun offer became official, Jacobs offer was finished. He had agreed to buy 3 million shares of Pabst. Over 5 million were tendered. It was a fully successful tender.

The next day, Jacobs received the welcome news that the Justice Department would not challenge his takeover this time. Everything was set. All he had to do was wait the ten days required by law, and he would control Pabst.

Heileman raised its offer to $27.50 a share and went ahead with its offer anyway. Timing was crucial here. Jacobs's deal was not yet consummated, and shareholders could withdraw tendered stock if they wished—and tender it to Heileman—up until midnight of November 26, the end of the ten-day waiting period.

Jacobs sued Heileman, Olympia, and Pabst, seeking to prevent the Heileman tender offer. If he could even delay Heileman until November 26, the Heileman tender would be moot. Jacobs would own the controlling interest.

On November 22, Heileman entered into a consent agreement with the Justice Department, laying out which Pabst assets it could keep. Heileman was now free to go ahead with its offer.

Jacobs raised his offer to $30 a share, $3 more than Heileman's, and raised the amount he would accept to 5.5 million shares. The increased amount was designed to remove uncertainty among the shareholders who had tendered as to whether their shares would be taken. As 5.3 million shares were tendered and the original tender was for 3 million, had the amount not been raised, 2.3 million shares—almost half—would have been returned to their holders. This might have led to a stampede toward Heileman to guarantee receiving something. By this time, the arbitrageurs were in the deal in a big way. Arbitrageurs are stock dealers who buy large blocks of stock on the open market for fractions below the tender price—giving a stockholder almost the same price as the tender but without having to wait to be paid—then tender the stock and make the small profit on each share, a big profit when millions of shares are involved. Arbs have no loyalty; their profits involve turning over the stock as quickly as possible with the least risk. Jacobs was making sure they would keep their stock tendered to him.

But a higher price does not always guarantee that you will win. Credibility is one question—does the raider have the money to really take over the company? No one doubted that Jacobs would buy the tendered shares, but how long would it be before he bought up the rest of the stock—if he did? Heileman had laid out a plan for the company. To many people, it was the more attractive offer because they knew from the start what was going to happen.

Jacobs raised his offer again—to $35—but by now the backroom negotiations had begun in earnest. On November 26, Jacobs announced that he was now backing a revised Heileman two-tier bid at $29 a share (the first 5.6 million shares submitted would receive $29 a share; remaining shareholders would receive $24 face amount in 15-percent ten-year notes). The fine print explained it all. Heileman was going to pay Jacobs's group $29 in cash plus $7.5 million in expenses. Heileman was buying Jacobs off, paying him to discontinue his bid.

It looked like it was all over. Jacobs's group would not get Pabst, but they would walk away with a profit of over $20 million.

Not all of Jacobs's partners were happy, however. Paul Kalmanovitz, a California multimillionaire with controlling interests in two closely held, small private brewers and one public brewing company (Falstaff Brewing Co.), and large real-estate holdings, had been one of the financial backers of JMSL Acquiring Co., the vehicle Jacobs was using to go after Pabst. The seventy-seven-year-old Kalmanovitz—once described by *Fortune* magazine as "wealthy and eccentric"—disagreed with Jacobs's decision to take the money and run. Not content to protest in private, he went public, charging that Jacobs had negotiated the deal behind his back. He threatened to sue to block the Heileman bid on antitrust law and securities law grounds. Kalmanovitz said he would do everything he could to keep JMSL in the bidding and charged that Heileman had offered him a $5 million "bribe" to withdraw from the bidding.

Three days later he announced he was preparing his own tender offer for Pabst, saying he was afraid the Heileman-Pabst combination would adversely affect one of his companies, General Brewing, which had operations in the northwest. On the first of December, he sent a telegram to Jacobs threatening him with legal action for "breach of agreement" and "interference... with our contractual relationships." Two days later he made a tender offer for Pabst. The two-tier transaction would pay $32 a share for 4,150,000 shares and $26 in 15-percent notes for the remainder.

Pabst and Heileman filed suit to block the tender. At the same time, Jacobs formally announced that JMSL had discontinued its tender offer.

For Pabst and Heileman, the fight was to go on. (Kalmanovitz was finally to take over Pabst in May of 1985.) For Jacobs, though, it was all over but the shouting. Legal suits and inquiries would continue for years, but that is part and parcel of the takeover game. Of the $20 million profit made by his syndicate, Jacobs personally had made $11.5 million before taxes—a nice consolation prize even if he didn't have Pabst. The deal had begun in November 1980 with the disclosure of his interest in Pabst. His part of it ended in December of 1982.

Jacobs keeps a reminder of that deal in his office. It is a model of a ship. The sails are made of cut-up Pabst beer cans.

ONE OF THE things that differentiates Jacobs from fellow raiders such as Carl Icahn or T. Boone Pickens is that Jacobs rarely concentrates on one deal at a time. While others may be buying shares in more than one company in preparation for future deals, they generally go after only one company at a time. There have been few times in Jacobs's career when he has not been making headlines in connection with more than one company.

While still engaged in the Pabst takeover attempt(s), Jacobs was also going after another target. The company was Kaiser Steel.

Kaiser was a classic takeover candidate. Its stock was selling for under $18 a share, but its book value was about $37 a share. It had recently taken very large write-offs for discontinued operations, which meant the balance sheet probably represented Kaiser's true value. Some reserves were carried at cost, including some 900 million tons of coal reserves. Carried on the books at $54 million, some experts put their worth as high as $200 million.

Kaiser had scared away other suitors, though. It had huge unfunded pension liabilities. It also had a medical plan that was so open-ended as to make it impossible to guess at its future cost: all employees with fifteen years or more at Kaiser *and* their wives and children were guaranteed lifetime medical coverage.

There were other negatives. Kaiser's coal-mining and steel-fabricating businesses were profitable, but basic steel production had lost $125 million in 1982; basic steel had been profitable only one year in the prior six. Nevertheless, Jacobs thought he saw value, and in December, just as Pabst was winding up, he began to buy. It is even possible that the potential he saw at Kaiser persuaded him to accept the Heileman offer over Kalmanovitz's objections. He may have wanted to free up his cash—and profit—to go after the bigger game of a steel company.

By February, Jacobs's group owned over 16 percent of Kaiser at a cost of $31.2 million—most of it, as usual, borrowed money. His average price was just under $26.50 a share. In May, he made a takeover proposal to Kaiser's management. It was turned down. Jacobs threatened a proxy fight. When he next made an offer late in the month it was accepted. He was offering $19.50 a share plus one share of a $25-face-value redeemable preferred stock for each share of Kaiser. Total cost: $278 million. But, as with most leveraged buyouts, most of the money would come from loans backed by the value of the corporation.

In June, a hitch developed. Jacobs's group was suddenly "unwilling" (to use Kaiser's phrase) to go ahead. Then, just as suddenly, the deal moved forward again.

There was little public explanation of the hitch, but behind the scenes a great deal of maneuvering had gone on. The hitch had developed because Jacobs's group had wanted to get the same deal for their 16 percent of Kaiser as they were offering for the rest of the company—in other words, they wanted Kaiser to agree to allow the Jacobs group to use the money they were borrowing against Kaiser to buy back the stock owned by the Jacobs group. Kaiser balked, then gave in.

Generally, when a group of investors buys stock in a firm and then takes it over with a leveraged buyout, the remaining shareholders are bought out with the borrowed money, leaving the takeover group the sole shareholders. Jacobs's plan was different, and that is why Kaiser required some persuasion to agree to it.

The money borrowed in an LBO is borrowed against the assets of the company being acquired. Thus there is little or no cost to the acquiring group beyond the cost of their original stock purchase. In Jacobs's case, his group had paid $31 million for the 16-percent interest they held in Kaiser. In a normal LBO, the proceeds of the LBO borrowing would have been used to buy all the shares of stock not already held by the buyer.

Had Jacobs's group followed standard procedure, KS Holdings (a company formed for this acquisition), would have paid $19.50

in cash plus securities for the outstanding stock, raising the money through the LBO. Adding the newly acquired stock to the 16-percent interest it already owned, KS would have owned Kaiser. Its cost would have been the $31 million KS had paid for its 16-percent interest.

But Jacobs proposed a different scenario. He wanted KS Holdings to be *included* in the leveraged buyout of shareholders. In his proposal, Kaiser, rather than KS, would make the LBO. The buyout would pay KS the same $19.50 a share for its 16 percent as other stockholders would receive. At $19.50 a share, KS's shares were worth $23 million. Since the buyout would be paid for with money borrowed at no cost to KS, the entire $23 million would go to reduce the cost of acquiring the stock in the first place. KS's cost would be reduced to $8 million.

Kaiser would then own 100 percent of its own stock while KS owned none. Kaiser would then merge with a subsidiary of KS Holdings and Jacobs's group would own Kaiser.

Jacobs was proposing that KS take over Kaiser, a $278 million deal, for a total outlay of $8 million. As the saying goes: Nice work if you can get it.

The merger agreement also guaranteed KS Holdings a first-year dividend of $5 million. Thus, at the end of the first year, the Jacobs syndicate's cost would be reduced to $3 million. Finally, if Kaiser's net worth remained above a figure specified in the buyout contract, KS would be guaranteed an *additional* $5 million payout.

It all seemed ideal. However, a clause in the contract allowed Kaiser to cancel if someone came up with a better offer. Someone did. Another group, led by J. A. Frates of Tulsa, Oklahoma, topped Jacobs's bid. At first, Jacobs resisted. He went into the market and began to buy stock, seeking to accumulate enough to block the Frates group. But soon thereafter, Frates and Jacobs began negotiations.

In the end, in return for Jacobs's support of their takeover proposal, the Frates group agreed to pay the Jacobs group a premium of $12-a-share more than the other shareholders would receive. Jacobs and his partners made a $30.8 million profit on the deal.

Not winning his tenders was proving very lucrative.

MINSTAR FINALLY LANDED a good-sized fish in 1983. While not quite as big as Kaiser or Pabst, it was still a nice catch. For $92 million, Minstar bought up Bekins Co., the fifth-largest household moving company in the country. Jacobs personally guaranteed the loan.

Bekins was a poor performer and widely held to be badly managed. (Shortly after he took it over, Jacobs charged that some Bekins managers were involved in a kickback scheme.) Bekins also had a lot of real estate on its books at far less than market value. Bekins holdings in California alone, on the books at $52 million, were estimated to be worth as much as $100 million.

A year later, Minstar went after another addition to its family. Jacobs bid for Aegis Corp., a Fort Lauderdale-based mini-conglomerate, in what he called "a pounce." For months, he quietly bought up shares of Aegis but stopped before he reached the 5-percent level that would require notifying the SEC. Then, on April 6, 1984, he announced a tender for Aegis stock. The etiquette of takeovers requires that the target company be notified before the public announcement, Jacobs called Aegis CEO Castle W. Jordan at 7 A.M. to tell him what was about to happen. According to Jacobs, he was prepared for the usual acrimonious response. Instead, Jacobs says, Jordan was philosophical, remarking that he had long dreaded receiving an early-morning notification call.

But that was the last pleasant surprise Jacobs had. Aegis sought out a white knight and found it in DMG Inc. A lengthy tug-of-war ensued, complete with the usual court cases. This time, though, unlike Pabst, Jacobs won in court and ended up getting Aegis for $58 million.

He was primarily after an Aegis division, Wellcraft Marine Corp., a boat-builder. After the takeover, Jacobs proved again that he and his managers knew their stuff when it came to running a company. Wellcraft was integrated with the rest of Minstar's boat division. Research and purchasing were combined, cost-cutting was emphasized, and a stock incentive plan was begun.

The result? In 1984, Wellcraft earned an operating profit of $12.3 million, up 224 percent from the 1983 results. "It was just a matter of managing their businesses better," Jacobs says.

The acquisition of Bekins and Aegis catapulted Minstar's profits and stock price. Minstar's stock price doubled on a 73-percent profit rise.

Ironically, the sharp rise in Minstar made *it* attractive to raiders. In early 1985, Leucadia National Corporation, a consumer finance company controlled by Ian M. Cumming and Joseph S. Steinberg, began buying Minstar stock, accumulating about 10 percent of the outstanding shares. Since Jacobs owned only about 30 percent of Minstar (his percentage had been higher, but financings in 1984 and 1985 had diluted his holdings), he did not have absolute ownership of the company. Leucadia could be dangerous; as *Business Week* put it, Leucadia "typically does not make passive investments." Leucadia said in an SEC filing that it had no intention of seeking control of Minstar, but everybody says that. It is not illegal to say you aren't interested and then, later, change your mind. Publicly, Jacobs was not worried. "If someone wants to buy our company, let them come forth if they can do better," he said.

Privately, however, he took action that looked remarkably like a takeover target seeking a white squire. On March 19, 1985, Minstar announced that Carl Icahn was buying 500,000 shares of Minstar at a cost of $8 million to $10 million. Jacobs had recently helped Icahn out in the multi-party raid on Phillips Petroleum; many observers felt Icahn was now returning the favor.

Unlike the pirates of old, at least some modern raiders stick together.

FOR IRWIN JACOBS, 1984 was a banner year. He was now, with Pabst and Kaiser behind him, a well-known raider. His actions in 1985 were to move him into select company. Soon his name was being mentioned in the same breath as Carl Icahn or Saul Steinberg. In the course of twelve months, Jacobs was to go after Walt Disney, Phillips Petroleum, Tidewater Marine, and Avco. He successfully took over Aegis. His investments in RCA were to make headlines despite repeated denials that he was interested in the company. Jacobs had now reached the big time, where even a hint of his interest in a stock could send rumors flying and prices climbing.

Jacobs next raid began innocently enough; in the beginning it wasn't even Jacobs's raid. It throws some light on the behind-the-scenes financing and profits of all the raiders—and their backers.

When Saul Steinberg went after Disney, one of the people approached to back him financially was Jacobs. Jacobs agreed to lend Steinberg $35 million. That this type of commitment may be considered routine in certain circles is demonstrated by the fact that immediately after signing the papers Jacobs took his family to Greece on vacation. It was while reading the papers in Athens that he learned that Disney had bought out Steinberg. He called his office to ask what was happening.

What had happened was that he had received a check for $570,000 from Steinberg. The money was Jacobs's fee for agreeing to lend the $35 million—money that was never lent, merely promised.

With most of the silent partners and backers in raiders' deals, this would have been the end of the story. The investor would have deposited his check and waited for the raider to call about his next deal. But Jacobs is himself a raider, and his outlook is different. Steinberg's interest in Disney sparked his own. He took a good look at the company and came to the same conclusion Steinberg had: Disney was considerably undervalued and poorly managed.

In the meantime, Disney's stock had gone down, a frequent occurrence after a company has paid greenmail. (Investors and speculators, disappointed that a takeover won't happen, dump the stock.) Taking advantage of the slump, Jacobs began buying stock, accumulating 5.8 percent.

The problem with trying to take over Disney was the presence of the Bass Brothers, the Fort Worth investors who had come to Disney's rescue during the Steinberg raid. The Basses were just as experienced in corporate-takeover strategy as Jacobs—the only thing that differentiates their deals from those of most raiders is that most of the Basses' deals are not hostile—and they can be formidable opponents.

Jacobs persevered, however, charging that Disney was badly managed and needed to be reorganized. Charged in turn with planning to dismantle the company, Jacobs responded that, if the company would be more profitable in parts than as a whole, it should be done. Like Pickens and Icahn in similar circumstances, he took the moral high ground, saying that he represented the individual shareholder against the interests of entrenched—and incompetent—management.

Disney tried a classic antitakeover tactic: taking over another company and loading itself up with debt to make itself less attractive, while at the same time putting substantial amounts of stock in friendly hands. Disney agreed to take over Gibson Greeting Cards for more than $300 million in cash and stock. Jacobs, who had by now accumulated 6.9 percent of Disney, charged that the Gibson deal was overpriced. He found a surprising amount of support for his position in the financial press, bolstering his position as a champion of the shareholder against management.

Jacobs threatened a proxy fight to unseat any Disney director who voted for the merger. Despite charges that he didn't have the financial backing to go after Disney (Jacobs responded, "There wasn't a one-percent chance that we couldn't put it together"), this time, unlike Pabst, he got at least the preliminary support he needed. Enough stockholders supported Jacobs to enable him to force Disney to call a stockholders' meeting. At the meeting, Jacobs planned to launch his proxy fight.

He was helped in this by both the Bass Brothers and Roy E. Disney—son of Disney co-founder Roy Disney (Roy was Walt's brother)—who owned 5 percent of Disney's stock. Although they did not give Jacobs any direct support, they too thought the Gibson deal ill-advised.

Disney backed down, paying Gibson $7.5 million as a forfeit for backing out of the deal. The outside directors of the company formed a committee to assess the future of the company. Clearly, Jacobs had been successful in putting on pressure.

Finally, Jacobs met personally with Sid Bass, offering to buy out the brothers. Bass not only refused but countered with an offer to buy out Jacobs. After some negotiations, Jacobs accepted an offer from the Bass Brothers that gave his group a profit of over $28 million. From beginning to end, Jacobs was in Disney for only four months.

Jacobs's (and Steinberg's) attacks on Disney ended up generating some *good* press for the raiders. In the aftermath of the deals,

Roy E. Disney returned to the board, and the Bass Brothers had a huge interest (over 25 percent) in the company. The Basses are shrewd operators and are not known for sitting with weak companies. Disney embarked on what most analysts felt was a long-overdue restructuring of a company that had coasted for too long. "I think Disney is better off than it's been in years," Jacobs says. "I have served a purpose in that company."

Many people would agree with him.

Jacobs keeps a Mickey Mouse phone in his office to remind himself of the deal.

A GREENMAIL BUYOUT in another company led to Jacobs's next big deal of 1984. Leucadia National Corp.—the same company that was later to buy into Minstar—went after Avco, a company with interests in consumer finance (Avco Financial) and aerospace (they make turbine engines) as well as other areas. As with Disney, after Leucadia bought off Avco, it saw its stock price drop. Jacobs bought up nearly 3 million shares.

At this point, everything was still cordial. Jacobs called Avco's CEO in November to discuss the possibility of making a bid for the company. Robert P. Bauman, Avco's CEO, made the mistake of being abrupt with Jacobs. He had no interest in Jacobs's proposal and let Jacobs know it in no uncertain terms.

It is not good policy to make a raider mad. "I was mad," Jacobs says. "Imagine! He thought it was his company!"

Whether Jacobs was truly annoyed at Bauman's assumption of possession or not, he kept buying stock. By the time he had 12.3 percent of the company, Avco was nervous, even though Jacobs had not yet made a bid. Avco went looking for a white knight. It found one in Textron, another high-tech firm with extensive defense interests.

Textron offered $47 a share for all of Avco's shares, then raised the offer to $50. Jacobs accepted happily and without protest. In three months, Jacobs's group made $31.9 million.

While all this was going on, Jacobs was making headlines in connection with a company he kept insisting he wasn't interested in. News that he had invested in RCA leaked to the financial press. Jacobs denied he had any designs on the company. "I never even had 5 percent," he says. He bought the stock, he maintains, as an investment, selling most of it later. Nevertheless, he made headlines—and, reportedly, a profit on the shares he bought and sold.

Another company he became involved with during 1984 was Tidewater Inc. Tidewater was one of the largest companies in the business of supplying services to offshore oil rigs, as well as having interests in oil and gas-drilling and other oil-industry-related business. With the decline in the oil industry, Tidewater's profits were suffering.

Many Wall Street observers felt that this time Jacobs was barking up the wrong tree. The recession—some feel it's an outright depression—in the oil industry didn't look like it was about to end anytime soon (it still doesn't). But Jacobs was undeterred. "You either believe there will be an oil and gas industry or you don't," he said. For about $37.5 million, Jacobs picked up 1.5 million shares of Tidewater. Jacobs made suggestions about selling off some of Tidewater's losing businesses, such as its Hilliard Oil and Gas subsidiary. Everything was, as Jacobs said, "very friendly, very amicable." In September, he signed an agreement with Tidewater that, in return for a full look at Tidewater's books, he would either make a friendly takeover offer or go into a standstill agreement until late in 1985. The standstill agreement restricted him to no more than 15 percent of the stock (he held 8.9 percent).

After looking things over, Jacobs did bid, offering $415 million for the 91 percent of the stock he did not own. Tidewater, though, had been looking for something more in the neighborhood of $500 million. Although everyone was still cordial, Tidewater rejected the offer. Jacobs was stuck with his standstill agreement until October 31, 1985.

He increased his shareholders to 12 percent and then watched the price of the stock go down. By the end of 1985, he was still holding the stock and had a loss of about $19 million. Meanwhile, Tidewater in September enacted a series of antitakeover moves over Jacobs's protests. Jacobs sued to have them rescinded. As 1985 drew to a close, both sides were in court, Jacobs was no longer bound by the standstill agreement, and Tidewater had scattered shark repellent far and wide. The results are still to be seen, but based on other deals where Jacobs has appeared to be the loser, no one is counting him out.

One other major investment in 1984 (spilling over into 1985) was Phillips Petroleum. Phillips Petroleum spent most of 1984 and early 1985 fighting off takeover attempts, first by T. Boone Pickens and then by Carl Icahn. Every time Phillips thought it had beaten a raider off, it seemed as if someone else's name cropped up in the newspapers. Jacobs picked up a piece of the action in Phillips twice. Though he was never a major player in the Phillips deal, he made profits both times he dipped in—and added to the nightmares of Phillips executives and board members each time.

Jacobs's major contribution to the action came in early 1985. Phillips agreed to buy out Pickens to get rid of him. Partly to pay for the buyout and partially as shark repellent, Phillips proposed a restructuring of the company. The restructuring was opposed by Carl Icahn, who had acquired a large position in Phillips. Icahn proposed a leveraged buyout of Phillips. Phillips said no and went ahead with its plans and scheduled a shareholder meeting to vote on the restructuring.

Jacobs and Ivan Boesky (an arbitraguer whose name crops up frequently in raids) lent their support to Icahn in his drive to convince shareholders to turn down the Phillips restructuring plan. They succeeded. Phillips was forced to negotiate to prevent Icahn from going ahead with his buyout attempt. In the end, Icahn and his partners were bought out, and everyone—Pickens, Icahn, Jacobs, Boesky—made a lot of money.

JACOBS'S NEXT DEAL illustrates once again his uncanny ability to change a losing situation into a winning one. On January 19, 1985, newspaper financial sections announced that Irwin Jacobs was on the prowl again. This time his target was Castle & Cooke.

Castle & Cooke was another ripe target for a raider, especially one who, like Jacobs, is convinced of his ability to take a sinking company and bring it back to profitability. Castle & Cooke was a food company, primarily known for Dole pineapple and fruits and Bumble Bee Tuna. The Honolulu-based company also had extensive real-estate holdings, some going back to land grants from the kings of Hawaii before the country was annexed by the United States.

But Castle & Cooke had fallen on hard times. In its last fiscal year (instead of a calendar year, Castle & Cooke used a fiscal year ending June 16), the company had reported a $77-million loss on revenues of $1.5 billion. In the quarter that ended December 29, 1984, it reported a loss of $35 million.

The president of Castle & Cooke, Ian R. Wilson, who had joined the company from Coca-Cola in February of 1983, had resigned in December. Finally, early in January 1984, the company, desperate for money, had agreed to sell its Bumble Bee Seafoods subsidiary to a group of investors that included some Bumble Bee executives.

Asset rich, financially troubled: Castle & Cooke was the classic raider target.

Jacobs's announcement revealed that his group had acquired 3.1 million shares, about 12 percent of the company. The announcement also said that the group was considering seeking control of Castle & Cooke, either alone or in company with a third party.

The announcement also said that Jacobs's group might sell some or all of the stock on the open market.

This failure to indicate his intentions is typical of Jacobs. "You can't predict what I'm going to do next," he says, "because there is no track, no character to it. Our big asset is our flexibility, being able to move on a moment's notice."

This is not necessarily a simple matter of a raider keeping his plans secret. Sometimes the plans aren't made yet. Later in 1985, *Fortune* magazine, speculating about Jacobs plans for ITT (see below), asked Carl Icahn if *he* knew what Jacobs was up to. Icahn replied that he didn't. "One doesn't always know oneself," Icahn added.

Eventually, Jacobs accumulated 14 percent of Castle & Cooke and made an offer for the firm. Castle & Cooke resisted and fought Jacobs to a temporary standstill. The company was aided by the fact that 20 percent of its stock was in friendly hands. Torray Clark & Co., a Bethesda, Maryland, investment company, had bought into Castle & Cooke when the stock was between $8 and $9 a share. They were in no hurry to unload, and they weren't interested in taking it over—either in partnership with Jacobs or without him. "That isn't our style," said Torray Clark president Robert E. Torray. "We are in Castle & Cooke as investors."

Torray Clark was known on Wall Street as a contrarian investment company—that is, one that invests its money contrary to prevailing trends and thinking. Interestingly enough, Torray Clark was holding a large block of Pabst stock at the time that Jacobs was trying to acquire the company. Torray Clark sided with management against Jacobs in that deal as well.

Making no headway, Jacobs finally signed a sixty-day standstill agreement.

Castle & Cooke took advantage of the breathing room to look for a white knight. It found one in Flexi-Van Corp., a container leasing company. Flexi-Van and Castle & Cooke agreed to merge.

Jacobs was not happy with the arrangement. Castle & Cooke's stock had dropped while the standstill agreement was in force and Jacobs's syndicate now had an $11 million loss; Jacobs had purchased most of his stock between $12 and $16 a share. The merger would make that loss permanent.

Jacobs filed suit to stop the merger and announced he would vote against the agreement. He also began to gather shareholder support to defeat it.

Jacobs had recently been quite successful in getting shareholders behind him in the Disney and Phillips raids, and this was no exception. Flexi-Van took it seriously. David H. Murdock, Flexi-Van's CEO (and a takeover artist of some note himself), traveled to Minneapolis to meet with Jacobs. It was beginning to look like a replay of Disney all over again—except that in Disney, Jacobs had gone to see Bass. Flexi-Van was coming to Jacobs.

Jacobs seems to do well at these negotiations. He and Sid Bass were able to come to a quick agreement, and the same held true with Murdock. Jacobs came out of the meeting with an agreement by Flexi-Van to pay his syndicate $16 a share for its stock. Castle & Cooke was then trading on the open market at under $12 a share, so Murdock was willing to pay Jacobs a substantial premium to drop out.

All told, after expenses the Jacobs group earned a profit of $7 million. They had invested $48.4 million (mostly borrowed; the expenses were chiefly interest) and held the stock from January through May.

For someone who had a paper loss of $11 million when Murdock arrived, a $7 million profit wasn't too shabby.

BY 1985, JACOBS'S Minstar had become a successful company, but it was still not as large as some of the prizes that had gotten away. In the spring and summer of 1985, however, Jacobs finally landed a prize. He took over AMF.

AMF's revenues were over a billion dollars a year. Its interests ranged from leisure-time products to industrial plants and equipment. It was also, like other raider targets, a company that has had its ups and downs.

Things began in earnest in April, when Jacobs had accumulated a 7.5-percent interest in the company. Jacobs then made his obligatory call to AMF chairman W. Thomas York. He expressed an interest in buying AMF's Hatteras boat division and mentioned that he might be interested in buying all of AMF.

It is quite possible that had York responded positively at that point nothing hostile would have taken place. The interest in the Hatteras boat division sounds genuine. Minstar's second largest profit center—after Bekins—was in its boat division, which Jacobs salvaged out of the wreck of Arctic Enterprises. It was the boat-building division that he primarily wanted when he took over Aegis. It is not unlikely that if York had said something like "we might consider selling Hatteras; why don't we talk about it?" AMF would be an independent company today.

But York didn't. He was not interested in selling any part of AMF. He also said, according to Jacobs, "We don't pay greenmail."

You shouldn't say that to Jacobs. Of all the raiders, he is most vehement in denying that he sets out to greenmail companies. "I don't want it," he says. "I don't believe in it. But," he adds, "I wouldn't necessarily refuse it if it were forced on me."

Jacobs tendered for 43 percent of AMF—12 million shares—offering $23 a share. With the 7.5 percent he already owned, 43 percent would give him absolute control.

AMF reacted quickly by spreading shark repellent. The company sent out its investment banker, Morgan Stanley, to beat the bushes for a white knight. Then it adopted a poison pill.

AMF put into place a rights offering to shareholders, triggered if a hostile buyout took place, that would allow shareholders to exchange their shares for a package of securities worth $23 a share, thus loading AMF up with debt. While not a very potent poison pill compared to some—many analysts in fact refused to call it a true poison pill, saying it was really a "fair price" offer—it was enough to make things difficult for Jacobs if allowed to stand.

AMF also alerted shareholders to the possibility that it would seek a white knight or white squire or might even go for a scorched-earth defense: AMF's defenses, a letter to shareholders said, might include "a business combination involving AMF, the sale of one or more of its businesses, or a complete or partial liquidation."

Jacobs, of course, filed suit to overcome the shark repellent.

Here, parenthetically, a question must be asked: What might Jacobs do to the company that would be so terrible that "a complete or partial liquidation" was preferable? AMF's answer was that it was protecting its shareholders. Jacobs, AMF said, was not guaranteeing that all shareholders would be treated alike. As AMF saw it, Jacobs was seeking 50.5-percent ownership. He had, AMF admitted, said he would acquire all the remaining AMF shares if his offer was successful. But, AMF pointed out, he didn't say how or when he would do it *and* he didn't guarantee he would do it at all. In fact, Jacobs specifically reserved the right to abandon the plan if he wanted—or needed—to.

Furthermore, AMF said, Jacobs had already let it be known that he did not expect to continue the dividend on the remaining AMF stock after his acquisition. AMF was laying out the specter that an AMF shareholder who did not tender—or was not accepted—in the first offer might find himself or herself a minority stockholder with no say in corporate affairs, no dividend, and, possibly, a limited market for shares.

AMF's scenarios were unlikely—Jacobs was, after all, interested in acquiring all of AMF, and a leveraged buyout was available to him to do it—but they were possible. Nevertheless, the whole thing became moot. On June 6, the Federal District Court held for Minstar. AMF's poison pill was dismantled.

Meanwhile, Jacobs began behind-the-scenes discussions with Maxxam Group, Inc., a New York-based real-estate company that had been invited by Morgan Stanley to make a friendly bid for AMF. Jacobs and Maxxam chairman Charles Hurwitz spoke on the phone while their representatives negotiated in New York. Unknown to AMF or Morgan Stanley—who still thought of Maxxam as a possible white knight—Hurwitz and Jacobs were cutting a deal: Maxxam would take over AMF, then immediately sell parts of it to Minstar.

If this sounds familiar, it is. Jacobs had cut just such a deal with Heileman at the time of his first tender for Pabst.

It was not to be, however. Hurwitz claims Jacobs backed out of the deal because he saw a better shot elsewhere. Jacobs says he and Hurwitz couldn't come to an agreement. Whoever is correct—and in this kind of deal, it's entirely possible both are—the talks collapsed on June 13.

That same day, Jacobs's lawyer—Stephen E. Jacobs (no relation) of Weil Gotshal & Manges—contacted AMF's lawyer, Peter A. Atkins of Skadden Arps. Jacobs (the lawyer) offered Atkins a new deal. Overnight, the two law firms negotiated and drafted a friendly takeover of AMF by Minstar.

Sudden switches like this are not unusual in takeover deals. It is always amazing how people who are vilifying each other one day can be bosom buddies the next.

On June 14, both boards approved the merger. Minstar would give $24 ($1 more than its previous offer) for each share of AMF up to 12.5 million shares. The shares Minstar already held would be included in that 12.5 million (shades of the aborted Kaiser deal). The remaining shareholders of AMF would receive a ten-year debenture worth $18.25—in 1995. In 1985, it was, therefore, worth considerably less.

To prevent the sort of thing that happened to him in the Kaiser deal (where the company found a better offer after everything had been agreed to), part of the merger proposal was a "crown jewels" guarantee. *Crown jewels* is the term applied to the heart of a company, its most profitable, most attractive divisions. In AMF's case, this was its leisure division: boating, bowling, and exercise equipment. Minstar was given an option to buy AMF's crown jewels for $300 million. If a competing bidder did come along, Minstar could exercise its option and the competitor would find it was bidding for a gutted company—still viable, but without its most attractive parts.

To finance the deal, a leveraged buyout of $525 million was arranged. From Jacobs point of view, it was a good price. AMF carried its assets on the books at $430 million; most analysts felt they were worth more than that if sold.

In August, AMF announced that it was selling certain divisions —Paragon Electric, AMF Scientific Drilling, AMF Tuboscope, and several others—all as going concerns, not as liquidated hulks. The yield from the sales was expected to largely eliminate the debt load.

The merger hadn't yet taken place. It wasn't to be voted on until October. Nevertheless, Jacobs was in control. The tender offer at $24 had, of course, been completed. Minstar Acquisitions—a subsidiary of Minstar—owned over 50 percent of AMF.

The results of the October voting were not expected to be a surprise.

Ironically, the spadework done by Morgan Stanley in looking for buyers when AMF was trying to fend off Jacobs was now aiding Jacobs in selling pieces of AMF: Morgan had already found lots of interested companies.

For years, Jacobs has smarted under charges that he was just a raider and a liquidator despite his protestations that his success with Minstar shows he is more than that. Now, unless he totally liquidates AMF, he has reached the big time in more than just raiding.

AS 1985 DREW to a close, Jacobs was making headlines once more. This time his target was ITT Corp. And once again, as with Disney, people were listening rather than protesting.

ITT today is the legacy of one man: Harold Geneen. Geneen was viewed as a management genius during his tenure at the top of ITT. He made ITT, then called International Telephone & Telegraph, into one of the more successful conglomerates. By the time he left ITT, there were over two hundred fifty companies under the ITT name.

The current chairman of ITT, Rand V. Araskog, felt it was his duty to pare down the company and bring it into the eighties, building on its successful high-technology and telephone companies (ITT is a major supplier of telephone services outside the United States). But everything did not go well for Araskog.

Critics of his tenure as chief executive say he has been too slow to take advantage of the deregulation of the U.S. telephone system. Others say he has diverted too much of the company's resources to an ITT project called System 12—a computerized switching system for telephone central offices that is behind schedule—while not only ignoring other areas but also diverting cash flow from other areas to System 12. Even his pruning of divisions has backfired on him; his critics portray him as dismantling the company instead of building it.

All this could have been handled had ITT's earnings stayed good. But they didn't. ITT has a high debt load: 64 cents of debt for every dollar of shareholder equity. This eats up a tremendous amount of ITT's cash flow in debt service and exaggerates drops in revenue when it gets translated into earnings per share. To make matters worse, the biggest generator of cash flow for ITT is its Hartford Insurance subsidiary. The property- and casualty-insurance industry is in the midst of the worst slump *this century,* cutting even further into ITT's cash flow. Shareholder unrest was growing as Araskog announced each year that earnings were worse than the year before. All told, earnings of the company slipped 40 percent between 1980 and 1984.

The real blow came in July of 1984. With Hartford's cash flow down substantially because of storm-damage claims, Araskog was forced to cut the dividend. In July, he announced a cut from $2.76 to $1.00.

The stock price dropped $10 a share in one day, and the public-relations chief of ITT had a heart attack in his office.

Irwin Jacobs began to buy. He hadn't planned anything; he just sensed a good situation. "You look at what you think is undervalued," he said, "and you let the situation command what develops."

Jay Pritzker, a wealthy investor who owns Hyatt Hotels and Braniff Airlines—but does not, he claims, believe in hostile takeovers—also began to buy ITT stock, eventually accumulating over 2 percent of the common in partnership with Philip Anschutz, a Denver oil man.

ITT began scenting the wolves in the underbrush. It started getting nervous.

Rumors and stories abound. One is that Pritzker proposed a leveraged buyout of ITT by himself, Anschutz, and ITT's management. According to the story, Araskog refused, even though he stood to make $30 million on the deal. Pritzker retired to the background (so far)—although Jerry Seslowe, the managing director of a Pritzker-Anschutz-owned investment advisory firm, continues to say that Pritzker is interested in the firm.

Jacobs, meanwhile, was accumulating stock. By the time of ITT's annual meeting in May of 1985, Jacobs had 6.2 million shares—4.4 percent of the outstanding stock. In April, while still buying stock, he proposed to ITT's management that ITT be broken up into three or four separate companies, each of which would be leaner and more competitive. He felt, he said, that the current mix of ITT companies was too unwieldy to manage effectively.

ITT said no. Jacobs repeated his suggestions at the May 16 annual meeting, attracting much press and shareholder attention. He and Araskog engaged in a spirited debate over what should be done to bring ITT back to full profitability.

The result of all this has been, even more so than with Disney, a flood of relatively good publicity for Jacobs. While speculation runs rife as to whether he will make a run at the company ("putting it in play" is the term the arbitraguers use), much of the press coverage—and Wall Street opinion—seems to feel that this time what he is suggesting might be the best thing for *all* the shareholders and that ITT's management is not representing the average stockholder.

What will happen at ITT is anybody's guess. Jacobs is increasingly blunt about ITT's management. ("I've had it up to my neck with them," he told *Fortune* in November. "Those guys are the biggest bunch of losers I ever met.") Araskog has managed to alienate Pritzker, who nevertheless has so far refused Jacobs's offer to join forces. ITT is adopting a bunker mentality; one director who suggested that Jacobs's liquidation proposal should be studied was asked to resign.

Almost anything could happen—and probably will.

TIMES ARE CHANGING, and the rules of the takeover game are getting tougher. The doomsayers have predicted that the increased use of shark repellent and antitakeover legislation will drive the raiders from the market. The antitakeover forces say they are a threat to the economy. How does Jacobs feel about it?

"People say, 'Kill the raiders, they're no good for the economy.' Well, not too long ago I told Carl and Boone that we all ought to go on strike for six months. If you took all the merger speculation out of the market, you wouldn't have a market."

And have the new rules made it too tough for raiders? "Nothing would please me more," he has said, "than for people to think the party's over—and then wake up one day and find all of us in the market at the same time."

4

The Wolf in the Oil Patch

T. BOONE PICKENS

WHEN HE HAS the time, T. Boone Pickens likes to hunt. He hunts birds, especially quail. He has a simple motto: "Never shoot anything you can't eat."

He also hunts companies.

SEPTEMBER 1984. PHILLIPS Petroleum Company, the tenth largest oil company in the United States, had a problem: it was very healthy. It had a billion dollars in cash in its treasury. But its stock was selling for only a little over $40 a share. At that low price, its very healthiness made Phillips a target for a raider. Analysts believed that the breakup value of the company—the price it would bring on the open market if sold piecemeal—was nearly double that, between $70 and $80 a share. And Phillips was nervous.

R. J. Reynolds Inc. was also nervous. Its stock was under-valued, too. Worse, signs indicated that T. Boone Pickens, chairman and president of Mesa Petroleum Co., was buying Reynolds stock.

Pickens's name is frightening to corporate CEOs and managements. He has made takeover attempts on one company after another—always firms in the oil business—aiming to merge them with Mesa. Like Steinberg's Reliance or Jacobs's Minstar, Mesa is both a thriving corporation and the vehicle for raids on other companies. And like Jacobs's claim that he pursues companies not for greenmail but to help build up Minstar, Pickens claims his pursuit of oil companies also has a purpose besides making money. His avowed intention has been to turn Mesa into an integrated oil company. Failing that, it seems, he simply wants Mesa to join the select group of companies known as "Big Oil."

Mesa Petroleum is entirely Pickens's creation. Formed in 1964, by 1984 it had sales of $413 million. It is primarily an exploration and production company, though, and Pickens wanted Mesa to be more than that. Integrated oil companies do everything from exploration to refining and wholesaling of oil products. Some, such as Exxon or Gulf, sell at the retail level as well, owning their own gas stations. (This is, however, no longer as true as it once was; many oil companies have closed or sold off their dealer networks.) They are enormous companies, with sales measured in the billions of dollars.

The big nonintegrated companies also talk in terms of billions, not millions. Mesa, profitable as it is, seems tiny beside them. Pickens wanted to join the club.

R. J. Reynolds, the world's largest tobacco company, might have seemed safe on the face of it from such a single-interest raider, but it wasn't. It also owned Aminoil, one of the nation's largest nonintegrated oil companies. If Pickens was stalking Reynolds, he was probably after Aminoil.

Reynolds's and Phillips's managements, independently seeking a solution, talked with one another and saw a way to solve both companies' problems. Reynolds chairman and CEO J. Tyler Wilson made a deal with Phillips CEO William C. Douce. Reynolds sold Aminoil to Phillips for $1.7 billion.

At first, Wall Street applauded. Wilson had gotten rid of a division that didn't mesh with the rest of Reynolds's consumer-oriented businesses. (Aminoil didn't even have any gas stations to marginally qualify it as consumer-oriented.) He planned to use proceeds to buy back Reynolds stock. This would drive up the stock price and make the company more expensive—i.e., harder—to take over.

Douce, too, got his share of kudos. He was credited with picking up low-priced resources and, by selling debt to finance the purchase, making Phillips less attractive to a takeover.

But soon there were second thoughts. Careful analysis of the deal indicated that Reynolds—spooked by the specter of Pickens—may have been in so much of a hurry to sell that they underpriced the deal. Phillips had discovered that Aminoil reserves (oil in the ground) may have been undervalued by as much as 25 percent. Had Reynolds taken the time for a careful valuation of Aminoil's assets, it might have gotten an additional $100 million. The deal didn't look as good for Reynolds on close examination as had originally been supposed.

Phillips, though, was also a loser, despite having gotten what appeared to be a bargain. Its stock price dropped 10 percent, to $38 a share, after the announcement of the Aminoil purchase, because speculators who had been hoping Phillips would use its cash to buy back its stock (driving up the price) sold out in disappointment.

Phillips, its stock price lower, was still vulnerable despite the new debt.

Worse, the new debt didn't increase the company's debt-to-equity ratio enough to deter a leveraged buyout—in part because of the upward revision in the value of the Aminoil assets. Phillips's debt-to-equity ratio, even after the acquisition, was only 35 percent—and on its liquidation value it was only 28 percent. There was plenty of room for a profit.

Phillips also had a large cash flow—so large that a raider using an LBO to take over the company might be able to pay off debt in five or six years even without selling off major assets or divisions.

All in all, Phillips was a very attractive target.

DECEMBER 4, 1984. Under the SEC 5-percent rule (anyone acquiring 5 percent or more of the stock of a publicly traded company must file with the SEC), T. Boone Pickens announced that a group he headed owned 5.7 percent of Phillips's stock. He also announced he would tender for 15 percent more. Pickens offered stockholders $60 a share for their stock, which was selling in the low 40s. His announced intention was to take control of Phillips and run it himself.

Phillips's lawyers hired a private investigator, Jules B. Kroll, to look for anything damaging about Pickens.

"Big Oil is a club," Pickens said, "and they'll do everything to keep me out."

The battle was on.

PHILLIPS WAS FAMILIAR with Pickens, not just from reading about him but as an opponent. In 1983, Phillips had taken over General American Oil of Texas, acting as a white knight to stop Pickens from getting GAO.

Phillips had no intention of allowing Pickens to succeed. By December 5, takeover specialists from Morgan Stanley & Co. were flying in to the Bartlesville, Oklahoma, headquarters of Phillips to plan a defense. Morgan Stanley is one of the most prestigious Wall Street investment bankers, and the firm is expert at takeover countermeasures. Many Morgan clients owe their continued independence to defenses Morgan helped them mount.

Pickens was no stranger to the tactics of the countermeasure game, either. In 1982, when Mesa tried to take over Cities Service, Cities Service countered Mesa with a Pac-Man defense. Cities came very close to succeeding though it ultimately fled into the arms of a white knight, Occidental Petroleum.

Pickens made his tender offer for Phillips on behalf of a partnership between Mesa and Wagner & Brown Co., of Midland, Texas. Wagner & Brown was privately held; they had no publicly traded stock and were thus immune to a hostile tender offer. Even if a Pac-Man defense were successful against Mesa, Pickens and Wagner & Brown could still go ahead with a takeover of Phillips. The result would be the same either way: Pickens would control both Phillips and Mesa.

THERE IS AN element of cloak and dagger in takeover confrontations, and this can sometimes, lead to situations that seem farcical to a detached observer—though they aren't comical at all to the participants. Phillips's and Morgan's defense teams rented a suite in the Helmsley Palace Hotel in New York City to use as headquarters. After several days, they were horrified to discover that the suite they had rented was across the hall from one rented by Pickens.

The Morgan-Phillips team immediately changed hotels. They also junked all the strategies they had previously decided upon. The reason? Their discarded notes and memos might give away too much, and they couldn't take the chance that the maids weren't taking their garbage cans across the hall to Pickens's suite.

PICKENS HAD NOW put Phillips into play and the arbitrageurs piled in.

Sometimes arbitrageurs—and market speculators—will bet a stock will go even higher than the tender price. In the case of Phillips, many Wall Street observers thought Phillips would look for a white knight. A white knight would have to offer more than Pickens in order to take over the company. So the price rose *above* what Pickens was offering. The arbitrageurs were looking for a *big* profit.

Between the arbitrageurs and the institutional investors (pension plans, insurance companies, mutual funds, etc., who own most of the stock in America's companies), less than half of Phillips's stock was in individual hands. A corporation can appeal to small investors on the grounds of loyalty or faith in the future. Institutions have a responsibility to get the best return on their investments; if offered a good price, an institutional investor will take it.

That wasn't always the case. Companies used to regard institutional investors as "friendly investors." Institutions invested for the long term and tended to hold stock longer than individual investors out for a quick profit. Most institutions could be counted upon to support management's decisions and to vote with management in proxy fights. When Saul Steinberg tried to take over Chemical Bank, the institutional investors helped to defeat him.

Times have changed, however. During the stock-market slump of the seventies, institutional money investors came under increasing attack from disgruntled customers—the people whose money was being invested, such as mutual fund shareholders or clients of bank trust departments—and from those charged with overseeing the performance of funds, such as pension plan trustees. The cosy world of the institutions was shattered as the performance of fund managers was challenged.

The fund managers themselves changed too. The compensation of fund managers is often linked, either directly or through bonuses, to the performance of the funds managed. This combination of unhappy customers and unhappy managers was a ripe situation the raiders of the late seventies and eighties were quick to turn to their advantage.

Institutions started asking whether it was to *their* advantage, not just management's, to support management slavishly. They began to notice that raiders offered a sure profit—and profits are the only way to boost fund performance. Suddenly, institutional investors could no longer be counted as "friendly hands."

Arbitrageurs are even worse from a company's point of view. They are in it just for the profit. You might convince an institutional investment manager he will get more if he waits. An arb is looking for a quick return. An arb won't—with interest rates high, *can't*—wait.

With so much stock in loose hands, Phillips was in trouble when it came to a fight.

BARTLESVILLE, OKLAHOMA, IS a small place, with a population of just under forty thousand people. Phillips is the largest employer in Bartlesville and has dominated the town since Cities Service moved to Tulsa in 1968, taking nine hundred jobs with it. By some estimates, at the time of Pickens's raid, two-thirds of the people in Bartlesville either directly or indirectly owed their livelihoods to Phillips's presence.

In many ways, Bartlesville is a company town.

Bartlesville people may have been far removed from the gray canyons of Wall Street—or even Pickens's headquarters in Amarillo, Texas—but they were not hicks. They knew what had happened in other cities when companies had merged or been acquired and when bustling headquarters had closed or become low-employment regional offices. The people in Bartlesville were prepared to fight to keep Phillips alive. Soon "Boone-busters" T-shirts appeared all over town, bearing Pickens's features in the familiar red and white "prohibited" symbol, a takeoff on the logo of the movie "Ghostbusters." Designed by A. J. Lafaro, a Phillips employee, they symbolized the town's feelings.

Pickens protested. He wasn't interested in dismantling Phillips, he said. He reminded people he was an Oklahoma native, that he started his career at Phillips (in 1951 as a geologist). He promised that he would move to Bartlesville and run both companies from there.

Still, the opposition grew. The opposition of a town, even a small one, can be a formidable obstacle in a takeover attempt. Colorful demonstrations, church prayer services, and T-shirts attract media attention. Media attention attracts politicians. Judges, too, have been known to be swayed by public opinion.

And judges and politicians often end up playing a part in takeovers. As Jacobs's attempts at Pabst illustrate, often a single legal decision—or even the threat of one—can cripple a takeover attempt.

In December, Mesa put its offer on the table. Pickens said he wanted 20.6 percent of the company and envisioned an eventual buyout that would, by using an Employee Stock Ownership Plan or ESOP (which had substantial tax advantages to the corporation setting one up), eventually allow employees to own up to one-third of the company. The ESOP idea was a direct appeal to Phillips's employees and management to go along with the deal.

Phillips wasn't interested. The company went on the offensive, charging Pickens with "intentional violations" of securities laws. It claimed Mesa had, by tendering for Phillips, violated a no-takeover pact Mesa made with General American Oil (now part of Phillips) in 1983. It tried other maneuvers as well. Eight percent of Phillips's worldwide cash flow came from its 37-percent share of the Ekofisk field in the North Sea; Phillips asked the Norwegian government to forbid Mesa to acquire it.

This was a variant on the ploy known as "selling the crown jewels," where it is arranged that in the event of a hostile takeover, the best parts of a company will be sold out from under the raider. It was a good move, but, unfortunately for Phillips's bid to remain independent, it raised other possibilities. Norsk-Hydro, an energy company 51 percent owned by the Norwegian government, had already approached Phillips with an eye to "purchase opportunities." Mesa was not the only company that might be interested in Phillips.

The sharks were gathering.

But Morgan Stanley had been busy. Phillips unveiled the defense Morgan had designed for it. Phillips offered to buy Pickens's shares of Phillips stock for a $75 million pretax profit, plus $25 million for expenses. Phillips had decided the direct approach was the best one.

Surprisingly—because most observers thought he would stick it out longer—Pickens agreed and abandoned his raid when many people thought he had the company in his grasp. Instead, he allowed himself to be bought off. Pickens claims he doesn't take greenmail, but in the case of Phillips, its hard to describe his actions in any other light—unless you accept the semantic argument that greenmail only exists if the intention from the beginning of the raid is to extract money, rather than to take over the company. Since Pickens probably did intend, at least at the beginning, to take over Phillips, under that narrow definition he did not commit greenmail. Wall Street wasn't that generous. It labeled the deal as greenmail, pure and simple.

Pickens, however, rejected the charges. He said the opposition not only of Phillips but of the people of Bartlesville had convinced him he couldn't win, so he was taking the consolation prize.

And, after all, $75 million was quite a consolation prize.

What happened to Phillips next is a good illustration of why greenmail is going out of favor. As with Walt Disney and Steinberg or Avco and Leucadia National, by paying greenmail, Phillips only attracted more sharks.

Phillips was not unaware of the perils of greenmail and began preparing some permanent shark repellent. It had to take into account that a lot of its shareholders were unhappy that Pickens was getting money and they weren't.

Douce, the Phillips CEO, announced a plan to take care of both the shark repellent and the unhappy shareholders. It was in the form of a corporate restructuring. Phillips planned to sell $2 billion in assets, load the company with debt (protecting against another takeover attempt), and set up an ESOP that would own 38 percent of the company. The ESOP would buy the stock from shareholders. All stockholders would get notes and subordinated debentures for 38 percent of their holdings. The deal was, Phillips said, worth $53 a share. As Pickens was getting $53 a share for his stock, Phillips claimed everyone was being treated equally.

Phillips also announced it would use the $1 billion in cash in its treasury to buy up Phillips stock on the open market, guaranteeing that the stock wouldn't drop below $50 for at least a year.

The market didn't agree. Analysts immediately began poking holes in Phillips's assumptions. Pickens was getting cash, they pointed out, while everyone else was only getting notes and bonds. Pickens was getting the deal for *all* his stock; Phillips was only offering to buy 38 percent of everyone else's holdings. Worst of all, most observers felt that the notes and subordinated debenture package wasn't worth $53 a share.

Far from holding in the $50-plus range, street estimates held that the remaining stock would sink into the low 30s once the deal was consummated. Armies are said to vote with their feet; Wall Street votes by buying or selling. On the announcement of the Pickens buyout and the restructuring, Phillips stock price dropped into the low 40s.

The arbitrageurs are estimated to have lost as much as $100 million.

Then the news broke: Irwin L. Jacobs, Carl Icahn, and Ivan Boesky, acting separately but with a common goal, had acquired 10 percent of Phillips. Their common goal? All three announced their opposition to the restructuring plan.

Phillips reeled with shock but gamely stuck to its proposal.

Icahn, who owned 4.8 percent of Phillips himself, offered a counterproposal. He proposed an $8.5 billion leveraged buyout of

Phillips, which translated to $55 a share in cash and debentures, $2 more than Phillips claimed its plan was supposed to be worth. As usual, Icahn's investment banker was Drexal Burnham Lambert, Inc., which confirmed the financing was available.

Phillips said no. It was still going to put its restructuring proposal to a shareholder vote on February 22.

Pickens, bound by the buyout agreement, remained on the sidelines. He could afford to wait. Phillips, whether its restructuring took place or not, would have to pay him $53 a share. He could only make more, not less, if someone else bought the company.

On February 22, 1985, Phillips's shareholder meeting took place. At the end of the day, however, Phillips did not release the results of the vote. Instead, Douce announced that the polls would remain open for five more days in the hopes Phillips would get the million votes it needed in order to pass the restructuring.

It was a forlorn hope. Press reports assumed Phillips would not be able to make the restructuring fly: if they weren't able to get the votes they needed by the time of the meeting (and obviously they hadn't; why else keep the polls open?), why should Phillips expect that five more days would make a difference?

The skeptics were proved correct. The final vote was 68.2 million yes, 52 million no or abstained. Although the majority of the votes had clearly been cast for the proposal, the corporate charter required the holders of more than 50 percent of the *outstanding stock* to vote their approval in order for a restructuring to proceed; 50 percent of the outstanding stock was 77.3 million shares. Phillips's management had only gotten approval from a majority of the stockholders who voted. It was not enough. They were over nine million votes short.

Icahn renewed his counterproposal. Phillips continued to reject it. There was speculation that Icahn might not be able to raise all the cash he needed for the buyout. Though Icahn and Drexal both denied they had problems, Phillips, clutching at straws, may have taken this as a hopeful sign.

On March 1, *The New York Times* announced it had learned that Sir James Goldsmith, another man whose name looms large in the takeover game, was considering joining in Icahn's bid.

Though Goldsmith didn't join in, the threat that he might seems to have provided the last straw.

On March 3—a Sunday—Phillips threw in the towel. They presented a new plan. They offered to exchange up to 72.2 million shares of their own stock for a package of debt securities. Based on the stock's price on Friday, the package was worth $56 a share, $1 a share better than Icahn's offer. In addition, they announced they would increase the dividend to $3 from $2.40.

The next day, Icahn agreed to be bought off. Phillips would not be taken over.

And Pickens, who had done nothing since signing his own agreement, picked up almost $14 million in additional profit.

THE PHILLIPS DEAL illustrates very well why takeover raids can be so profitable and why critics of the raiders say their activities are destructive. The bottom line on the raid looks like this:

- Mesa and its partners made a profit of almost $90 million plus expenses.
- Icahn's syndicate got $75 million plus expenses.
- Drexal Burnham Lambert, Inc., got $14 million in fees.
- Morgan Stanley got at least $10 million for its services. (Had the restructuring plan gone through, they probably would have earned at least $35 million.)
- Phillips stayed independent, but the debentures it issued to buy up its stock left it with an $8 billion debt—80 percent of its total capital. Any dip in oil prices before sufficient assets were sold would make it difficult to pay the new dividend. It would have to sell $2 billion to $4 billion in assets to bring the debt down to a manageable level.
- The employees of Phillips, including those who lived in Bartlesville, faced job shifts due to the sale of the assets—possibly more severe than if Pickens had taken over Phillips in the first place. Ten percent of its work force was offered early retirement in an effort to cut costs.
- Phillips CEO William C. Douce, whose purchase of Aminoil probably triggered the raid and who had seen his restructuring plan rejected by shareholders, announced his retirement.

In general, it looks as if the results of the Phillips raid were disastrous to Phillips—ammunition for the forces that oppose the raiders. But a question must be asked: What if Phillips had entered negotiations with Mesa for a merger? How much of the damage to Phillips was, in a sense, self-inflicted because of a desperate desire to stay independent *at any cost?*

It's a difficult question to answer. Pickens probably would have used a leveraged buyout to take over Phillips, which would have loaded Phillips with debt, but Pickens would have also merged it with Mesa, raising the asset side of the scale as well as increasing the income available to service the debt. He probably would have pared down Phillips's businesses, selling less attractive ones—also to pare down debt—but Phillips was doing that anyway. Why fight Pickens?

The answer may lie in a simple fact: No one knows what Pickens would do if he took over one of the companies he has gone after. T. Boone Pickens, arch-raider of the oil patch, has never successfully taken over an integrated oil company.

HIS FULL NAME is Thomas Boone Pickens, Jr. The Boone refers to a distant kinsman, a certain Daniel Boone of Kentucky and points west. In the tradition of the oil business, Pickens was born within sight of oil wells, on May 22, 1928, and grew up in the little town of Holdenville, Oklahoma. Holdenville is the county seat of Hughes County and has a population of just over 6,000 people today. It was considerably smaller when Pickens was growing up.

East central Oklahoma is cattle country, fertile pasture land drained by the Canadian River. The Canadian was important in the opening of the west, since it flows all the way from New Mexico through Texas and Oklahoma until it joins with the Arkansas River and flows into the Mississippi. This is also, though, the land of the dust bowl of the thirties.

Thomas Boone Pickens, Sr., was an independent oil man. Like many another independent in the wide-open early days of the oil business, he bought and sold oil leases—the rights to drill on pieces of land. And like many another independent—then and now—he made and lost a fortune doing it. The gambling instinct is a necessity to an independent oil man (Pickens senior also bet heavily on college football games), and his son seems to have inherited it in full.

His mother was almost the opposite. Described as a practical woman, Grace Pickens didn't make decisions without considering everything first. During World War II, she ran Holdenville's gas-rationing program. Pickens feels he got the best of both worlds.

"I was very fortunate in my gene mix," he has said. "The gambling instincts I inherited from my father were matched by my mother's gift for analysis."

His father called him T-Bone.

Pickens was in high school when his family moved to Amarillo, Texas. Amarillo sits almost at the midpoint of the Texas panhandle, that section of the state that pokes north into Oklahoma. This is high plains country, and Amarillo is considered, unofficially of course, the capital of the panhandle. Pickens played basketball at Amarillo High School. Although Pickens was then only five feet eight inches tall (he now says he is five-foot ten), he played guard on the Amarillo team, all of whom seem to have been of less than optimum height for basketball players. Nevertheless, they made it into the semifinals of the state tournament and Pickens won a basketball scholarship to Texas A & M. He went because of the scholarship. He says today that he had no particular idea in mind of what he wanted to do with his life.

He played there for only one year, however—he broke an elbow and lost his scholarship. He transferred to Oklahoma State and renewed courting his high-school sweetheart, Lynn O'Brian. They were married when he was twenty and she was seventeen.

Pickens had by then decided what he wanted to do and majored in geology. He spent two years on the dean's list, then graduated in 1951 and went to work for Phillips Petroleum.

In Oklahoma Phillips looms larger than many of the bigger firms. Its headquarters are there, and it must have seemed a logical choice for an Oklahoma State graduate. His father was working for Phillips at the time, as a lease broker, and no doubt that had an influence on Pickens's choice.

Phillips sometimes has trouble recruiting personnel because of the size and isolation of Bartlesville. To someone from the east or west coasts or from Houston or Dallas, a town of forty thousand far from any large cities is not always an attractive place to live. An unnamed executive of TRW, the second largest employer in Bartlesville, told *U.S. News & World Report* in 1984 that, when recruiting, "the first visit is the hardest to get anyone to make. The next obstacle is to get the spouse to come."

But to someone brought up in the rural Oklahoma of Holdenville, Bartlesville was no obstacle. Besides, times were tough in the oil industry. Out of the fifty graduates in Pickens's class at Oklahoma State, Pickens was one of only four who got work in the oil industry. There were worse things than living in Bartlesville. Boone and Lynn Pickens settled into the life-style of a young well-site geologist and his wife in a company town.

He hated it. Pickens felt smothered. No one wanted to listen to his ideas—which was not surprising. In the oil industry a college degree is considered only the beginning of an education. Years of experience are needed before big companies will risk millions of dollars on the interpretation of a smudge on a seismic chart. The independent drilling companies are almost all staffed by younger men whose restlessness and impatience have caused them to leave the safety of pension plans and steady paychecks to work "where the action is"—leavened, generally, by a few older and wiser heads who've seen it all.

Pickens was one of those restless, impatient young men. One day, about four years after he joined Phillips, his wife casually remarked, "If you hate it so much, why don't you quit?" Pickens went back to his office and gave notice. He received a $1,300 lump-sum payment from Phillips's profit-sharing plan and used the money to buy a station wagon. He filled it up with exploration gear and set out to find oil.

He was at it for a year before he managed to get financial backing. In 1952, his wife's uncle came up with a $50,000 line of credit. Pickens negotiated another $50,000 from other sources and by 1956 had formed the Petroleum Exploration Co.

And he found oil and gas, attracting investors. The company grew, but Pickens himself became a workaholic. He paid little attention to his family—he and Lynn had four children—and

Lynn had no interest in his work. The marriage collapsed and finally ended in divorce in 1971.

But in the meantime, he had taken Petroleum Exploration public. Under its new name, Mesa Petroleum, its stock began trading in 1964.

Pickens has done well for Mesa. Some of his finds are almost legendary. One such was an investment in some Canadian drilling sites that Pickens paid $35,000 for in 1959. Petroleum Exploration used the income from the wells drilled on the sites to drill new wells. Twenty years after the sites had been purchased and fourteen years after Petroleum Exploration became Mesa Petroleum, in 1979, Mesa sold its Canadian operations—founded with the $35,000 investment—to Dome Petroleum for $600 million.

Even more than the money Mesa made on the deal, the timing is a credit to Pickens's judgment. In 1979, Canada was regarded as fertile ground for American oil companies, with lots of opportunity for growth and discovery. By selling out, Pickens was bucking the prevailing wisdom in the industry and on Wall Street.

Shortly after Mesa pulled out, the Canadian government announced a new energy policy that favored Canadian companies at the expense of foreign—including American—ones. The move took everyone by surprise—even giants like Shell and Gulf. Mesa was happily out of it, sitting on its $600 million.

While Mesa was growing, Pickens acquired a new wife, Beatrice. Pickens had known Beatrice at Oklahoma State. After college, she married one of his fraternity brothers, but after four children, her marriage, like Pickens's to Lynn, fell apart. She was divorced in 1969. She married Pickens in 1972.

Unlike Lynn, she not only shares Pickens's hobbies (she likes to hunt quail and is almost as good a shot as her husband, who has picked up a number of markmanship awards) but is interested in his work. Shortly after they were married, Beatrice enrolled in a geology course at Amarillo College. She got an A. She usually accompanies her husband on his business travels, doing anything she can to help out, even if it means running the slide projector at presentations. Pickens often talks out ideas with her before running them by his corporate staff. In 1975, he named a new oil find in the North Sea after her.

(The North Sea finds that Mesa made provide another instance of Pickens's acumen. In 1979, Pickens sold Mesa's holdings in the North Sea, picking up $65 million. Then the British put a new tax on North Sea oil production, cutting into the profits of a lot of companies—but not Mesa's.)

Pickens has an easygoing manner that causes him to be described as "a classic country boy." He is anything but. When not engaged in business, he can be found on his forty thousand-acre ranch north of Amarillo. It is a working ranch, running about twenty-five hundred head of cattle. He hunts, fishes, and rides for relaxation—and plays gin rummy with old friends from high school.

He also has a dry sense of humor that occasionally expands into pranks. In college, he was known for tossing water-filled bags from hotel windows when the basketball team was on road trips. He has risen above water bags but still plays tricks. A long-time friend and card-playing buddy once accompanied Pickens on the corporate jet to Toronto. Pickens told him they were going to San Francisco. The friend had never been to either city and didn't realize where he was until he tried to get to Fisherman's Wharf from a downtown Toronto hotel.

That Pickens's easygoing manner is deceptive is perhaps best illustrated by his eating habits. While denying that he is a "fitness nut," Pickens jogs regularly and plays a competitive game of tennis (he has an indoor court at home). He also plays racketball at the end of every day when he's at Mesa headquarters (playing in a court that's part of the fitness center he had built there for employees). Nevertheless, he finds it necessary to watch his weight. He religiously counts calories (no more than 2,000 a day) and balances what he eats, but the way he does it is revealing: he generally leaves half the food on his plate.

There are few people with the willpower to do that consistently. Pickens is one of them.

PICKENS BEGAN HIS pursuit of other companies in 1969. Mesa went after Hugoton Production Co., an oil company twenty times the size of Mesa, and took it over. Hugoton was merged with Mesa and Mesa's exploration and production operations were greatly expanded as a result. But Pickens's next attempt was not as successful. He bid for Southland Royalty in 1970 but was repulsed.

In 1973, he was successful again, taking over another small oil company, Pubco Petroleum. In 1976, he went after Aztec Corporation, yet another oil and gas company, only to be outbid by Southland Royalty Corporation, the target of his failed bid six years earlier.

As the seventies drew to a close, Mesa Petroleum was known on Wall Street as a profitable oil and gas company, though not one of the "majors" as the big oil companies were known. Pickens's name would have been virtually meaningless to all but those who followed Mesa and knew him as its CEO. The year 1979 was to change all that.

In 1979, Pickens created the first royalty trust.

The idea came to him, he says, while he was lying awake in bed in his home in Amarillo, Texas. It was 3 A.M., but he woke his wife to tell her his idea. "I said to Bea," he told an interviewer, "'I think I've got it figured out,' and I got up and wrote some things down. Then we started checking it out and, by golly, it worked."

What he had figured out was the answer to a problem he saw confronting not just Mesa but many oil companies, including the majors. An oil company's stock price reflects its earnings, and the earnings come from profits on the sale of oil and gas. But oil and gas are not produced in a manufacturing sense; they are extracted, just as coal is mined. No matter how much oil a company owns, eventually the last drop will be pumped from the ground. If a company doesn't find more reserves, it will, eventually, be out of business.

But to find reserves, a company must spend huge amounts of money on exploration, land acquisition, and drilling. The more of the cash flow that is spent on exploration, the smaller the company's profits after expenses—and the lower the share price and dividends that are paid to a shareholder. Thus oil companies—and other extractive industries—are in a perpetual bind. If they maximize profits, they will eventually liquidate the company—

slowly, it is true, but surely. If they spend more money on exploration, the company's stock price will go down with no guarantee that oil will be found.

Pickens's plan was a way of getting at least some of the profits directly into shareholders' hands. He formed Mesa Royalty Trust and issued shareholders—including himself—one share of the trust for each share of Mesa stock. The trust owns a big chunk of Mesa's former properties and does no exploration. Thus it can pay out all its cash flow after expenses as a dividend to shareholders. The trust will, of course, eventually liquidate itself, but in the meantime it will have paid out a lot of dividends.

Mesa, on the other hand, was left with fewer reserves. While this cut into cash flow, it also lowered the amount of new oil that had to be found each year to replace the oil taken from the ground, making it easier to keep from liquidating the company. Paradoxically, though the company now had fewer assets, its stock value (after adjustment for the spinoff) was enhanced because the rate at which reserves are replaced is considered an important element in the valuation of oil stocks.

Like Citicorp's invention of the bank holding company, Mesa's creation of the royalty trust was a brand-new wrinkle in an old business. Pickens was suddenly a name everyone knew. He used his newfound notoriety to publicize his opinions about shareholder rights and corporate democracy.

And under that banner of corporate democracy, Pickens was about to launch his career as a raider.

BY 1981, THE OPEC-inspired oil price rise was slipping—the high prices of the seventies had resulted in a rush to find new reserves at the same time as oil-consuming nations found ways to cut demand. The consequences were a worldwide glut of oil. Partly as a result of the decline in the oil markets, demand for natural gas was down as well.

About 80 percent of Mesa's reserves are in natural gas. Mesa began to cap its wells one by one as demand slumped. Something had to be done to increase Mesa's earnings.

Pickens began to stalk the oil patch for takeover targets.

Pickens's critics say he is a master at greenmail and has used the proceeds from his raids to bolster Mesa's earnings during a slack time for the oil and gas industry. Pickens admits—proudly—that his raids have aided Mesa's bottom line, but he rejects the idea that his raids have had no other purpose. Although his last successful takeover was Pubco in 1973, he maintains that all of his raids have been bona fide attempts to take over other oil companies and merge them with Mesa.

By Pickens's calculations, in 1982 it cost Mesa $17 per barrel to find oil. He looked at the stock prices of major oil companies with large reserves and figured they could be taken over for a price equivalent to about $3 a barrel of reserves. "It has become cheaper," he said, "to look for oil on the floor of the New York Stock Exchange than in the ground."

His first run was at Supron Energy, a medium-size oil and gas firm in which Mesa had owned stock since 1978. Supron got away, eventually being acquired by a then-unusual consortium of two large corporations, Allied Corp. and Continental Group Inc. Pickens made a net profit of better than $22 million. The raid that put him on the map, however, was his next: Cities Service.

CITIES SERVICE WAS an integrated oil company more than twenty times Mesa's size in 1982. Although the sheer effrontery of Mesa's bid made headlines across the nation's financial pages, the difference in size between the two companies was to prove Mesa's undoing in the deal. Mesa simply didn't have the financial resources to hold the line against the tactics Cities Service choose.

Pickens was still new in the takeover game in 1982, and he made no secret of his intention to go after Cities Service. Mesa didn't have the money to mount a takeover by itself, so Pickens was discussing a syndication with Louisiana Land & Exploration Co. and Freeport-McMoran Inc., both energy firms like Mesa. There is no question that Mesa's intent was to acquire oil and gas reserves; had greenmail been the intention, there would have been no need to bring in partners. Pickens was doing exactly what he said he was doing: prospecting for oil on the New York Stock Exchange.

But Cities struck before Mesa was ready. First it threatened

Mesa's partners with takeovers, then it went after Mesa itself with a preemptive bid. It was a classic use of the Pac-Man defense. Mesa was forced into tendering for Cities stock even though Mesa wasn't ready and didn't have enough money to successfully counter Cities' moves. Ironically, just as it looked as if Mesa might be gobbled up by its target, it was saved by a white knight—not an investor in Mesa, but one that came in to help Cities Service.

Despite what looked as if it might be a successful Pac-Man defense, Cities was not feeling secure. Lawsuits could still unravel everything, and Mesa was still fighting, picking up Cities' stock. Cities' executives were also well aware that one tender attempt, even if successfully beaten off, often results in other hostile offers. Cities decided to take the sure way out offered by a white knight. Gulf Oil agreed to take over Cities Service. Mesa, exhausted by the battle and assured of a profit, agreed to the deal.

Though Gulf Oil later backed out of the merger—prompting an immediate lawsuit by Cities Service—Cities was able to find a substitute paladin in Occidental Petroleum. Mesa, which had seemed in danger of going down in flames, ended up with a profit of $44 million on an investment of $182 million. After expenses and taxes, Mesa ended up taking home a net profit of almost $13 million.

It is obvious, in retrospect, that Pickens badly misplayed his hand in his attempt on Cities. He tipped the target off long before he was in a position to defend himself, let along mount a convincing attack. He made a profit—and press reports, focusing on the profit, made him look like a genius—but he failed in his attempt to acquire reserves for Mesa. As an anonymous "prospective Mesa partner" told *Business Week* in October of 1982, "Boone got good press and looked like a genius, but the deal was poorly constructed and poorly executed."

It is difficult not to conclude that Pickens was lucky to get out of the deal whole, let alone with a profit.

It is also interesting to see what became of Cities Service after its takeover by Occidental Petroleum. A dispassionate observer, noting the way Cities fought tooth and nail against Mesa, would have to assume that Cities was afraid of the consequences of being taken over by Pickens and saw a white knight as a better alternative. Yet the post-takeover activities of white knight Occidental once again raise the question: Was Cities so much better off as part of Occidental than it would have been as part of Mesa?

Soon after the takeover, Occidental sold off Cities Service Gas Co., a Cities subsidiary, for $530 million. It disposed of a copper division for $75 million. It terminated a joint chemical venture with the Italian energy group ENI (which had been losing Cities money), picking up another $176 million. In fact, by the spring of 1983, virtually all Cities Service assets except its reserves were either sold or on the block. Occidental had no choice: it needed the cash.

Occidental had raised over $4 billion through bank loans and preferred stock and note sales in order to purchase Cities. Though it had paid back $1 billion of the bank loans (in a dramatic gesture, Occidental's chairman Armand Hammer turned over a check for $1 billion to Manufacturers Hanover in January of 1983), it still faced total cash needs of $800 million just to cover its interest payment and to keep up its dividends. With oil prices continuing to slip, Occidental eventually ended up selling parts of its own divisions to stay afloat.

Could a takeover by Mesa have been any worse? At least Pickens had shown a talent for finding reserves and selling them at the right time—no mean feat in the oil industry. Yet Cities preferred dismemberment by Occidental to ownership by Pickens. Why?

It is a question without an answer. At the time of the attempted takeover, Pickens was not regarded as a greenmailer or takeover artist. He was simply an oilman running a medium-sized company who wanted to take over a bigger one. Such ambitions are not uncommon. He had a reputation as an innovator as a result of the royalty trusts he had created. He made no threats about dismissing Cities management. Still, Cities management reacted as if he were proposing to sell them into bondage.

The answer may lie in something Pickens said: "Big oil is a club." Like the Wall Street establishment that overwhelmed

Steinberg when he went after Chemical Bank, the big oil companies—and many of Pickens fellow independents—don't like people who break the rules. Pickens had a reputation on Wall Street and in the press as a champion of shareholder rights and as a savvy oilman who'd built a company from scratch. To other oil companies, though, he was a pirate, an outsider despite his credentials, because he was engaged in *hostile* takeovers. "Engaging in hostile takeovers like this is buccaneering of the worst kind," the chairman of Apache Corp., a large independent, told *Business Week,* when asked to comment on Pickens's run at Cities. And Chevron chairman George Keller said, "Pickens does not break any laws doing what he does. But he breaks tradition." Pickens himself has said that former friends who run big oil companies will no longer speak to him.

He angers the members of the "club" with statements like "Chief executives, who themselves own few shares of their companies, have no more feeling for the average stockholder than they do for babboons in Africa," and "It infuriates me to see them invest their own money in Treasury bills rather than work to improve the value of their companies' stock."

Given that many analysts feel that most big oil companies are trading at less than half their breakup value, Pickens's criticisms of oil-company management would seem to have some truth to them. In 1984, for another example, *Fortune* magazine listed what it felt were the seven worst acquisitions of the previous ten years. Four of the seven on the list were made by oil companies, including Mobil's disastrous $1.86 billion purchase of Montgomery Ward, which was losing money when Mobil bought it and continued to do so *after* Mobil bought it. Other oil companies have done as badly. Atlantic Richfield had to take a $785 million write-off of its investment in Anaconda. Exxon, after years of trying and oceans of money, dropped out of the office-products business. It also hasn't done so well with its purchase of Reliance Electric.

The list goes on. There is plenty of support for Pickens's contention that oil companies are badly run. All he is asking for, he says, is to be given a chance to show if he can do better. "I would show them how I could make their stock dance," he says.

Maybe what Big Oil is afraid of is just that. After all, if Pickens *did* show he could run one of the giants better than current management, it would make all the members of the club look bad, wouldn't it?

In any case, no one seems inclined to let him try.

DESPITE HIS CLOSE escape in the attempt on Cities, Pickens was still out to buy reserves. The Cities deal was over by the middle of 1982. Mesa then went after General American Oil.

Unlike Cities Service, General American Oil was a company just slightly smaller than Mesa. This time, Mesa would have the resources to stay the course. This time, it looked as if Mesa would win.

The raid was kept under tight security until December 20, 1982—Pickens had learned from his mistakes. Then Mesa made a bid of $520 million for 51 percent of General American Oil—$40 a share for each of 13 million shares—and announced its intention to offer about $38 in stock or debentures to the remaining holders if the tender was successful and Mesa and Pickens gained control of GAO.

GAO's stock had traded for only $24 a share as recently as the summer of 1982, so the $40 bid looked good. Once again, however, a Mesa target wanted no part of Mesa. GAO chairman William P. Barnes announced that GAO was looking for a white knight. It also began putting in place a package of antitakeover actions, including elements of both scorched-earth and poison-pill defenses.

GAO announced that it would tender for 13 million of its own shares, offering $50 a share. At the same time, it announced it would spin off major assets of the company. Since the stock repurchase would cost $400 million, the result would be a company loaded with debt and with much of its value gone—a classic scorched-earth defense. The poison pill—a small one as these things go, but potent when combined with the scorched-earth plan—went into effect with the declaration of huge severance benefits for anyone fired as a result of a merger.

Wall Street investors, scenting the possibility of a bidding war, sent the stock up to $48 a share. But analysts soon began to find holes in GAO's armor.

First there was the question of where GAO was to get the $400 million. Challenged, the company admitted it might not be able to buy back more than 8 million shares. That amounted to only a third of GAO's stock. The outlook for the shares GAO didn't purchase was not good. Street estimates predicted that GAO stock would drop to the low 30s, where it had been trading before Pickens made his tender. Thus, even though Mesa's offer was for considerably less than GAO's $50, those GAO shareholders not fortunate enough to have their stock bought at the $50 price would be in worse shape than if they tendered to Pickens at $40—or even than if they waited and took $38 after takeover.

To make matters worse, no white knight appeared. The stock price soon fell to $42 a share. The betting was that Pickens would either raise his tender to $42 or $43 a share—in which case most analysts felt he would get the company—or that he would take what he could at $40, then wait for the stock price to drop and tender again at a lower price. Either way, short of GAO liquidating itself (and there wasn't enough time to put a liquidation in motion before Mesa's tender expired), most analysts felt that GAO was about to become part of Mesa. Pickens's offer expired on January 11. On that date, all shares tendered would belong to Mesa.

On January 7, GAO and Mesa announced that they had signed a standstill agreement and that Mesa was dropping its offer. Speculation was rife as to why Mesa was pulling out. The only answer seemed to be that Mesa had decided that GAO's scorched-earth-poison-pill defense was too good.

On January 10, the financial pages of the newspapers announced that Phillips Petroleum would take over General American Oil. Literally at the last minute, GAO had found its white knight.

Phillips offered $45 a share for all shares of GAO. Mesa, bound by the standstill agreement, could not enter a bidding war even if it wanted to. Once again, Pickens had failed in his attempt to find new reserves the easy way.

Nevertheless, in the takeover game, failure can be good for the bottom line. Mesa's profit on not taking over General American Oil was a net of $25.3 million. Its investment had been just under $32 million.

Why did Pickens back out when the street thought he could

win with just a little more effort? One arbitrageur was quoted as saying, "If Pickens upped his offer to $42 or $43, he could probably have my stock." Yet he stepped aside and gave GAO and Phillips time to work out their own deal.

Possibly, even after three negative experiences, Pickens still thought there was an easy takeover target out there somewhere, so he backed off when his quarry fought back, preferring to spend his energies elsewhere. The fact that he was offered substantial profits on both Supron and Cities may have made the decision easier. It was only later, after *all* his takeover deals had failed, that Pickens was accused of being a greenmailer.

In 1983, Pickens was still learning the takeover game and was very lucky that he made, rather than lost, money in the process. The conclusion is easier to accept when it is remembered that some of his greatest coups in building Mesa—selling out of Canada and the North Sea just ahead of sudden changes in government policy—seem also to have been guided by luck or intuition. No one has seriously suggested that when Mesa got out of Canada, Pickens had any more information about the upcoming "Canadianization" of the oil industry there than did the big companies.

In his takeovers, the same luck (or sense of timing) seems to have been present.

It is strange that no one accused him of greenmail. The oil industry was outraged that Pickens was making hostile tender offers, but no one doubted he *was* trying to take over the companies. Yet Pickens never pursued a target as tenaciously as some other takeover specialists who *were* accused of greenmail—and worse. Irwin Jacobs made repeated attempts to take over Pabst and was vilified as an opportunist and greenmailer. Pickens walked away as soon as he was offered money and was called a champion of shareholder rights.

Assuming, then, that his reputation *was* correct—that he wasn't after greenmail—why did he give up so easily, especially when he seemed to have what he wanted in his grasp and only had to reach a little further?

Perhaps Pickens was simply an inept and still inexperienced takeover artist—but a very lucky one.

His next "success" tends to support that conclusion.

SUPERIOR OIL WAS one of the giants. Though perhaps not in the same class as Exxon, it had over one billion barrels of oil and gas in the ground. For years, though, Superior had been wracked by behind-the-scenes in-fighting that had, occasionally, surfaced in the financial press.

Superior Oil was founded by one of the legends of the oil business. William Keck, always known as Bill, is still regarded as one of the greatest—if not *the* greatest—wildcatters of all time, a man who supposedly could tell if there was oil in a drilling sample by tasting the dirt. Superior built the very first offshore-drilling platform. Bill Keck built Superior into one of the best oil companies in the world.

Keck had two sons and a daughter: William, Howard, and Williametta. Williametta was never considered a contender for running the company—in the fifties, few women were considered fit to be corporate executives, let alone chief executives, and in the oil industry it was more like "none' than "few." The conflict between William and Howard, however, was never far from the surface. Both men had been brought up learning the business like their father had, working on the wells in the tough, dirty, and dangerous jobs of tool pushers and roustabouts. Drill pipe is heavy, and the drilling doesn't stop when new pipe is added; many veteran drillers are missing fingers and toes. It is hard, physical work with no margin for error.

One thing neither son learned was how to compromise. In 1959, Bill Keck tried to solve the problem by selling the company to Texaco: if he no longer owned the company, he wouldn't have to choose one son to run it. The deal fell through on antitrust grounds. Bill Keck had to make a choice and did. In his will, he gave power over the family holdings to Howard B. Keck.

Howard Keck saw to it that his brother and sister were neutralized. Williametta was kept away from the company altogether; William, the elder brother, was allowed to work for Superior but given no real authority. Howard ran the company virtually as a one-man show.

He was also publicity shy and uninterested in a broad shareholder base or in answering questions from security analysts, which helps to explain why Superior was far less known to either the general public or to investors than were companies far smaller. The stock traded at high prices—over $500 a share in the late seventies—and no effort was made to lower the price through stock splits in order to make it more attractive to smaller investors. Howard Keck liked things just the way they were.

But Howard Keck was not immune to age. Although the board of directors three times waived the company's requirement of mandatory retirement at age sixty-five, he could not go on forever. His son had become a banker, turning his back on the company, so he had to look elsewhere for a successor. He began to bring in people from oil companies such as Exxon and Mobil to take on more and more of the day-to-day managing of the company. In 1981, he retired as chairman, but continued to control the family's stock.

His successor as chairman, Fred Ackerman, a former Exxon executive, took charge quickly—and promptly alienated a large chunk of Superior's management by imposing an Exxon-style structure on what had been a rather free-form management team (under Keck, Superior didn't have a planning department or even a tax department). Within a year, nine of the top twelve executives of Superior had left the company, including Joseph Reid, the president and CEO. Superior's drilling results also began to suffer.

In this rather tense atmosphere, the family squabbles broke out again. Relations between Howard and Williametta (now Mrs. Day) had never been good. (She still tells interviewers how Howard killed her pet ostrich some sixty years ago, and she once sued him for refusing to use family funds to build a mausoleum for their father.) Now, with Superior's management in turmoil, she was afraid that Howard would use his influence to refuse another takeover offer such as the one Texaco had made in 1959. Mrs. Day had long felt her brother wasn't managing family funds to maximum effect.

In 1983, Williametta Keck Day announced that she would solicit proxies to force the board to consider takeover offers. Should she win, it would be an open invitation to other oil companies to buy out Superior for its reserves.

In March of 1983, Pickens bought a 2-percent stake in Superior Oil.

Superior's management, reacting both to Mrs. Day's proxy

fight *and* to Pickens's investment, enacted a series of anti-takeover moves, including staggered directors' terms, and once again waived mandatory retirement for the now seventy-year-old Howard Keck so he could stay on the board.

When the shareholder vote came up, Mesa voted its stock with Mrs. Day. She won, with 55 percent of the vote.

Shortly afterward, Pickens met with Mrs. Day at her home in Santa Barbara. The accounts of the meeting are, to say the least, lurid, with Pickens recalling that Mrs. Day accused her brother of bugging her home and insisted on sitting in the pool house to avoid eavesdroppers. Pickens presented her with a plan to reorganize Superior and spin off reserves to shareholders. They failed to reach agreement. Pickens says it was because he was looking out for shareholder interests and Mrs. Day was after revenge on Howard Keck. Mrs. Day says she was angered by a Pickens statement that he didn't think there was much oil left to be found on Superior's properties. In any case, both refused to have anything to do with the other after the meeting.

Pickens says that while he and his wife were driving down the hill after the meeting she asked him what he was going to do next. He replied, "I am going to get out of this deal as quick as I can."

He did. He called Superior chairman Fred Ackerman and arranged a secret meeting, in the best cloak-and-dagger fashion at an abandoned Army airfield outside of Waco, Texas. With Pickens's jet parked beside Ackerman's, the meeting was held in Ackerman's plane because the temperature was 115 degrees and Pickens's plane's air conditioner wouldn't work on the ground without an auxilliary power unit—not readily available at an abandoned airfield. Again Pickens presented his ideas for maximizing shareholder value. Ackerman was more receptive. The following Tuesday, Pickens met with Superior management and representatives of Morgan Stanley, Superior's investment bankers. No one was impressed with his ideas.

Two days later, they called him back and offered to buy his stock. Pickens says he was only too glad to get out. He was offered $42 a share for his Superior stock, and he took it, giving him a profit of $31.6 million. The stock was then selling for $35 to $36. Pickens had been paid a substantial premium to go away.

Told of Pickens's deal, Mrs. Day said, "I should have pushed that Lear-jet cowboy into the swimming pool while I had the chance."

Superior was later taken over by Mobil, but only after much more family feuding. Howard Keck and Superior sued each other; Keck launched his own proxy fight; heavy antitakeover measures were instituted, and Mrs. Day began to doubt she had done the right thing; but Pickens was long gone—with the money.

The Superior Oil play (it was never really a raid) is often pointed to by his admirers as one of Pickens's better deals. He got in, got out again, and made a lot of money in the process. People who think he is a greenmailer point to it as proof that he is one—and, on the surface, the facts appear to support them. If, that is—and it's a big if—you discount the sincerity of Pickens's attempts to offer a restructuring plan to benefit shareholders.

It's important to remember that Pickens never threatened a takeover or anything else. If his suggestions were genuine—and, except for diehard critics, no one seems to doubt they were—Pickens was simply acting in a normal fashion for a large shareholder concerned about the direction the company was taking. It is part of management's job to listen to large shareholders, even if they don't like them. What Pickens did was normal business practice.

Being bought out at a higher price than was available to other shareholders, though, *does* look a lot like greenmail. But, once again, the answer may lie in another direction. According to Pickens himself, he miscalculated badly in buying into Superior and simply took the first good offer to get out.

In an interview Pickens gave in March of 1984, he was surprisingly candid about misjudging the situation at Superior. "We felt it was a squabble between a brother and a sister and something would very likely happen. . . . We were going along believing that the stockholders would vote with Mrs. Day, which they did, and that would force the sale of Superior Oil Co., and we would just participate." So far, he sounds a lot more like an opportunist—which is what most investors try to be—than a greenmailer. But then he continued, "Frankly, we did not do a good job of evaluating the value of Superior Oil Co. We believed it was worth probably twenty percent to thirty percent more than it was actually worth."

When talking in millions of dollars, 20 percent to 30 percent is a lot to be off. That is how a lot of people lose money in the stock market. No wonder Pickens took the money and ran.

1984 WAS THE year of Gulf Oil. The profit on the Gulf Oil raid was *$760 million*. Shareholders who owned Gulf stock at the start of the raid saw its price rise from $41 a share in October 1983 to $80 a share in March 1984, the price Chevron agreed to pay to take over Gulf. Pickens made a lot of shareholders happy and ended up on the cover of *Time* magazine.

As a result of the Gulf raid, Pickens became perhaps the best known of the raiders. People who have never heard of Steinberg or Jacobs know who T. Boone Pickens is.

Gulf Oil was too big for Mesa to go after alone. Pickens instead formed a consortium called Gulf Investors Group. Gulf Investors' backing was impressive. Among others who invested in it were G. Michael Boswell, CEO of Sunshine Mining, and the Belzberg Brothers (Samuel, William, and Hyman Belzberg), head(s) of a family-owned financial conglomerate in Canada and themselves famous (or notorious) for raids on U.S. and Canadian companies. Within a few months, Mesa had acquired 8.3 percent of Gulf and Gulf Investors Group had picked up an additional 4.1 percent for a total investment of about $790 million. The intention was to raise the investment, eventually, to 15 percent of Gulf's outstanding stock. The cost would be nearly $1.1 *billion,* with Mesa supplying $700 million of the total.

This time Pickens had really entered the big time. Gulf was *Big Oil, seventy-five* times the size of Mesa Petroleum.

It had also long been the worst managed of the big oil companies. Its exploration and new production activities had failed for years to equal depletion, and its reserves had declined substantially.

Gulf had been the victim of both external and internal problems—not all of them of its own making. In 1975, Gulf lost both its Venezuelan and Kuwaiti drilling concessions. In 1976, its then chairman, Bob Dorsey, left the company in the wake of a messy political payoff scandal. It got caught up in Westinghouse's uranium lawsuits and was charged with being part of a consortium that had artificially raised uranium prices; Gulf ended up paying damages to Westinghouse. Jerry McAfee, Dorsey's successor, tried to rebuild the company slowly and cautiously, but ended up being little more than a caretaker. Between 1975 and 1982, Gulf's U.S. oil reserves fell more than 40 percent. Foreign reserves dropped even more when the loss of the Venezuelan and Kuwaiti concessions were added in.

James E. Lee, who replaced McAfee as Gulf's chairman and CEO, was far more vigorous. Needing a big hit to end the slow liquidation of reserves the company faced, he redirected Gulf's exploration program toward high-risk ventures in offshore and Arctic drilling (all recent *big* fields have been found either offshore or in the Arctic). He also shook up the company, reorganizing management and cutting personnel an astounding 25 percent. And he began using company cash flow to buy back Gulf stock, a method of increasing per-share earnings, thereby increasing the stock price.

Lee accomplished a lot in his first two years, but he had not yet turned the company around in 1984. It was simply too big for anyone to make that much of a change that quickly. Worse, despite some obvious successes in his rebuilding program, the stock price was still too low.

From a raider's point of view, the company looked like a good target. Lee's accomplishments seemed to point to a possibility that the company *could* be turned around, and the stock, at around $40 a share, was selling for far below appraised estimates of its value (one appraisal put the potential value of Gulf's shares, based on its assets, at $114 per share).

Pickens, of course, had his standard solution: form a royalty trust from Gulf's domestic properties and distribute shares to stockholders. By his estimate, the combined value of the royalty-trust shares and the ex-trust distribution stock would be better than $60 a share. This would be far better for shareholders and would, not incidentally, give the Pickens group a profit of around $220 million.

WHEN PICKENS BEGAN taking over other companies in the seventies, his purpose was, quite plainly, to build Mesa. As his targets got bigger and bigger, Pickens talked more and more about his desire to run a large, integrated oil company.

By the time of the Superior Oil deal, however, a new element had made its appearance and grown until it dominated Pickens's public thinking. One of the reasons Williametta Keck Day gave for refusing to deal with Pickens was, she said, that Pickens had told her he didn't think there was any more oil to be found by exploration. The remark was widely reported, but, at least in the press, no one seems to have recognized the significance of it.

T. Boone Pickens had made himself a multimillionaire by finding oil. Suddenly, in the early eighties, he was making public and private statements that it wasn't worth looking for oil any more. Most observers seem to have assumed that he was merely rewording his often-quoted remark that it was cheaper to find oil by buying companies than drilling for it. But there is a difference between saying it is cheaper to find oil one way than another and saying that *there is no longer oil to be found.*

Which leads to Pickens's proposals to use royalty trusts. Royalty trusts can maximize cash flow to shareholders and eliminate double taxation of dividends (income flows through the trust to the trustholders; it is taxed only once, when received by the holder—there is no tax at a corporate level). This is one of the attractions of Pickens's plans for Superior, for Gulf, or for Cities Service. The disadvantage, however, is that a royalty trust will eventually liquidate itself because it does not replace reserves it depletes.

Pickens makes a good argument that companies such as Gulf were liquidating themselves anyway so they might as well form trusts that will "waste" less money in taxes. There is, however, an unspoken corollary to Pickens's "there isn't any more oil to be found" statements that also applies to royalty trusts: If there really *isn't* any more oil to be found, then money spent attempting to replace reserves is also being wasted.

No doubt Pickens doesn't expect to be taken literally when he says there is no oil. But he does seem to mean that in a time of falling oil prices and increasing exploration costs, exploring for oil is no longer worthwhile.

"The oil and gas business doesn't lend itself to heavy exploration activities," he said in late 1985. "Finding costs are too high, there's a lack of markets for natural gas, and uncertainty for oil prices." Heavy exploration activities, though, are what large oil companies are all about. Therefore, he seems to be saying that the best thing to do with big oil companies is to liquidate them.

He never uses the word liquidate, but he does talk a lot about the need to "reorganize" big oil. And perhaps he's right. Smaller companies don't need huge finds to make a significant difference on the bottom line; the future of the oil industry in a world of decreased prices and increased costs may lie with the smaller independents. But reorganizing big oil is a very different goal than picking up reserves for Mesa or showing big oil managers that he could run an integrated company better than they could.

Somewhere along the line, Pickens seems to have radically changed his intentions and ambitions. Or perhaps that is what he meant all along when he said he wanted to run a big company. Maybe he had this vision of a reorganized oil industry from the start, but no one picked up the clues.

Or possibly they did—consciously or unconsciously. Maybe it's the reason oil company executives now treat him like a leper and want no part of him as a shareholder.

To men who have dedicated their whole lives to looking for oil, a bona fide oil man who no longer believes looking is worthwhile is a heretic.

And no orthodox community of any kind—religious, scientific, or commercial—likes, or even tolerates, heretics.

WHEN PICKENS MADE his proposals to restructure Gulf, he expressed a hope that Gulf would go along, since Lee had stated publicly that he was sensitive to Gulf shareholders' unhappiness. Instead, Gulf geared up for a fight. Lee declared, "We're going to defend management's actions vigorously." Harold Hammer, a Gulf executive charged with overseeing the companies defense, added that the royalty trust was "a dumb idea that would mutilate Gulf Oil."

There is a difference between the defenses a small company can muster and those of a giant such as Gulf. One of Gulf's first defensive moves was to negotiate an addition of $4 billion to its line of credit, giving it a total credit line of $6 billion. That's a large fighting fund. It raised its quarterly dividend from 70 cents to 75 cents—anything that makes shareholders happier tends to make them vote with management.

Lee quickly called a special shareholders' meeting for December 2. "I wanted a referendum on Boone Pickens taken at a time not of Boone's picking," Lee said. The agenda was straight out of the antitakeover handbook: consider moving the company's state of incorporation to Delaware (a state where challenges are harder to make), and consider changing the voting rules to make it more difficult for Pickens to gain a seat on the board of directors.

Gulf also showed that it, like Chemical Bank in 1969, was a member of the establishment. Within a short time, four banks that had dealings with both Gulf and Mesa withdrew multi-million-dollar lines of credit from Mesa.

The battle lines were clearly drawn.

Throughout November, Gulf shareholders were bombarded with letters, bulletins, and newspaper advertisements expressing the views of one side or the other. "Important Message to Gulf Shareholders," read a Pickens ad, signed by him "On Behalf of the Gulf Investors Group." James Lee, Gulf's chairman, took a more folksy approach. Under a headline that read, "Important Message to All Gulf Oil Corporation Shareholders," came the line, "Dear Fellow Gulf Shareholder."

The debate, once you got past the emotionalism and name-calling, centered on whether a royalty trust would work for Gulf. Pickens, citing his successful experience at Mesa, said it would. Lee and Hammer said it wouldn't, pointing out that a big, integrated oil company was different than a small, unintegrated one. Analysts on the street were split.

The oil industry wasn't. Executives of the other majors saw Pickens's plans for Gulf as a threat to them all. Other large independents were equally opposed, but for different reasons. Most were afraid that an attack on a company such as Gulf would focus unwelcome Congressional attention on the oil industry, in general, and mergers, in particular.

The attention generated on Wall Street by the raid was already great. At a meeting held in the Waldorf Astoria in New York, over two hundred analysts and money managers showed up despite a pouring rainstorm to hear Pickens say he would not cut any separate deals with Gulf. Pickens had taken a stand: He would not accept greenmail.

On December 2, Gulf shareholders voted with management against Pickens. Pickens challenged the vote in court and failed. Gulf reincorporated in Delaware and put its defenses in order.

Pickens had predicted that if he lost, Gulf stock, which had risen from $35 to $45, would fall back to $35. Instead, after an initial sag down to the $42 range, it slowly went up to more than $50. Wall Street was betting that Pickens was not finished.

One explanation for the continued strength of Gulf's stock price lay with the arbitrageurs. Gulf was not popular with the arbitrage community; many of them had lost heavily when Gulf backed out of the merger with Cities Service, and that bit of emotion may have helped sway them into staying with the stock in hopes that Pickens—or someone else—would make a tender offer. Also, had there been any doubt about the undervaluation of oil stocks, it had been put to rest when Texaco offered $10 billion for Getty Oil. Applying the same kind of per-share valuation (based on such things as cash flow and appraised value of reserves) to Gulf would result in a price of $80 a share. A lot of people were willing to bet a lot of money that Gulf might go that high.

Gulf seems to have underestimated Pickens throughout the raid, and nowhere is that more apparent than immediately after its successful proxy fight. When Gulf dropped to $42, the Pickens group was sitting with a paper loss in the stock, which made keeping the bank financing that had funded the purchases difficult and expensive. The group was also vulnerable to such anti-takeover actions as the issuance of new shares (diluting their position) or the acquisition by Gulf of another company. If new stock were issued for the purchase, it would also dilute the stock. (Disney tried this in its abortive purchase of Gibson Greeting Cards.) Instead, Gulf ignored the advice of its investment bankers (Solomon Bros. and Merrill Lynch) and ignored Pickens.

Once the stock price crept up past Pickens's break-even price, much of the pressure was off him. Also, as it became apparent to the investment community that Gulf was not about to counterattack (Gulf could easily have made a Pac-Man bid for Mesa, given the difference in the companys' sizes), it became easier for Pickens to find financing for another attempt.

Pickens's search was considerably smoothed by, of all things, another big oil company. As in all raids, the presence of one shark tends to attract others. People who might never have considered looking at another company see a raid in progress and begin to wonder whether making one themselves might be a good idea.

In this case, the man with the idea was Robert O. Anderson, the chairman of Arco. He called Lee and suggested that Arco take over Gulf for $70 a share. The total package would be $11.7 billion.

Since the Texaco-Getty deal had shown that not only was the financing available from the banks for a deal of that magnitude but also that the federal government would not intervene on antitrust grounds just because of the size of the companies involved, this was a real offer. Lee turned Anderson down, but details of the offer soon appeared in the newspapers.

It was all Pickens needed. If Arco also saw worth in buying Gulf, Pickens must be on the right track. It gave him credibility. If he could pick up enough Gulf stock to force a takeover, he should be able to get the money to do it.

At the time, he was trying to raise $3 billion through Drexel Burnham Lambert. (More on that later.) He abandoned the attempt and, instead, sold $300 million worth of Mesa securities to Penn Central Corp. He was mortgaging his own company to the hilt. This was more than just betting the rent money; this was betting the farm.

It was not what you would expect of a greenmailer. The conclusion is inescapable: Pickens wanted Gulf, not greenmail.

He tendered for 13.5 million of Gulf's 165 million outstanding shares, offering $65 a share. While success in the tender would not give him control, it was likely that many more than the 13.5 million would be tendered. With Arco's offer making headlines, Pickens envisaged no difficulty in raising additional money once shares began pouring in—and the number of shares tendered for can always be raised once the bidding begins.

Gulf panicked. After months of not taking Pickens seriously, they were faced with the possibility that by March 14, the end of his tender, he might control the company. Hurried defensive moves were tried but failed.

Gulf was hampered in its defense, in part, by a residue of hostility on the street. When Gulf backed out of its takeover deal with Getty, the price of Getty's stock dropped. A lot of investors and arbitrageurs lost money. Those same investors were not about to go out of their way to help Gulf avoid Pickens. Pickens was the beneficiary of the hostility. While it was the Arco deal that provided the justification for the price he wanted to pay, the hostility to Gulf made it easier to raise money.

Pickens had become a juggernaut that could be turned aside in only one way.

On February 24, Lee announced that Gulf was for sale. He hoped a non-oil company would be the buyer—thus keeping Gulf intact as a separate entity—but this hope soon died. No one but an oil company would want oil reserves badly enough to pay $70 to $80 a share (Gulf's asking price) for the company.

So desperate was Gulf management that they opened their books to potential suitors, asking only that those admitted to look agree not to launch spoiling raids if they lost the bidding.

Arco (formally Atlantic Richfield), Socal (formally Standard Oil of California), Unocal (formally Union Oil), Standard Oil of Ohio (which hadn't changed its name), and Allied all agreed to the terms. Mobil was the only one of the majors who opted out, claiming the price was too high.

While the examination was going on, Gulf was approached by Kohlberg Kravis Roberts & Co., an investment banker. Kohlberg Kravis proposed a management leveraged buyout of Gulf, taking the firm private by paying $87 a share for 51 percent of the shares and paying for the rest with preferred stock and debentures.

It probably would have worked (Kohlberg Kravis was to take the giant consumer goods company Beatrice private with a similar deal late in 1985), and it was, at least potentially, the deal that would have given Gulf's shareholders the biggest payout, but it was too complicated for already-rocky Gulf's board of directors to deal with. It would require too much refining before it could take place and Pickens was breathing down their necks *now*.

Arco offered $72 a share, Socal $80. Socal won, hands down.

Gulf agreed to merge with Socal, and Pickens abandoned his tender; $80 a share was too rich for him to overbid.

Gulf's managers were given big golden parachutes; Gulf employees whose jobs were in jeopardy were assured of generous severance benefits; Socal's and Gulf's investment bankers split about $60 million in fees, and Gulf's shareholders received $80 a share for their stock.

The arbitrageurs made a lot of money, the best revenge for the losses they suffered when Gulf pulled out of the Cities Service deal.

Mesa and its partners made $760 million.

Pickens had made a killing and became the most famous raider of them all.

A BIG QUESTION still remains. What would Pickens have done if he had taken over Gulf?

In March of 1984, *Fortune* magazine reported that it had obtained a copy of a highly confidential solicitation, circulated by Drexel Burnham, that had been sent out when Drexel was seeking money for Pickens to mount a tender offer—before Arco's bid spurred Pickens to mortgage Mesa and go for broke. Although the company in the solicitation documents was code-named "Grey," as *Fortune* put it, it was "unmistakably Gulf."

The documents outlined a takeover of the target company. After takeover, the company *would be broken up and the pieces sold off.* The solicitation suggested that the pieces would all be sold by 1986—within two years—and the return to an investor (assuming a takeover price of $55 a share) would average between 27 percent and 88 percent compounded, depending on sale prices.

By the time *Fortune* acquired the document, Gulf was already up to $57 a share, and Pickens was preparing his go-for-broke bid at $65, but it nonetheless gives a remarkable look at Pickens's intentions. The solicitation doesn't mention keeping reserves. It says nothing about showing the world how a major oil company should be run. It simply envisages breaking it up and selling the pieces for the most money possible.

Had Irwin Jacobs been the author of the plan, no one would have been surprised. But it doesn't sound like the public image of

Pickens the oil man, champion of the little shareholder, seeker after reserves, the man who is sure he knows how to run an oil company.

Instead, it sounds like a man who no longer believes in big oil. His reorganization of the oil industry seems, at least on the basis of the solicitation, to mean the liquidation of the oil industry.

ONE OF THE companies that was invited to look at Gulf was Unocal, the thirteenth largest oil company in the United States. Its chairman Fred Lloyd Hartley, was sixty-eight years old in 1985 when he faced T. Boone Pickens directly.

The later part of 1984 and the early part of 1985 were occupied, for Pickens, by the conclusion of his raid on Phillips Petroleum. Because of the intervention of other raiders, Pickens's group ended up making even more money than greenmail would have given them, since the final form of the restructuring paid shareholders, including Pickens, more than his original agreement would have. The extra money was to come in handy. Pickens had already turned his attention to another target.

It is possible that he abandoned his raid on Phillips because he saw a better opportunity at Unocal. Unocal had a far better debt-to-equity ratio than Phillips, and its domestic oil and gas reserves were stronger. With opposition so high at Phillips and a better target near at hand, he may have simply given up on Phillips. Whatever his reasons, early in 1985 a consortium called Mesa Partners II began buying Unocal stock. By early March, the partnership had accumulated nearly 10 percent of the outstanding stock in Unocal.

Unocal reacted with predictable hostility, but Pickens remained, at least publicly, unfazed. The investment, he said, was "strictly for investment purposes."

Unocal's annual meeting was scheduled for the end of April. Unocal immediately put in motion rules that would make it more difficult for Pickens to nominate, let alone elect, a slate of rival directors.

Late in March, Mesa Partners II spent $322 million to purchase 6.7 million more shares of Unocal. The partnership now owned 13.6 percent of the company. Under the new rules, however, only the original 9.8 percent could be voted at the shareholders' meeting; the cutoff date for voting was holders of record as of March 14.

With the annual meeting looming on the horizon, Pickens launched a proxy fight in an attempt to unseat Hartley. Hartley indicated that Unocal would unveil an antitakeover plan at the meeting.

Hartley made no attempt to conceal his attitude toward Pickens. Both men were called to testify in April at the House Ways and Means Committee hearings about takeovers. Meeting in the hall outside the committee room, Pickens offered his hand to Hartley. Hartley responded with a snarled, "Go away."

"Fred, you're talking to your largest stockholder," Pickens replied.

"Isn't that a shame," Hartley responded. Later he told reporters, "I decided that he wasn't entitled to shake my hand."

Inside, in his testimony, Hartley continued his attack. "Mr. Pickens has somehow created a speculative frenzy that has convinced his camp followers that there's easy money to be made in attacking oil companies and to hell with tomorrow." He continued, "Too many fine oil companies have already been destroyed, or nearly so, by Mr. Pickens and his ilk. The beneficiaries of Pickens's actions are not America's energy consumers, America's security, or even small shareholders, but rather only a handful of shareholders—and, of course, Mr. Pickens.

"If the Russians had somehow quietly managed to murder five of the country's leading oil companies," he added, "and were stalking the rest, I'm certain that Congress would be in an uproar, demanding action. But murder it has been and murder it may be."

Pickens generally kept his testimony on a less personal basis, but he did stray off into an attack on Hartley's executive perks. Pointing out that Unocal's corporate jet was equipped with a piano, Pickens said it was there for the use of "the guy in the back," indicating Hartley, who was sitting some rows behind the witness table. "The piano cost $500," Pickens went on, "but it cost $50,000 to install it aboard the airplane. Who paid for all this? The shareholders."

Hartley was blunt in his response. The piano had been a gift from grateful employees, he said. Pickens statements were "the same old crap."

Later, after the Unocal raid was history, Pickens sounded almost hurt about Hartley's attitude. In an interview in *Barron's,* Pickens said, "He called me a Commie, a barbarian, all kinds of stuff. I mean, that was his thanks to somebody that had put a billion dollars in his company. I wouldn't consider doing that, even if somebody I didn't like came in and bought a billion-dollars worth of Mesa stock."

Pickens lost the proxy fight, and Unocal put into place its defenses. And here is where the Unocal deal becomes unique.

Pickens began a tender offer for Unocal, offering $54 a share in cash for enough shares to give his group a majority ownership and $54 in debt securities for the rest. Unocal countered with a bid for its own shares, offering $72 a share in debt securities for 50 million shares of stock—29 percent. If Unocal's offer was successful—and with Unocal offering a third more than Pickens, it most likely would be—Unocal would be saddled with a huge amount of additional debt: $3.6 billion worth. This would make a leveraged buyout of Unocal almost impossible.

The new wrinkle was that Unocal excluded Mesa's stock from eligibility under the offer. Mesa could not tender its stock.

Mesa sued. In a Delaware district court, it won. The court held that Unocal could not discriminate against one group of share-holders. Unocal appealed but lost again in the appeals court. Unocal did not give up. It appealed to the highest court with jurisdiction, the Delaware Supreme Court—but, meanwhile, covered its bets by offering to buy Pickens out. Pickens walked out of the meeting.

On May 17, the Delaware Supreme Court ruled that Unocal could discriminate against Mesa Partners II. It held that Unocal was acting legally under the "business judgment rule" against a "grossly inadequate, coercive, two-tier, front-end-loaded tender offer." Looking at Pickens's recent takeover attempts, the court ruled that his presence in the partnership led to "a reasonable inference that its principal objective is greenmail."

Pickens had the ground abruptly cut out from under him. Had

he been able to tender Mesa Partners' stock to Unocal, the partnership stood to make about $178 million. Instead, with the probability that Unocal stock would drop after the offer back to the low 30s, Mesa Partners would lose over $300 million.

Although Hartley had Pickens over a barrel, he agreed to negotiate. Pickens was still suing in federal court, charging that Unocal had violated securities laws in changing the voting rules before the annual meeting, and a win there would reactivate Pickens as a threat. Pickens and Hartley quickly agreed to a deal. Unocal would buy 32 percent of Mesa's stock in the buyback (other investors would get to exchange 38 percent of their stock).

The arithmetic worked out as follows: Mesa Partners had paid over $1.1 billion for their stock. They would receive $574 million on the exchange, leaving them with 16 million shares. At the time of the deal, Unocal shares were trading at about $33 a share for unexchanged shares. At that price, Mesa stood to lose $20 million. With interest expenses and legal fees added in, analysts figured Mesa's pretax loss at nearly $100 million.

It was a figure to give even the most sanguine raider pause. When asked about the loss, Pickens responded, "You can't hit a home run every time you come to bat."

IT IS CONCEIVABLE that Pickens will eventually come out whole. Unocal announced it would use one of Pickens's ideas after all and spin off partnership units that will own 45 percent of Unocal's U.S. oil and gas reserves—a variation on the royalty trust. If the combined price of the partnership units (shares) and the ex-distribution Unocal shares are high enough, Pickens could still come out ahead. But his group will have been stuck with Unocal stock for over a year before they can get out, and interest and legal expenses will continue to mount.

Mesa, astoundingly enough, posted a *gain* on its investment in Mesa Partners II—of $83 million—but careful analysis showed that the gain was strictly on paper, the result of creative manipulation of the IRS code and corporate financial rules. A surer indication, most people felt, was that Pickens, who had been voted a $18.6 million bonus by Mesa directors after the Gulf raid and had gotten $5.5 million after the Phillips raid, received nothing—other than his regular salary—after Unocal.

Unocal may have been the victor, but it wasn't celebrating. Like Phillips before them, the cost of victory was Pyrrhic. Unocal, once proud possessor of an excellent debt-to-equity ratio, had saddled itself with debt. It was committed to spinning off 45 percent of its reserves. It would no longer be the company it had been before the raid.

As Fred Hartley said in a speech to the Natural Gas Processors Association annual convention in Houston in 1985: "We have a new word in our vocabulary called restructuring. What all this comes down to is simply withdrawing the warm blood of equity and replacing it with cold water and debt."

IN THE WAKE of Unocal, speculation was rife about what Pickens would do next. The answer came late in August: Mesa Petroleum was going to be restructured. Taking a leaf from Unocal's book—but applying it to the whole company, not just 45 percent—Mesa was going to cease being a corporation and become a partnership.

The plan would be carried out in two stages. In December 1985, Mesa shareholders would receive one partnership unit for each share of stock. For the next year, the units would trade simultaneously with the stock. After that, a second partnership unit would be exchanged for the stock. Mesa's shareholders would now be partners in the company. Double taxation of dividends would end and, theoretically, everyone would make more money.

Especially T. Boone Pickens. Pickens gets a 1-percent management fee (maximum in any one year is $1.8 million) plus a 4-percent acquisition fee for any new properties he finds that the partnership buys. He also continues to participate in profit sharing.

Pickens stands to make almost $25 million if he cashes in his stock options and could make nearly $60 million more by selling off part of his 7-percent interest in the partnership (his agreement as general partner says he must keep at least 2 percent, leaving him free to sell off the remaining 5 percent).

Pickens says, however, that the profit figures are illusory. In order to get the $25 million from cashing in his stock options, he would have to exercise the options—and that, he says, would cost him too much (he estimates he would have to borrow $50 million).

Instead, the options will be converted into partnership shares. By his calculations, he will end up with 90 percent of his assets in the Mesa partnership—and, he adds, he has no intention of selling.

Pickens feels this should reassure Mesa stockholders that the restructuring isn't a way for him to get his money out and leave them behind. So what *is* the purpose of the partnership? Consider this exchange between Pickens and *Barrons* in September of 1985 about the then-upcoming vote on Mesa's restructuring:

Q. So there's a Boone Pickens emancipation provision in that proxy?

A. It clearly says in there that I'll be general partner and look after the partnership business, but it will also give me freedom to do other things.

What other things might Pickens do? One of the things he has already done is to testify before the SEC about the Delaware Court decision. The SEC seems inclined to forbid discriminatory treatment of shareholders. That would lift the specter of the Unocal decision from Pickens's shoulders. The Delaware court, by specifically identifying Pickens as a greenmailer who could be discriminated against, puts Pickens at some risk if he tries another takeover under the present rules. If the SEC takes action to effectively nullify the Delaware court ruling, Pickens would be right back in the game.

"Somebody said the other day," Pickens says, "that Boone Pickens was probably going to get out of the oil industry. Well, that somebody doesn't know what he's talking about."

WALL STREET DID not have long to wait to see whether Pickens was a man of his word. In January 1986, he made a hostile offer for KN Energy Inc., a natural-gas distribution company, after its board rejected his initial friendly overtures. Mesa had first approached KN in 1983—and had been rejected then as well. This time, though, Pickens seemed to be more intent on pursuing the deal, despite KN's hostility.

Less than a month later, the papers carried the announcement that Pickens was after still another company, Pioneer Corporation, an oil and gas producer headquartered in Amarillo, Texas. (*The New York Times* pointed out that if a merger took place, moving costs would be low—the headquarters buildings of Mesa and Pioneer are only two blocks from each other.) The bid for Pioneer was friendly, and Pioneer management seemed inclined to agree. Ironically, Pickens may have snatched Pioneer away from another raider. Irwin Jacobs already had a 14-percent stake in Pioneer and had made a $700 million offer for the rest of Pioneer's shares. Pickens's offer was higher than Jacobs's and Jacobs lost the fight. In March Pickens and Pioneer announced that Mesa would acquire Pioneer in a stock swap.

KN was still studying the situation.

The ink was barely dry on the Mesa restructuring when Pickens made these bids. As KN and Pioneer show: whose who wrote off Pickens after Unocal have another think coming.

5

A Cautionary Tale

ASHER EDELMAN

ASHER EDELMAN HAS been a raider since 1982. In that short time he has scored big twice. Those big scores led to the public trappings of success as a raider—mention in *Time* magazine, articles in *Barron's,* and profiles in the *Wall Street Journal.* Compared to the years it took a Pickens or a Jacobs to attract that much attention, Edelman arrived with a bang.

But all is not always roses in the life of a raider and Asher Edelman's story illustrates that well. Like T. Boone Pickens, Edelman has made some mistakes. So far, unlike T. Boone (who, until Unocal, always seemed to come out ahead even when he shouldn't have), he hasn't managed to make his mistakes pay.

Worse, he's alienated Wall Street in the process. That can be costly. The Street's hostility to Gulf Oil, incurred after Gulf backed off from acquiring Getty, hindered Gulf's defense against Pickens. Gulf was a huge firm with a lot of clout. Raiders such as Edelman, who have to convince the Street to side with them in a raid, are doubly handicapped if the Street starts out hostile.

What's most surprising about Edelman having alienated the arbitrageurs is that he, of all people, should know better.

He is one.

ASHER EDELMAN GREW up in the New York City suburb of Lawrence. Lawrence is one of the "Five Towns," a group of villages that make up a wealthy enclave on the south shore of Long Island near the Nassau County-New York City border.

The border marks more than a political demarcation. On the Nassau County side, where Edelman lived, are expensive homes and streets lined with shops and boutiques selling to the rich, the well-to-do, and the merely affluent. On the New York City side are modest homes, poor apartments, and stores that sell inexpensive appliances and food. People in Lawrence who work in the city drive to work or ride the Long Island Rail Road; the branch line that serves Lawrence is considered one of the best the L.I.R.R. runs. People on the other side of the border ride the Rockaway line of the New York City subway. It is a long ride on the subway to the city and at night a lonely—and often dangerous—one.

Interestingly enough, the area of the city nearest to Lawrence is Far Rockaway. Carl Icahn and Asher Edelman grew up within a mile of each other.

Edelman went to Bard College, a small school located among the rolling hills that border the Hudson River midway between New York City and Albany. He took his degree in economics. After graduation, Edelman worked in various jobs in the brokerage industry both in New York and Europe. In 1969, he co-founded a small brokerage house, but it didn't work out. It folded in 1974 amid disagreements with his brother (and co-founder) John Edelman. The breakup led to lawsuits. Over the next few years, he found his true metier. Working through partnerships, he committed himself to one of the more esoteric and misunderstood areas of finance: arbitrage.

Arbitrage has a history that dates back to the Middle Ages. It developed along with—and sometimes ahead of—the financial markets we take for granted today. It exists wherever something is traded regularly, whether the trade is in stocks or bonds, currencies, precious metals, or oil.

Edelman began with hedge arbitrage, probably the oldest and certainly the safest form of the business. Today, hedge arbitrage relies on virtually instantaneous communications and networks of people. It requires split-second decisions and can involve large amounts of money invested for tiny returns.

Tiny returns, that is, that accumulate into big returns.

The classic illustration of hedge arbitrage is of a stock that trades on two different stock exchanges that are open at the same time: Paris and London, New York and London, New York and the Pacific Stock Exchange in California, for example. An arbitrageur, looking at the trading on the tape as it occurs, sees that XYZ company is trading at 10 in New York and at 10¼ on the Pacific Exchange. The arbitrageur buys stock in New York at 10 and simultaneously sells it for 10¼ on the Pacific Exchange. The profit is the quarter point differential less costs.

The buy in New York will tend to push the price up there, while the sale on the west coast will do the opposite. Thus, one result of the arbitrageur's action is to smooth out the differences between the two markets.

Of course, the actual transaction is not as simple as the explanation makes it seem. To make a profit, the arbitrageur has to be a member of both exchanges or have an arrangement with a member (otherwise, brokerage commissions would eat his profit). He has to have people in place to make the trades. He must know, as he buys the stock in New York at 10, that he can still sell it in California at 10¼.

And he has to buy and sell in sufficient quantity to make those tiny profits meaningful.

After cutting his teeth in hedge arbitrage, Edelman moved on to currency and convertible bond arbitrage. Currency arbitrage is a bit trickier, as it involves differences in exchange rates and a transaction may include more than two currencies—a trade exchanging lira into pounds into dollars into lira again would not be unusual. Convertible-bond arbitrage is a little more straightforward.

Bonds that are convertible into other securities—as well as convertible stocks—trade with two separate pressures on their prices. One is the value of the bond as an income vehicle, which is related to interest rates and the creditworthiness of the company backing the bond. The other pressure is the value of the security into which the bond is convertible. If, for example, a bond is convertible into 10 shares of stock and the stock is trading at 50, the bond has a conversion value of $500—regardless of its value as an income vehicle. If the bond is selling for $475, it can be purchased at that price, converted into stock, and the stock sold for $500, a profit of $25 before expenses. This is, simply, what a convertible arbitrageur does. Again, the reality is more complicated. Conversion rights are often hedged with caveats and frequently cost money (the bond, for example, might give the right to convert into 10 shares only upon payment of $10 a share for the stock). The arbitrageur must, once again, know his markets and be able to execute trades at the favorable prices.

Despite extensive computer aids and systems to alert arbitrageurs to opportunities, arbitrage is still a field that requires talent. The market is an ever-changing place, and the arbitrageur is playing those changes. Like the commodity pits, it is no place for the fainthearted.

Edelman was good at it and, by the end of the decade, he was able once again to found a brokerage firm—two of them, in fact. In 1977, he started Arbitrage Securities. Later, in 1980, he started up Plaza Securities. He still controls both of them.

But despite his success—or, perhaps, because of it—the tamer forms of arbitrage held his interest for only a little while. In the late seventies, he began to dabble in risk arbitrage. By the time he launched his first raid, risk arbitrage accounted for 40 percent of the profits earned by Arbitrage Securities and Plaza Securities.

Anyone who has owned a stock in a company being taken over is familiar with the market side of risk arbitrage. Glance at a paper soon after a merger or takeover is announced and look at the price of the stock of the company being acquired. If the takeover price is at 20, the stock will usually be trading at slightly less than 20. If the deal looks solid, the price might be 19⅞. If the deal looks shaky, it might be trading at some lower price—the shakier the deal, the lower the price.

If the stock owner merely holds his or her stock until the deal is consummated, the stock will be taken in at $20 a share. But suppose the stockholder doesn't want to wait? It might be a month or more before the stock is taken. The investor might reason that 19⅞ now, less commission, is better than 20 two or three months down the road. And that 19⅞ is cash in hand. A sudden threat of antitrust action or a breakdown of the deal might prevent the payment of the $20 and the stock might slip back to its lower pre-merger price. The investor might never see that $20.

But who would be willing to buy the stock for 19⅞? An eighth of a point is a tiny profit, especially when it requires waiting for a month or two to collect as well as taking the risk that the deal might fail. The buyer is the risk arbitrageur.

Here is where arbitrage really becomes an art, requiring a gambler's instincts in addition to the best possible access to information. The biggest profits come from buying into a stock at the lowest price—in other words, when the deal is least likely to come off. The arbitrageur must judge the situation, decide what the risks are versus the rewards, and then start to buy.

Fortunes have been made this way. They have also been lost. Edelman made a lot of money in risk arbitrage. Today, Arbitrage Securities and Plaza Securities have a combined equity of about $60 million. That's after whatever profit distributions have been made to Edelman and his other partners (Plaza Securities, for example, has seventy partners). Arbitrage has been very good for Asher Edelman. His personal fortune is estimated at over $40 million.

EDELMAN IS A good-looking man with dark hair, piercing eyes, and rather sensuous lips. He is married and has three children. He is reticent not only about his personal life; he also prefers to conduct his business affairs out of the limelight.

One area in which he does not hide his light under a bushel, however, is his art collection. Edelman is an inveterate collector of modern and contemporary art. His collection includes works by Picasso, Jasper Johns, Jean-Michel Basquiat, and Ad Reinhardt. Asked about his seeming eagerness to make a mark in the art world, Edelman replied, "I actually think that I've had an influence on certain contemporary artists."

Like most dealmakers, Edelman works hard, usually sixty hours a week. He tries to devote at least half that time to pursuing new deals. He normally works out of his offices at Plaza Securities, on New York's Fifth Avenue, where he can gaze out the windows at Central Park. One mark of eccentricity is that he often commutes to work in a chauffeur-driven jeep.

Edelman hasn't always worked such long hours. Before getting into takeovers, he used to spend months at a home he owns in Sun Valley, Idaho, skiing in the winter or hiking in the summer. Resorts like Sun Valley and Aspen attract entrepreneurs in their forties and fifties who have worked hard all their lives, made money, and are now prepared to sit back and enjoy it, playing as hard as they once worked, secure in the knowledge that should they lose everything they can always earn more. Edelman, with some $40 or $50 million under his belt, easily fit that mold.

But it wasn't enough. Like all the raiders, Edelman can't, or won't, just rest on his laurels.

Risk arbitrage must have begun to seem tame; for a dealmaker, any business that allows months to be spent away from the office would be too tame. In addition, as Edelman explains, by the early eighties too many other firms were crowding into the arbitrage business. "I began to look for an alternative that would have the kind of risk/reward that I wanted to accomplish," he says.

The answer was literally right in front of him. "Why not," he asked himself, "be a mover instead of betting that other people will be the movers?"

In 1982, at the age of forty-two, he became a mover. He may still indulge in a weekend's sailing—another of his hobbies—or go to Sun Valley to hike or ski, but since 1982 he has been in the thick of the action. He has gone from the unsafe world of risk arbitrage into the even less safe world of takeovers.

UNITED STOCKYARDS CORPORATION is not the sort of company generally associated with such high-risk pursuits as arbitrage and corporate takeovers. Its stock-exchange symbol is COW.

Appearances can be misleading. United Stockyards marked Asher Edelman's first foray into corporate raiding as a player rather than a hanger-on. It proved to be extremely lucrative.

In 1982, United Stockyards was part of a larger company called Canal-Randolph, a New York-based commercial real-estate firm. The company's stock sold for $26 a share.

Once Edelman decided to go into raiding on his own, he began looking for companies that seemed undervalued. All raiders follow much the same procedure in searching out raids. They—and their staffs—research companies, comparing asset ratios and debt loads and looking for corporations with hidden assets such as appreciated real estate carried at acquisition cost rather than current value. Canal-Randolph was one of the companies that met Edelman's parameters. Edelman decided the stock was worth a lot more than $26 a share. In fact, by his calculations, the company had a breakup value of about $85 a share.

Most raiders use a variety of methods—proxy fights, hostile tenders, etc.—to go after a target company. Until recently, Edelman worked exclusively by the proxy fight. Working through Arbitrage Securities, Plaza Securities, and a partnership set up just for the deal, Canran Associates I, he accumulated 20.8 percent of the outstanding stock in Canal-Randolph. He then announced in March 1983 that he planned to oust the board of directors at the next shareholders' meeting, and began soliciting proxies for his slate of directors.

Canal-Randolph's plans to fight back almost immediately fell afoul of the SEC, resulting in a typically bizarre set of SEC consent decrees. It turned out that a company called Rea Brothers PLC, a London-based brokerage firm headed by Canal-Randolph chairman Sir Walter Saloman, held 28.5 percent of Canal-Randolph. It also turned out that Rea Brothers had never bothered to notify the SEC that it owned more than 5 percent of Canal-Randolph—as is required by law. In a suit the SEC filed against Rea, it charged that Rea was *nine years* late in filing the required notification.

Rea countered that, as a brokerage firm, it was merely holding the stock for investors. The SEC pointed out that most of the stock Rea held was registered in the name of Walsa (Nominees) Ltd. Walsa stood for Walter Saloman, Rea's—and Canal-Randolph's—chairman.

It further turned out that Rea had agreed with another London firm, Montagu Investment Management Ltd., that Montagu would purchase shares of Canal-Randolph and vote them with management against Edelman. Canal-Randolph had neglected to tell its shareholders—or anyone else—about this cozy little arrangement.

The ways of the SEC, however, are not always scrutable by lesser mortals. No charges were filed against anyone for the nine-year "oversight," and all parties were allowed to sign consent degrees. The SEC also managed to find grounds to charge Edelman and *his* partners with violations of the disclosure laws, alleging that in June 1982 Edelman made plans to make a tender offer for Canal-Randolph and take over the company. Although the plans never came to fruition, the SEC somehow seemed to feel that Edelman should have made them public.

Edelman likewise signed a consent degree.

It is hard to escape the conclusion that the SEC wasn't really interested in pursuing criminal charges against Saloman and Rea, so they found a reason to charge Edelman, which allowed them to report that both sides in the dispute had equally violated disclosure laws—thus justifying their allowing both sides to sign consent decrees. How not reporting a plan that was abandoned without being put into operation equates with concealing for nine years a quarter-interest in a publicly traded company is something the SEC declined to explain.

The disclosures didn't help Canal-Randolph's management. Edelman had already made a convincing presentation to stockholders, promising that if his slate was elected to the board, stockholders would get more for their stock than the current market price. The SEC disclosures discredited management, undermining their claims that sticking with them would be more beneficial. Edelman garnered enough proxies to elect his slate to the board. He took the title of vice-chairman.

Edelman frequently becomes vice-chairman, rather than chairman, of companies he acquires, but the title is something of a misnomer. It is Edelman who is in control.

Using his new control of the board, Edelman promptly began to liquidate the company. United Stockyards was spun off to shareholders, becoming a separate company. Since Edelman's group owned nearly 30 percent of Canal-Randolph at the time of the spinoff, he retained the same percentage of United Stockyards. The rest of Canal-Randolph was sold off piecemeal. By 1985, most of the company was gone, with the proceeds distributed to shareholders.

Edelman's investment had been just under $23 million. Estimates of his profit on the deal range from $25 to $30 million.

Edelman calls his fight with Canal-Randolph the toughest fight he has had with management in his four deals, but, like other raiders before him, his former adversaries have a way of turning up later on as supporters. Raymond French was the head of Canal-Randolph during its fight against Edelman. He now heads United Stockyards and is considered, as one newspaper put it, a "close associate" of Edelman.

Politics is not the only area of endeavor that makes strange bedfellows.

EDELMAN'S NEXT MOVE was into an entirely different field: computers. The shakeout in the computer industry in the early eighties was large-scale and across the board. Software houses, makers of large computers, makers of personal computers, service companies—companies of every stripe were in trouble, with the exception of a few market leaders. Even those that weren't in bankruptcy often sold for less than book value. For a raider such as Edelman—a man out to liquidate, rather than run, the company he acquired—it seemed an ideal hunting ground.

His first target was a small business-computer maker: Management Assistance. Based in New York, Management Assistance had been one of the high flyers of the seventies. By the early eighties, however, more and more personal-computer makers—including giant IBM—were invading the market for small business computers. Management Assistance lagged behind. In 1979, the company earned $19 million. By 1984, year-end results showed a *loss* of $17 million.

Edelman looked beyond the numbers and liked what he saw. Several Management Assistance divisions seemed to him to have value beyond what the company's market price reflected. One division, Basic Four Information Systems, though losing money like the rest of the company, seemed to have good potential. Edelman saw the possibility of converting the division into a distribution company that would sell not just Management Assistance machines but also those of other manufacturers. As such, it could be sold for a good price despite its current losses.

Another division, Sorbus Service, looked even better. Sorbus repaired microcomputers. "It seemed to me," Edelman said, "something that on its own would sell for more than two times what Management Assistance as a whole was selling for in the marketplace."

That's the kind of numbers that make corporate raiders salivate.

Once again, Edelman used the mechanism of the proxy fight to go after the company. He acquired 10 percent of Management Assistance's stock, then launched his fight. After a bitter, six-month battle—during which management's anti-Edelman advertising became so vicious that Edelman sued for libel—he won four seats on the ten-member board of directors, replacing those directors most hostile to him. The result was to give him effective control of the board. Once again he took the title of vice-chairman.

In January 1985, the Sorbus and Basic Four divisions were sold—Sorbus to Bell Atlantic Corporation and Basic Four to a private investor, Bennett LeBow—beginning the corporate liquidation. In February, Management Assistance began sending liquidating dividends to all shareholders (liquidating dividends differ from regular dividends in that when the last dividend arrives, the company no longer exists). The dividends are still coming in, but the best estimates expect the total to equal at least $26 a share by the time the company is completely liquidated.

When Edelman first began buying stock in September 1983, the stock sold for $11 a share. His total investment was about $15 million. His profit? About $11 million.

A footnote to the Management Assistance takeover reflects, once again, how former enemies have a way of becoming friends. When Edelman won his proxy fight and was appointed vice-chairman, he got to name four directors to the board. One of the men he named was Dwight D. Sutherland. Sutherland had been one of the Canal-Randolph directors who had to resign to make room for Edelman's nominees on *that* board of directors.

EDELMAN WAS STILL small potatoes next to Pickens or Steinberg, but the Management Assistance deal, following as it did on the heels of the successful liquidation of Canal-Randolph, attracted a lot of attention. After all, Pickens and Icahn and other raiders had started small too.

Small, of course, is a relative term. The profits earned by Edelman's syndicates on the two deals had totaled between $35 million and $40 million—with more, perhaps, still to come—on total investments of about $38 million. That's a 100 percent or better return between late 1982 and early 1985. An amount like $38 million is only small compared to something like Pickens's killing on Gulf.

The problem with a growing reputation as a money-maker is that you have to keep doing it—any slip is regarded as a sign of grave failure and causes a loss of confidence. Headlines proclaimed that Pickens and his partners, for instance, may have lost as much as $100 million on the Unocal deal, but that figure still pales before the nearly *$1 billion* in profits his groups made prior to Unocal.

An ordinary investor who lost only $1 for every $10 he made would be considered a genius. Yet everyone jumped on Pickens's failure, predicting it would be the end of him as a raider.

Edelman had now entered that same rarefied atmosphere. Had he made his deals in the seventies or earlier, he might not have come under public scrutiny so quickly—Icahn, Jacobs, and Pickens were all active and successful for quite some time before their names became household words. (Steinberg, of course, became instantly notorious when he went after Chemical Bank.) Edelman did not have that leisure, however. His deals came in the midst of the incredible notoriety generated by the media fascination with corporate raiders.

Unfortunately, just as he was being touted as the new *wunderkind* of raiding, he stumbled.

IT WAS EDELMAN'S next two takeovers that tarnished his image: Mohawk Data Sciences and Datapoint. Like Icahn with TWA, many observers feel that Edelman has become mired long-term in what was supposed to be a short-term turnover. One magazine headlined its article on the subject: "Raider Asher Edelman Gets Trapped in the Executive Suite."

Edelman was led to investigate Mohawk in much the same way a shark might follow the smell of blood in the water—several executives of Management Assistance who left during and after the takeover went to Mohawk. It was only natural that Edelman would give the company a look.

What he saw seemed to be a repetition of what he had found at Management Assistance. Mohawk made, sold, and serviced minicomputers, just like Management Assistance. Also like Management Assistance, the service division was profitable while the manufacturing and sales divisions were not. It looked as if he could repeat the same scenario: sell the service division intact and restructure the sales division and sell it as well. "All it takes is some smart marketing," Edelman said at the time. "Those are assets I can sell."

Mohawk, like Management Assistance, had once been a high-flier. The company, based in Parsippany, New Jersey, was twenty years old when Edelman came on the scene. Some divisions still made money: Mohawk's subsidiary, DEK Identification Systems, makes identification cards for most state motor-vehicle agencies, and another subsidiary, Qantel Corp., dominated the market for custom minicomputer systems. But other areas of the company were in disarray for the same reason so many computer companies fail—because Mohawk hadn't kept pace with developments in the industry. It had failed to modernize—to introduce new models—and it was being left behind. In the fiscal year ending April 30, 1984, it had revenues of $400 million and posted a loss of $53 million. That worked out to an enormous $3.65 per share on the minus side.

A lot of that loss, however, was nearly $50 million in write-offs resulting from the closing down of two divisions. Both the divisions had been losing money, dragging down the more profitable sections of the company. Without the losing divisions and with the big write-down—and its effect on the company's stock—out of the way, Mohawk looked as if it had potential.

Mohawk offered another attraction to a raider. Part of its

financial difficulties stemmed from poor management: high overhead, too many employees, and research costs far too high for the results the company was getting. (For the price, Mohawk shouldn't have been falling behind.) For a liquidation-oriented raider, those are easy fixes. Streamline the company, cut fat, eliminate costs, and then, once profits begin to appear, sell quickly. It's not necessarily a bad thing for stockholders—look at the results at Management Assistance—nor is it necessarily bad for the company. Instead of one firm that's losing its shirt through bad investments and inefficiencies, the liquidator creates several firms that can run profitably either alone or as part of a different company.

There is, of course, a human cost—jobs lost or uprooted, etc.—but the same thing would happen if the firm continued into bankruptcy and closed, with the difference that then no one would still have a job. At best, a receiver would liquidate the firm by selling off the parts just as Edelman proposed to do.

And Mohawk was perilously close to that state. Mohawk had acquired a lot of debt—$180 million worth—making acquisitions that didn't pan out ($23 million of that $50 million write-off had been for one of those acquisitions, a California manufacturer of computer equipment). With losses piling up, Mohawk had violated the loan covenants on much of that debt. It was deep in talks with a group of banks on a way of renegotiating the debt. If the talks failed, the banks could push Mohawk into bankruptcy.

In the fall of 1984, Mohawk was selling for about $11 a share. Edelman calculated that if he broke the company up and sold it, he could net about $23 a share. By the time Mohawk realized what was happening, Edelman owned 8 percent of the company at a cost of $12.75 million—$10.85 a share. He was its biggest stockholder.

The Management Assistance liquidation was in progress while he bought, so Mohawk management could see exactly what Edelman had in mind. Surprisingly, they weren't totally in disagreement with Edelman. His ideas seemed the best way out for the company, and management was trying to come up with a plan to sell off divisions and restructure the company even before Edelman bought in.

Where they did disagree was in who was going to run the show. The chairman of Mohawk, Francis P. Lucier, was the retired chairman of Black & Decker. He had just finished taking over the company after the board caused the resignation of his predecessor, Ralph P. O'Brien. O'Brien had run Mohawk for nine years. Lucier, at least at first, wanted to try his own hand at mending the company.

Edelman, using his stock as leverage, made two offers. He would form a new company along with Mohawk management (*some* Mohawk management) and take over Mohawk for $250 million in securities. Given Mohawk's problems with its debt load, it wasn't a very realistic plan. Alternatively, he wanted to control the board.

Then Edelman's recently acquired reputation came into play. The stock began to go up, eventually reaching a high of 16¾. Edelman—who now claims he thought the stock was too high—sold about 13 percent of his holding, 160,000 shares, on the open market at prices between 14 and 16. That cut his holdings by only a fraction—to 7.7 percent—but recouped $2.25 million of his investment. He was still Mohawk's largest shareholder.

Mohawk decided to do it his way. He was appointed vice-chairman of the company. The arbitrageurs and speculators who had driven the stock up over 16 settled down to wait for him to repeat his performance at Canal-Randolph and Management Assistance.

Edelman had miscalculated. Mohawk had bigger problems than he had thought. Soon after he got involved, the company took another big write-off—$45 million. The stock sank slowly back to 11.

"There's no question," Edelman says, "that I made a mistake in my initial evaluation of Mohawk."

WHILE STILL ENMESHED in Mohawk, Edelman went after a second company. Datapoint was almost a twin of Mohawk. In the seventies, it had great success with local area-networking, a method of linking several small computers into one network within a company or area. It was, in fact, one of the pioneers in the field. But, like Mohawk and Management Assistance, it faltered during the 1982 recession and never recovered, while other companies moved ahead, eliminating Datapoint's lead. Worse, during the 1982 fiscal year it was revealed that 1981 sales had been overstated. 1981 earnings had been $49 million. 1982 produced earnings of only $2.4 million. Though they recovered thereafter ($8.1 million in fiscal 1983 and $26.4 million in 1984), the company's credibility was in doubt. Faced with competition that was now technologically *ahead* of it, Datapoint's future looked bad.

Edelman began to buy up Datapoint's stock in November 1984. In January 1985, he offered $23 a share for the company. Datapoint rejected the offer—not surprising, since Edelman admitted publicly that Datapoint was "a good candidate for a liquidation." By February, Edelman had accumulated 2 million shares at an average price of 17¾ and picked up options for an additional 223,000 shares.

He then moved to pick up enough consents to oust the board of directors and replace it with his own nominees.

Datapoint was not without defenses. Ever since consents had been revealed as a raider weapon, companies had realized the need to defuse them. Datapoint had put in place a requirement that forty-five days had to pass before consent votes could be counted (a time-gaining device) and barred the voting of consents altogether while the company was involved in litigation. The bylaw changes should have held Edelman off.

They didn't. Edelman sued in Delaware (Datapoint's state of incorporation). He had better luck with a Delaware court than Pickens did in his fight with Unocal. The court invalidated Datapoint's bylaw changes.

Datapoint was naked before his attack. It threw in the towel, and Edelman became chairman of the company in March 1985.

Then came the abrupt about-face that began Wall Street's alienation from Edelman. Datapoint's stock price had risen because of expectation that Edelman would repeat the strategy so successfully carried out at Management Assistance and Canal-Randolph. Edelman's own public comments and SEC filings had

led to the same conclusion—on March 1, in fact, he had specifically told the SEC that he would sell Datapoint to someone other
than himself or a member of his group. But by April, he had
changed his mind.

"I'm doing the thing that I think makes most sense for shareholders," Edelman said. "After all, I am the biggest shareholder."
What Edelman saw as best for the shareholders was to cut costs
and run the company as a going concern, rather than to liquidate
it.

The problem from the Street's point of view was that Datapoint after Edelman's takeover didn't look any better than it did
before he took it over. The action in the stock had all been in
anticipation of a liquidation and quick profits. Without that possibility, the stock quickly lost value. The arbitrageurs lost money
in droves.

Edelman's only explanation of his change of heart was that
new products Datapoint was readying for introduction would
turn the company around. No one at Datapoint, though, would
talk about the new products. All Edelman would say was "I saw a
technology I didn't expect to see."

THERE WAS SOME speculation that Datapoint's computer-service
division would be spun off or sold—TRW, a Cleveland-based
high-technology firm was reportedly interested in buying the
division—but most speculation centered on another possibility.
Rumors abounded that Datapoint's service division would be
merged with Mohawk's computer division and the two firms
would then be spun off or sold.

It was beginning to look as if Edelman had gotten into Datapoint in the hopes it would help pull him out of Mohawk.

Mohawk, meanwhile, was still in trouble. The stock price slid
below Edelman's cost, giving him a loss on the deal—even with
the profits from the stock he had sold at its high figured in.

On April 9, 1985, Edelman confirmed the rumors. Instead of
trying to sell the service division, the crown jewels of Datapoint,
which might have returned a good chunk of cash to the
company—and stockholders—the division was going to be spun

off to shareholders. As with the Canal-Randolph spinoff of United Stockyards, Edelman would maintain his percentage interest in the spun-off company and would therefore control it. He further announced his intention to merge the spun-off company with Mohawk's service division.

Datapoint's service division possibly could survive on its own; Mohawk's probably couldn't. By merging the two, Edelman undoubtedly hoped to create a single company that could survive. Datapoint's stockholders wouldn't necessarily benefit, but Mohawk's would. The unsalable service division would now be part of a profitable company, making the shares worth more.

And Edelman, of course, was the Mohawk shareholder with the most to gain.

Datapoint's shareholders, though, weren't particularly happy about the idea. Most observers felt that adding the Mohawk service division to Datapoint's would weaken the new company rather than strengthen it. In an effort to placate investors, Datapoint began to buy back its stock on the open market, taking advantage of the drop in the stock's price. This would, it was stated, benefit shareholders by propping up the price and increasing earnings per share. As such, it is a common strategy for publicly traded companies. It also had the effect of increasing Edelman's control. With less shares outstanding, his shares represented a larger percentage of the total.

To the further consternation of the Street, Edelman announced that he expected to earn an investment banking fee for cleaning up Datapoint. Shareholder sentiment began to mount against the merger of the two service divisions.

Edelman went ahead with the spinoff of Datapoint's service division anyway. The new company, Intelogic Trace Inc., had Edelman as chairman and largest stockholder. Talks with Mohawk about the merger went on, but shareholder opposition was making the merger seem much less likely.

By September, Mohawk's stock price had dropped to 1¾ from its high of 16 and the company was reporting fiscal 1985 losses of $181 million. And Mohawk was in default on its bank debt.

Datapoint's stock price also had dropped from its high of 21.

The combined value of the stocks of Datapoint and the spun-off Intelogic was only $14 a share; Edelman's cost was about $18 a share.

And no one appeared interested in the other parts of either company.

The basic problem seemed to be that, unlike Management Assistance, the service divisions and sales divisions of Mohawk and Datapoint handled only the companies' own products. As such, they were not good candidates for life on their own in the same way Management Assistance's had been. In addition, the combination of the takeover with the ongoing problems of both companies was scaring away customers. The erosion of the customer base was, in turn, adding to the bottom-line troubles— especially at Mohawk, awash as it was in red ink.

Edelman stayed tough in the face of mounting criticism. "Everybody will have to suffer Asher Edelman operating a computer company," he said. "It is not my intention to liquidate. I can't say it any plainer than that."

Meanwhile, TRW finally came through with a bid for Intelogic. To the incredulity of the Street, Intelogic's board—led by Edelman—rejected an offer by TRW to buy Intelogic for $177 million, equal to $9.50 a share. People who had hung on, expecting him to start liquidating the company and sending out some dividends, were furious. Intelogic announced that since it expected some shareholder opposition to its rejection of TRW's offer, it would begin its own buyback of shares. For up to 4 million of the 18.5 million shares outstanding, Intelogic offered a package of notes and preferred stock. The package was a complicated one and gave Intelogic the option of redeeming the package at any time for a $10 face amount, 15 percent subordinated note due in 1995—in other words, a junk bond.

At the same time as the rejection, Datapoint announced that Edelman wanted to take the company private through a leveraged buyout worth $6 a share. With it came a statement that put paid to any further speculation that Datapoint would be liquidated. The buyout, Edelman said, "will ensure the continued control and ownership that our customers are looking for. This makes it pretty evident that I'm here to stay."

About the only good news, from the Street's point of view, was that Intelogic had called off the talks to buy Mohawk's service division.

As 1985 drew to a close, Edelman was spending more and more time in San Antonio—Datapoint's headquarters—running the company and trying to get it back on the rails. Peat, Marwick & Mitchell & Co. resigned as Datapoint's accountants; Standard & Poor's Corp., the bond-rating agency, put Datapoint on its "credit watch" list, and the company was intangled in lawsuits with John C. Butler, a former Sperry Corp. executive who had been recruited by Datapoint only to be fired one month later (he had differed with the board over the Intelogic spinoff).

As for Mohawk, one respected Wall Street analyst made a succinct prediction: "It's a dead duck."

No matter what happens at Datapoint and Mohawk, it will be a long time before Edelman regains the confidence of the Street, so crucial to the swift completion of a raid.

Nevertheless, Edelman should not be counted out. As he himself said in September 1985, when asked if he would liquidate Datapoint, "Anything is possible."

In raiding, it usually is.

THE RISE IN stock market prices in 1985 and early 1986 saved part of Edelman's investment. Intelogic's stock price went up sharply along with the market. As a result, the combined value of Datapoint and Intelogic, by early 1986, had exceeded his acquisition cost. Edelman was finally showing a profit.

Mohawk, however, still showed a loss of over $5 million.

Edelman remained undaunted. Late in March 1986, it was revealed that a group Edelman headed had accumulated 1.1 million shares of Fruehauf Corporation, a Detroit-based manufacturer of truck trailers, cargo containers, and auto parts. Before the end of the month, Edelman had made a takeover proposal to the Fruehauf board. He offered to buy Fruehauf for $41 a share— $860 million. The stock price went up sharply on the news, then declined again a week later when the board rejected Edelman's offer.

What will happen next remains to be seen, but if the past is any guide, Edelman will once again launch a proxy fight in an attempt to gain control of Fruehauf's board.

Or he may try something else, such as a hostile tender. Just because he's never done it before doesn't mean he won't do it now.

Anything is possible.

6

The Knight Who Won a Crown

SIR JAMES GOLDSMITH

IN 1980, SIR James Goldsmith was trying to buy Diamond International Corporation. Diamond didn't want to be bought. They began looking for a white knight. At a meeting with the board of directors, Goldsmith asked, "What about me? I'm white, and I'm a knight."

The directors weren't impressed. They kept trying to fight Goldsmith off.

It didn't work. Goldsmith won.

It wasn't unusual. He rarely loses.

IN AN EARLIER period, Sir James Goldsmith wouldn't be included in a list of raiders. Had the general public been aware of him at all, he would have been considered a financier—or a robber baron—in the mold of John D. Rockefeller or J. P. Morgan. Not only doesn't a British knight fit the image of a raider, but Goldsmith also heads a chain of interlocking companies through which he makes his raids. As a result, he doesn't come across as a lone outsider chasing after helpless corporations, seeking greenmail rather than control.

But the activities of Icahn and Pickens and Steinberg and others have focused media attention on those who take over companies, and distinctions have begun to blur. Today, if you're in the business of taking over companies through hostile take-overs, you're a raider. By those standards, Sir James eminently qualifies. The basic difference between him and other raiders is his wealth. Some estimates put his personal holdings at $900 million. Others think that is an underestimate.

Goldsmith is an interesting person, a study in contrasts. At one and the same time he is described as flamboyant and camera-shy. He is an English knight and a French chevalier of the Legion of Honor. He first gained notoriety when he eloped with Isabel Patino, the heiress to a Bolivian tin fortune. He was twenty. After her death, he married Ginette Levy, a Frenchwoman. Despite having two children with her (plus one from his marriage to Isabel), he was obviously not ready to settle down. The British newspapers, not known for their reticence when a scandal is scented, gleefully chronicled the fact that while his wife and children lived in Paris, he kept a mistress—who had two children (his)—in London. At one point he took both families on vacation to the Mediterranean island of Sardinia at the same time. He kept the two groups discreetly separate, commuting between them by speedboat. In 1978, he finally divorced Ginette and married a third time. This time his bride was Lady Annabel Vane Tempest Stewart Birley—his English mistress. They have since had one more child.

Lest anyone think that after three wives and six children he had *now* settled down, *Fortune* magazine reported in 1983 that "in the last several years he has had a young French companion in the United States." The magazine added a quote from Gold-smith's brother, Edward (a well-known British scholar and envi-ronmentalist, usually known as Teddy): "Jimmy's a natural tribal polygamist."

Goldsmith has houses in Paris and London, but when in New York, he stays at a place in the East Eighties maintained, according to most reports, by that "young companion." (Goldsmith used to be quite open about his mistresses, but in recent years he has grown somewhat more discreet.) When he travels, he brings his butler with him.

James Goldsmith was born in Paris in 1933, the son of Frank Goldsmith, a well-known hotelier, and Marcelle Mouiller. His parents were socially acceptable and, while not rich, were reasonably well-to-do.

Frank Goldsmith was the descendent of a wealthy German family who had been bankers in Frankfurt since the late eighteenth century. In the 1880s, however, anti-Semitism increased dramatically in Frankfurt as Prussian influence dominated the newly unified Germany. The Goldschmidts, as they were then known, gave up banking and moved to England, anglicizing their name in the process.

Frank Goldsmith was born in England. He studied at Magdalen College, Oxford (where James's brother, Edward, was later to go), served in the British army, reaching the rank of major, and was later a Member of Parliament. Eventually, he went into the hotel business.

Young James went to Eton, and although his brief entry in *Who's Who* lists him as a graduate of Eton, he actually dropped out at the age of seventeen. He spent most of his time there enjoying himself—he liked to gamble—and was not very interested in studying.

Goldsmith took a job as a cook at the Palace Hotel for a year, then enlisted in the British Army as a private. His talents were soon recognized (helped, certainly, by the fact that, though a dropout, he *had* been to Eton), and by the time he left the army two years later he was a lieutenant.

Fresh from the army, he bought the French rights to a British rheumatism cream for $200 and started a company. It was 1953 and Goldsmith was twenty. Three years later, he sold the company for $300,000 and used the money to buy a diet-biscuit company that also did well. In small business circles, he was beginning to have a good reputation.

It was while he was getting started in business that Goldsmith began his public career in the sensational press. Setting up the pharmaceutical company wasn't the only thing he did in 1953. That was also the year he eloped with Isabel Patino. Her father, Antenor Patino, known as "the Bolivian Tin King," did not look kindly on Goldsmith's courting of his eighteen-year-old daughter. Goldsmith and Isabel took off for Scotland in a borrowed Rolls-Royce, making headlines across much of Europe and South America.

Their life together was to be tragically short, however. Within a year, Isabel had given birth to a daughter, Maria Isabel. Shortly afterward, she died.

Goldsmith began hitting his stride as an empire builder in the early sixties. In 1964, he began buying companies with two shared traits—they were all the same type of businesses, either candymakers or chains of shops that sold candy, newspapers, and tobacco, and they all were failing. "I bought what I could get," he said later.

Six years later, Cavenham Ltd., the holding company he had formed, was making a small profit. It was a remarkable achievement given the state of the companies he had bought, but more was to come. The British stock market went wildly bullish in 1971 and 1972, and Cavenham's stock went up with it. Taking advantage of the high price on his stock, Goldsmith quickly bought up nine companies, mostly for stock, and catapulted Cavenham's profitability.

From here affairs begin to get murky. Goldsmith's holdings are scattered throughout a variety of firms incorporated in different countries (a tactic more common in Europe and the Far East than in the United States). In 1976, Goldsmith's French company, Generale Occidentale, began buying up the publicly traded shares of Cavenham. Cavenham's shares were depressed due to the publicity surrounding a criminal libel suit Goldsmith had filed against a British magazine called *Private Eye*.

Private Eye is a satirical gossip magazine with a well-deserved reputation for skewering public figures. It never refers to anyone by name, using, instead, nicknames easily recognizable by those "in the know." Goldsmith's nickname was "Goldenballs." In its reporting on Goldsmith, however, the magazine went too far. It reported that "Goldenballs" had been a business associate of Roberto Calvi. Calvi was an Italian banker, often called "God's

Banker" because of his ties to the Vatican, whose affairs had begun to unravel in tales of fraud and links to organized crime in Italy and the United States. (In a still-unsolved mystery, Calvi was discovered hanged under Blackfriar's Bridge in London in 1982.)

The catch was that *Private Eye* had apparently dreamed the connection up for its sensational value. Goldsmith *hadn't* been an associate of Calvi's, business or otherwise.

Goldsmith, who is quick to go on the offensive when he feels he has been wronged, went after *Private Eye* with a vengeance. The magazine quickly backed down, admitting that its charges were false. Goldsmith wasn't satisfied—even after *Private Eye* publicly apologized—and brought the first criminal libel suit filed in Britain in thirty years against the magazine. He won, and *Private Eye* had to pay substantial damages.

While the case was proceeding, Generale Occidentale kept buying up Cavenham stock on the cheap. English institutional investors—as easily, if not more easily, spooked than their American counterparts—seemed only too glad to dump the stock. Goldsmith was able to increase his ownership of Cavenham at bargain prices. At the same time, the center of gravity of his empire shifted from England, where Cavanham was located, to France, the home of Generale Occidentale, since Generale Occidentale now controlled Cavenham.

Generale Occidentale was not long to remain the center of his empire, however. By the late seventies, the reign of the Gaullists in France was clearly on the wane. Goldsmith is a staunch conservative and didn't like the way the wind was blowing. He began shifting the focus of his ownership from Generale Occidentale (France) to General Oriental (Hong Kong). General Oriental eventually ended up with some 25 percent of Generale Occidentale and 30 percent of a second French company, Trocadero Participations. Trocadero in turn owns another 34 percent of Generale Occidentale. Goldsmith also owns 30 percent of Trocadero outright, besides the 30 percent he owns through General Oriental; thus he retains control of Generale Occidentale, but Generale Occidentale is now owned by a company located outside France.

Actually, confusing as all this sounds, it only begins to detail the complexities of Goldsmith's convoluted, interlocking owner-ships. Even General Oriental isn't directly owned completely by Goldsmith. Instead, it is owned partly by a Panama company called Compania Financiera Lido and partly by a Lichtenstein Foundation called Brunneria Foundation. Brunneria, to compli-cate things further, owns 60 percent of Compania Financiera Lido (Goldsmith owns the other 40 percent). The makeup of Brunneria is not clear; Lichtenstein's banking and securities laws make the Swiss seem like blabbermouths.

While he was setting all this up, however, Goldsmith wasn't neglecting the businesses themselves. Aided by the acquisitions he had made in the early seventies, by 1981 the Cavenham-Generale Occidentale combination had become the third largest food conglomerate in Europe, behind Unilever and Nestlé, with sales of over $6 billion.

In 1982, Goldsmith turned his sights to the United States.

Goldsmith, like many other wealthy Europeans, saw the Unit-ed States as a less hostile—and economically more secure—environment for investing then Europe or Asia. France was socialist and busy nationalizing banks and large industrial firms. Italy was wracked with terrorist attacks and kidnappings of wealthy individuals. The antibusiness, radical environmental Green Party was growing in influence in Germany. British industry was still dogged by labor unrest, low productivity, and outmoded management techniques. Hong Kong, the wide-open British colony where much European capital had fled, was about to begin negotiations with China that could result in the Chinese taking over the colony.

The United States, on the other hand, though deep in a reces-sion, was showing signs of getting inflation under control. The value of the dollar was rising. Most of all, it had one of the most stable governments in the world. For all its problems, the United States looked like an attractive place to be.

Goldsmith began selling off his holdings. By the middle of 1982, after selling his largest company, the supermarket chain Allied Suppliers (for $183 million), his only major interests remaining in Europe were a 50-percent interest in Aspinall Holdings and a 99-percent interest in Groupe Express. Aspinall Holdings owns a

London gambling club run by Goldsmith's friend (and co-owner) John Aspinall. Groupe Express is the French company that owns *L'Express,* the Paris-based weekly newsmagazine.

Goldsmith had no intention of selling *L'Express.* The newsmagazine had always been a conservative voice in the French media; after the Socialists beat the rightists, led by President Valery Giscard d'Estaing, Goldsmith announced that *L'Express* would campaign even harder for the conservative point of view. (During the 1981 election campaign, he fired a senior *L'Express* editor for running a cover that was less than flattering to Giscard d'Estaing. "I had to get rid of those people at *L'Express* unwilling to fight for what I believe," Goldsmith said.)

Goldsmith makes no secret of his conservatism (some would say ultra-conservatism). In a 1984 address to the National Strategy Information Center in Washington, D.C., he made his views very clear. Speaking of the differences between the West and the Soviet Union, he said, "Many of us still want to believe that the problems that separate us are problems that can be resolved by negotiation and mutual good will. But unfortunately we must realize that we cannot find lasting peace through negotiation because what the Soviets really want we cannot negotiate. We cannot cede to them the right to progressive imperial conquest. We cannot negotiate away our freedom. We must face the fact that the antagonism between our two civilizations is not superficial but fundamental and that we are condemned to this state of affairs for the long term. There is no easy solution, no quick fix. The only way to peace is by doing whatever is necessary for both sides to realize that war cannot be won."

L'Express was not the only conservative newsmagazine Goldsmith had owned. In 1979, he had founded *Now!* in Britain. The newsmagazine, right-leaning like *L'Express,* lasted only two years before folding. Goldsmith, however, seems to regard being a press baron as something desirable. In 1983, he tried again, this time near his more successful *L'Express*—in Paris. He bought a failing magazine called *Lire,* hired a French talk-show host to be the editor, and brought several experienced people over from *L'Express.*

Goldsmith seemed enthusiastic about its prospects, despite his failure with *Now!*, and offhandedly said the *Lire* project would cost only a few million dollars. His optimism proved correct. By 1985, *Lire* was the largest literary magazine in France.

Encouraged, Goldsmith added one more magazine to his French press holdings. He founded *Paris Express* in 1984. His announced intention was to turn it into a Paris version of *New York* magazine—a chatty, informative magazine dedicated primarily to the city itself.

Except for his press holdings, however, Goldsmith's activities had now moved across the Atlantic.

ACTUALLY, GOLDSMITH HADN'T waited until 1981 to begin investing in the United States. As early as 1973, he had bought into the Grand Union company.

Grand Union is a supermarket chain headquartered in Elmwood, N.J. Like many other supermarket chains, Grand Union was under pressure from a combination of factors: changing demographics (its stores tended to be in areas that often were no longer prime locations) and competition from discount chains such as Pathmark. Goldsmith, of course, had built up his holdings in Britain from just such marginal or failing businesses. Nevertheless, from 1973 to 1978, he left Grand Union alone.

In 1978 everything changed. In 1977, he had begun selling his British holdings. With his attention turning to the United States, Goldsmith became actively involved in running Grand Union.

The company began buying regional chains in the Sunbelt and simultaneously opened stores at a great rate. By 1982, Grand Union, which had previously been primarily a northeastern firm, had nearly nine hundred stores (double its pre-1978 numbers) blanketing the eastern half of the United States and Canada. Unfortunately, though sales had rocketed to $4.1 billion, earnings had not followed. In fact, earnings in the 1982 fiscal year had actually fallen 30 percent compared to 1981. The expansion had not done what was expected. "We screwed it up," Goldsmith admitted.

Rumors began to circulate that the chain was for sale, but Goldsmith quickly squelched them. Grand Union, he said, was not for sale. "I have great hopes for it," he said in 1984, "and besides, it's fun."

The company quickly retrenched, selling or closing half of its stores and pulling back to the northeast and a few stores along the eastern seaboard in the south. In addition, he embarked on an expensive campaign to upgrade Grand Union's image. He hired Milton Glaser, a well-known New York graphic artist, to redesign both Grand Union's stores and its private-label packaging. He pledged that every store would meet any competitor's prices. The makeover would, he admitted, be costly. In 1983 he predicted it would be 1985 or 1986 before the firm returned to profitability. (After losing money in 1984, Grand Union did show an operating profit in 1985.)

Still, he remains relentlessly unbowed despite it all. In a 1984 interview, he told *Business Week* magazine, "We managed to turn a dull but fairly profitable chain into an exciting lossmaker."

His other U.S. ventures were to prove considerably more lucrative.

IN 1980, DIAMOND International was a very large corporation that few found interesting. To describe it as a "forest products and packaging mongrel," as *Fortune* did in 1983, is almost an understatement. Diamond International made matches, cans, plastic pumps, and paper. It owned sawmills and millwork plants. It owned 1.7 million acres of trees.

It also was not going anywhere. Earnings rose and fell from year to year without attracting a great deal of attention. Diamond was just another name on the stock market.

Goldsmith began buying stock in Diamond in 1977 until, by 1980, he owned 5 percent of the company and had to announce his interest. Then he made a tender offer for 40 percent of the stock. He had the money: He had begun selling off his European holdings and had lots of cash and no debt. With Diamond's stock going nowhere, no one anticipated that Goldsmith would have any difficulty picking up the stock he wanted—his offer looked too good to shareholders sitting with Diamond.

Diamond reacted quickly. Afraid that with 45 percent of the

stock Goldsmith would move to gain control, the board of directors negotiated a standstill agreement with him. Goldsmith agreed that he wouldn't buy any more of Diamond for five years. Diamond's board also began looking for a white knight, prompting Goldsmith's remark that *he* was both white and a knight.

Many observers were puzzled by Goldsmith's interest in Diamond, since the company had been a very ordinary performer for many years. But Goldsmith had apparently been attracted to Diamond as an asset play. Diamond carried its timber acreage on its books at historical cost, a common practice in the timber industry. That cost was $24 million. By the early eighties, that same acreage was worth, by some estimates, over $700 million. That's the kind of undervalued asset a raider looks for.

Diamond's efforts to find a white knight (other than Goldsmith) were dealt a heavy blow in 1981 when earnings declined badly. The board, making the best of a bad deal, amended the standstill agreement to allow Goldsmith to tender for the rest of the company. He bid $44.50 a share and the board accepted. Goldsmith had himself a forest products company.

His cost was $661 million. Despite Diamond's lack of sex appeal, $661 million was not a bad price when you consider that Goldsmith acquired a company with $1.3 billion in sales from its operating divisions and perhaps $700 million in timber.

What was even more clever about the deal is that it didn't actually cost Goldsmith anything.

Goldsmith purchased Diamond International using a typically Byzantine group of holding companies that owned pieces of each other. The $661 million came partially from a bank syndicate (led by Citibank) that came up with $436 million, while the rest, $225 million, came from Generale Occidentale, which Goldsmith controlled. In return for lending the money, Generale Occidentale got 37 percent of the profits.

Generale Occidentale is a publicly traded company in France; Goldsmith's ownership is a controlling one—more than 40 percent—but it is not absolute. Thus, when Generale Occidentale lent money to General Oriental to buy Diamond, Goldsmith had arranged for a publicly traded company he controlled to lend money to a company he owned so that the company he owned could buy Diamond. In return, the publicly traded company—Generale Occidentale—got a share of the profits.

But Goldsmith himself never had any money at risk.

A further wrinkle also shows Goldsmith's abilities—or rather, in this case, those of his investment bankers—at creative financing. Getting that Citibank-led loan had not been easy. Goldsmith's takeover of Diamond was a leveraged buyout—only, no one had wanted to lend him the money against Diamond's assets. Diamond's assets were mostly trees, the banks reasoned, and, in the recession, no one wanted trees.

Drexel Burnham Lambert, the firm that was to virtually create junk-bond financing, came to the rescue. They persuaded Travelers Insurance to issue a put on 30 percent of Diamond's trees in return for a payment of $12.5 million.

A put is a kind of option. Unlike most options, which give an investor the right to buy something at a stated price for a limited time, a put gives an investor the right to *sell* something at a stated price for a limited time. Travelers, in return for the $12.5 million fee, had agreed to buy 30 percent of Diamond's trees at a price of $250 million at any time Goldsmith wanted up until the end of 1984.

With a guaranteed buyer for at least some of Diamond's assets, the banks were willing to lend the money Goldsmith needed.

As it turned out, there was no risk. Sir Jimmy's timing was perfect.

In August 1982, the stock market began to rally. In an upwardly moving market, the value of companies goes up as well. By December, Goldsmith was able to start selling portions of Diamond for far more than he had paid for them.

Goldsmith broke Diamond up into organic sections. Some he sold to other corporations, some to private syndicates, and one, Calmar, was sold by a public offering. All told, Goldsmith sold off divisions worth close to $600 million.

Diamond's debt load, which Goldsmith had, of course, assumed in taking over the company, was only about $160 million. (Diamond had itself sold a couple of divisions just before Goldsmith's takeover, thus reducing its debt.) By the end of 1983, Goldsmith's cost had been reduced to under $225 million.

And, besides a few small remains of sold-off divisions (17 percent of Calmar, 20 percent of Diamond Match), Goldsmith still owned the timberland. All $700 million plus of it.

Goldsmith announced that he would hold the forest lands until timber prices went up again. In the meantime, he went shopping for some more American companies.

BEFORE GOLDSMITH'S TRIUMPH with Diamond, he was just another European investor expanding into the United States. His purchase of Grand Union was perfectly understandable—Goldsmith had made his fortune in the grocery business. The fact that he wasn't doing so well with his purchase was simply proof that doing well in Europe didn't mean you could do well in the United States. If any real attention was paid to him, it was only because of his notoriety in non-business affairs.

Diamond International changed all that. Wall Street had to sit up and take notice of anyone who could take over a basically unappealing company and end up ahead by some $500 million. Like Irwin Jacobs's feat with W. T. Grant, Goldsmith's dismantling of Diamond for such a large profit was completely unexpected.

People who can do that become topics of conversation.

They also move into that rarefied arena where the mere mention of their names can send stock prices soaring and board members to get tranquilizers.

In 1984, Goldsmith proved the value of his newly won reputation. Working in partnership with Jacob Rothschild—a relative who often invests along with Goldsmith—Goldsmith picked up an 8-percent-equity position in St. Regis Paper. Like Diamond, St. Regis was a forest products company—in St. Regis's case, concentrated primarily in paper products.

Goldsmith proposed to St. Regis that it merge his Diamond International timber lands into St. Regis in return for a 25-percent interest in the company and a seat on the board. Though he claimed to have no intention of dismantling St. Regis, the company's board, with the specter of Diamond's dismemberment before it, reacted quickly. They offered to buy Goldsmith out for $150 million.

Goldsmith took the money. There is no indication that he intended to greenmail St. Regis, though there *were* charges. (Goldsmith responded to the charges by saying, "St. Regis was a failure, not a success.") Nevertheless, he was too savvy an investor to refuse money when it was offered, given St. Regis's hostility. Diamond and St. Regis weren't the only forest products companies suffering from low stock prices. Goldsmith was perfectly happy to take the $150 million and look for another place to play. At least $50 million of the $150 million was pure profit.

(St. Regis, spooked by Goldsmith, went looking for a white knight even after it had bought him out. The company found one and late in 1984 merged with Champion International, another paper and packaging materials concern.)

Goldsmith's next target proved equally unwilling and equally lucrative. Continental Group—the old Continental Can Company—also wanted no part of Goldsmith. Goldsmith pressed ahead nonetheless, offering $2.5 billion for Continental. He was outbid, however, by a syndicate led by David Murdock, a West Coast investor and occasional raider. Goldsmith, nevertheless, got another consolation prize. He made a $35 million profit on the shares of Continental he had picked up before Murdock entered the picture.

The $85 million he made on the two failed takeover attempts was to come in handy on his next deal.

AS EARLY AS May of 1984, rumors were circulating that Goldsmith was interested in Crown Zellerbach. Goldsmith refused to confirm or deny the rumors, but after his successful attempt at Diamond and his unsuccessful (but profitable) tilt at St. Regis, no one was surprised at the rumors. Zellerbach was another forest products company and, like Diamond, was not a favorite of investors. Perhaps, observers reasoned, he was going to try his Diamond tactics on another forest company.

And he still had all those trees. The timberland that was most of what was left of Diamond was a valuable resource that when merged with another timber and paper company, could make the combination a stronger economic unit. So people began to watch Crown Zellerbach.

It came, then, as quite a surprise when Goldsmith filed with the SEC, stating he had acquired more than 5 percent of Colgate-Palmolive.

Colgate, a diversified consumer products firm, was about as far from being a timber company as one could get. Then, after making the filing, Goldsmith got quiet again. He made no further moves on Colgate.

On December 13, 1984, the financial press carried the news that Sir James Goldsmith intended to buy between 15 percent and 20 percent of the outstanding shares of Crown Zellerbach.

The notification was a requirement of the Antitrust Improvements Act of 1976, known as the Hart-Scott-Rodino Act after its sponsors. The act mandates notifying both the SEC and the company involved whenever an investor, individual or corporate, is about to buy a large portion of a company's stock. Crown expressed its complete surprise at the notification. They, like everyone else, had discounted the early rumors of Goldsmith's interest after he bought into Colgate.

Another reason for Crown's surprise was that the company had just put into place a series of antitakeover measures designed by the Wall Street law firm (and takeover-antitakeover specialists) Wachtell, Lipton, Rosen & Katz. Crown naturally expected that the measures would discourage a raider. They were somewhat taken aback when they didn't.

Goldsmith may not have been deterred, the speculation ran, because the antitakeover provisions were under attack in court. Wachtell, Lipton had advised several clients to put the particular package Crown used into place and one of those clients— Household International Inc.—was being sued over them in the Delaware Supreme Court on the grounds that it denied shareholders the right to consider a tender. Perhaps Goldsmith was counting on the provisions being overturned. (If he was, he would have been mistaken. The Delaware Supreme Court later upheld Household.)

Given the capricious nature of court rulings, it seemed unlikely. Surely Goldsmith could have waited until after the court ruled before he moved.

There *was* one clue to Goldsmith's intentions—and several

publications noted it in passing in their coverage—but no one drew the proper conclusions from it. It is only in hindsight, now that the deal is done, that the clue makes sense. *The New York Times,* for one, reported that Colgate, the other object of Goldsmith's interest in 1984, was also a Wachtell, Lipton client and had adopted the same antitakeover provisions. Nevertheless, neither the *Times* nor anyone else could figure out the connection.

The key lay in the heart of the Wachtell, Lipton package: a poison pill. Simply enough, Goldsmith had figured out a way to use the Wachtell-designed poison pill to his own advantage.

IN 1984, CROWN Zellerbach was 113 years old. It had extensive timber lands in the Pacific Northwest and in the South. Its divisions made paper, containers, and specialty plastics. It also had a small computer division. Its timberlands alone were more than twice the size of those Goldsmith had acquired through his purchase of Diamond International.

But, like other forest products companies, Crown had been badly hurt by the recession. With housing starts at record low levels, the demand for timber was anything but strong. In 1982, Crown had reported a year-end loss of $112 million, partially caused by write-offs from discontinued operations.

In 1983, it had recovered somewhat. Earnings for the year were nearly $89 million, and predictions for fiscal 1984 were even better. In the wintry days before Goldsmith's announcement, though, other large forest product companies had reported their fourth-quarter earnings—and none of them looked good. International Paper, Boise Cascade, and Champion (the company that had absorbed St. Regis) had also taken large write-offs to reflect the loss of value of leases and the closing of plants. Crown had not yet reported fourth-quarter results, but its third quarter had been disappointing. As a result, despite Zellerbach's rosier outlook, stock prices for the company—and the entire forest products industry—were low.

Not for long, at least as far as Zellerbach was concerned. On the day the news broke that Goldsmith intended buying into the company, Zellerbach's stock price soared 5¼ points, to $34 a share. It was the seventh most active stock that day.

Investors were naturally interested in a company in which Sir Jimmy was interested. Anyone who had owned Diamond or St. Regis or Continental when Goldsmith came in had made money. Expectations were that, whatever his plans for Zellerbach, they would make money for investors as well.

RAIDERS ARE NEVER still. In March 1985, the speculation surrounding Goldsmith's plans for Zellerbach was temporarily eclipsed by the intrusion of another company into the headlines. On another part of the business pages—in some cases, on the same page with news of Zellerbach—columns had been reporting the ongoing battles between Pickens and Phillips, and Icahn and Phillips. Suddenly, on March 1, *The New York Times* announced: "Goldsmith in Talks with Icahn." The *Wall Street Journal* put it a bit more clearly: "Icahn Is Seeking Goldsmith's Help in Bid for Phillips."

Icahn was then involved in his ultimately successful bid to force Phillips to amend its recapitalization plan. The news that Goldsmith might join him was electrifying. Phillips had already fought Pickens to a standstill. Irwin Jacobs was acquiring stock. Super arbitrageur Ivan Boesky was known to have a large position in the stock. Phillips did not need another raider added to the equation.

As it turned out, nothing came of the talks, at least publicly. Goldsmith may have contributed money to an Icahn syndicate, but as the membership lists of such syndicates are kept secret, there's no way to know. His public participation wasn't really necessary, however. Just the fact he was considering joining in Icahn's bid added to the pressure Icahn was putting on Phillips.

Goldsmith had really reached the major leagues. When a big-league raider such as Icahn uses your name to scare a giant corporation, you've arrived.

As if anyone had any doubts.

BY APRIL 1985, Goldsmith had acquired 8.6 percent of Zellerbach's stock. He then made an offer, at $42.50 a share, for up to 19 million shares of Zellerbach. The cost would be $807.5 million. If successful, he would own more than 78 percent of Zellerbach. He also threatened a proxy fight to unseat the board of directors if they didn't rescind the poison-pill provisions they had set up in 1984.

The Zellerbach poison pill was a simple one. In the event anyone bought 20 percent or more of the outstanding stock, or made a tender offer for 30 percent or more of the outstanding stock, the poison pill would take effect. The pill would give holders of Zellerbach stock the right to buy, for $100, $200 worth of any company that then took over Zellerbach. (Contracts or rights issued by a company are binding on any successor company that acquires it.) A raider who took over Zellerbach would find himself forced to sell stock at, basically, half-price to Zellerbach's shareholders.

Goldsmith's tender offer took the poison pill into account. It was a conditional tender that wasn't to take effect unless the poison pill was removed. Therefore, it wouldn't trigger the poison pill under the 30-percent-tender provision because, technically, there would be no tender so long as the poison pill was still in place.

The betting on the street, though, was that if Crown seemed to be losing the proxy fight, it would look for a white knight. Most analysts expected a takeover to occur at a price of $50 to $55 a share.

ZELLERBACH COUNTERED WITH a restructuring plan calculated to appeal to investors. Zellerbach, the board decided, would be split into three companies. One, which would own the timberland, would be a partnership that would liquidate itself—much like the royalty trusts pioneered by Pickens in the oil industry. The second company would be comprised of Zellerbach's packaging operations, including its plastics division. The remainder would be called Crown Zellerbach and keep only the paper products divisions.

Goldsmith rejected Crown's proposed restructuring and continued his demand that the poison pill be removed, pointing out that it was detrimental to shareholders since the provision could effectively prevent a white knight from coming in and giving shareholders a better price than the restructuring would offer.

The stockholder meeting was held, and the proxy fight came to a head. Goldsmith lost. Zellerbach claimed an "overwhelming victory" and crowed that some two-thirds of the votes cast had been in favor of management. Nevertheless, because voting was under cumulative voting rules (with four seats up for election, each shareholder got four votes and could vote once for each of four directors, four times for one director, or any combination thereof), Goldsmith was able, by voting all the votes accruing to his holdings for himself, to secure a seat on the board. It was a small victory that had no effect on the rest of the board's plans. Zellerbach's chairman claimed that the overall vote showed that the board "already had a mandate" to go ahead with its plan.

To put pressure on Zellerbach's board, Goldsmith continued buying Zellerbach stock (he had withdrawn his tender offer when the board announced the restructuring), increasing his ownership to 19.9 percent. A purchase of only a small amount of stock would now trigger the poison pill.

The pressure on Zellerbach was to use a provision of its poison-pill arrangement to buy back the rights from shareholders. The key was that Zellerbach was permitted to do so only up to the point a public announcement was made that someone had acquired 20 percent of the company. After that, the rights were irrevocable. Zellerbach and Goldsmith were now playing a very expensive game of chicken. If Goldsmith bought more stock, the poison pill would be triggered, and there would be little possibility of getting a white knight interested in Zellerbach. The company would simply be too expensive to take over.

Zellerbach refused to budge, and Goldsmith made his announcement. He now owned, he said, more than 20 percent of Zellerbach's outstanding stock. He thus became the first investor in Wall Street history to trigger a poison pill.

Goldsmith's willingness to trigger the pill came from a novel interpretation of the pill's effectiveness. The Wachtell, Lipton-designed pill made it prohibitively expensive for anyone to acquire Zellerbach. But Goldsmith announced that he didn't intend to acquire Zellerbach. He would simply buy enough stock to *control* the company—thus allowing himself, within limits (the rights of minority shareholders are partially protected by law), to do as he pleased with the firm. And by triggering the pill, he made it impossible for Zellerbach's board to prevent his buying in; any white knight would also find it prohibitively expensive to acquire the company.

Zellerbach had backed itself into a corner.

Lawyers who specialize in corporate takeovers immediately began to redesign pills with similar provisions before others could take advantage of the weakness Goldsmith had found. New provisions were added to pills invoking them even if a bidder only sought control instead of merger. For Zellerbach, though, it was too late.

(The legality of the new pills that sought to avoid the Zellerbach problem were immediately challenged, and the outcome is still in doubt. For that matter, many feel any poison pill is illegal, and challenges to its use, even in unmodified form, go on. Even though Goldsmith triggered Zellerbach's poison pill as a means of pressuring the company, he himself maintains they are an illegal infringement on corporate democracy.)

Crown continued to act as if nothing had changed. It continued to press its restructuring plan and refused to deal with Goldsmith. Goldsmith responded by continuing to buy and, by July of 1985, he owned over 50 percent of Zellerbach.

Zellerbach's board still ignored him. They cited another of their antitakeover provisions which held that Goldsmith could neither oust management nor change the corporate bylaws so long as he held less than two-thirds of the stock. Since Crown's board held staggered terms, Goldsmith, they maintained, couldn't even oust any of the board members. (Goldsmith himself, of course, had been a board member since May—but he was only one vote among thirteen.)

Zellerbach was ignoring the man who held more than half its stock.

It was an interesting situation, a Wall Street version of a Mexican standoff. Without buying more stock, Goldsmith couldn't seem to influence Zellerbach's actions. On the other hand, his majority position made it doubtful Zellerbach could proceed with its plan to restructure the company. Under that plan, an exchange offer would be initiated and shareholders could exchange their Zellerbach stock for shares in the three proposed new companies.

Board meetings at Zellerbach at that point must have been interesting. Goldsmith, with over 50 percent of the stock, would have been sitting with directors who outnumbered him 12 to 1 yet represented less stock than he owned. The restructuring plan, which Goldsmith opposed, had passed the board and was awaiting SEC approval.

Then Crown announced that its second-quarter earnings had fallen by 34 percent. Simultaneously, it announced that Crown and Goldsmith were "engaged in discussions to resolve matters between them." Both sides agreed to call off, for the moment, the various lawsuits each had filed against the other.

On July 25, 1985, Sir James Goldsmith became chairman of the board of Crown Zellerbach. The former chairman of Crown, William T. Creson, kept his positions as president and chief executive officer. Instead of Goldsmith swallowing the poison pill, the pill had exploded in Crown Zellerbach's fce.

GOLDSMITH'S VICTORY DID not stop the Street from its favorite pastime—speculating on what would happen next. The big question, of course, was Now that Goldsmith had gotten Zellerbach, what would he do with it? Analysts made exhaustive reports on Zellerbach's assets, discussing whether the timber holdings could be sold, given the depressed values in the industry and whether Zellerbach's plants were worth anything (some analysts held that of Zellerbach's thirty-odd paper and container plants, only two were). Zellerbach, it was pointed out, was not configured like Diamond. Diamond's plants and divisions had each been specialty outfits, easily sold on their own. Zellerbach's were integrated, making breakup difficult. The Monday-morning quarterbacks were quick to point out that Goldsmith might be in trouble.

As usual, Goldsmith wasn't. In December 1985, he announced that Crown had come to an agreement with the James River Corporation to make a $766 million stock swap. James River, itself a forest and paper products concern, had dealt with Goldsmith before. In 1983, it had paid $149 million for the paper and pulp product divisions of Diamond International.

The agreement with James River was a complicated one, but one thing remained clear. Goldsmith would end up with Crown Zellerbach's container and computer operations. He would also end up with its timberland. Added to that of Diamond International, the total value of the timberland Goldsmith would control could be as much as $1.6 billion.

As 1986 opened, bankers and brokers were still arguing about the potential profit Goldsmith might realize out of Crown. The difficulty in estimating the value of the timberland was the main problem; with prices depressed, sale of any part of it might be difficult. But Goldsmith seems in no hurry to divest himself of any of his trees. He may sell off some of Crown's other divisions in the future—estimates indicate he might be able to realize as much as $550 million that way—and if Diamond is anything to go by, he probably will. His costs in acquiring Crown were nearly $700 million. A $550-million sale would leave him in much the same situation as at Diamond, with a huge chunk of assets at a cost of about $200 million dollars.

The only remaining question is if—and how soon—prices for timberland will rise. Until then, Sir James Goldsmith will own a lot of trees.

7

Crying All the Way to the Bank

VICTOR POSNER

Taking the worst possible case, the one in which his corporate empire eventually goes completely down the tubes and he himself is in jail on the pending tax fraud charge, Posner could still console himself somewhat on being America's only centimillionaire jailbird.
—*Forbes,* April 8, 1985

I'm a genius.
—Victor Posner, 1969

VICTOR POSNER IS a very secretive man. When he arrives at the headquarters of his empire—a converted beachfront hotel in Miami Beach called the Victorian Plaza—his bodyguards call ahead and the lobby is cleared before he enters. Unlike Howard Hughes, though, Victor Posner hasn't withdrawn from the world—but a lot of corporate executives wish he would.

203

In 1985, DWG Corp, the centerpiece of Posner's chain of inter-locked companies, earned $5.6 million, despite a loss in the fourth quarter. Victor Posner, DWG's chairman, president, and CEO, was paid $8.1 million in salary—$2.5 million more than the company earned. Even by Posner's standards that was enor-mous. In 1984, DWG only paid him $1.9 million.

Of course, Posner has always paid himself well. The best estimates put his total salary and bonuses from 1979 to 1984 from the companies he controls (including DWG) at more than $24 million. He paid himself $6.2 million in 1982 and $10.4 million plus stock options in 1983.

Posner does believe in sharing the wealth, though. His son, Steven (age forty-two) is paid over $1.3 million a year as vice-chairman of some nine of Posner's companies.

Other Posner kin are taken care of as well. His twenty-three-year-old daughter, two years out of college, is an executive of at least seven of Posner's companies and, apparently, is running Evans Products. Posner's brother Bernard and ex-brother-in-law Melvin Colvin (Posner divorced Colvin's sister over forty years ago) are kept gainfully employed. His daughter Gail Posner Cohen (Stevens's twin sister) has only recently dropped off the payroll.

Then there's Posner's fiancée, Lisa Mottram. Ms. Motram was made a vice president of Securities Management Corporation, Posner's holding company, in 1985. Ms. Mottram was nineteen (in 1985, Victor Posner was sixty-six).

Of course, lots of other raiders—and ordinary corporate execu-tives, for that matter—keep family members on the payroll; Saul Steinberg's brother, for instance, is an executive of Reliance Group and other companies Steinberg has an interest in. And a nineteen-year-old fiancée looks less sensational when compared to Jimmy Goldsmith's open affairs or the accusations Steinberg's second wife made during their rather messy divorce. If Posner were as successful as Goldsmith, perhaps no one would pay any attention beyond an occasional footnote.

Unfortunately, Posner has only been successful if you define success as how much Victor Posner—and family—have made.

While many raiders have been accused of having only their own self-interest at heart, Posner has, more than any of the others, been charged with the mismanagement and looting of the corporations he has acquired. And now, unlike Sir Jimmy or Saul Steinberg or Irwin Jacobs, some observers feel Victor Posner's empire is coming apart.

AT THE AGE of thirteen, many boys discover girls for the first time. Victor Posner discovered real estate.

Posner, according to the official biography his companies used to put out, was born in 1918, the son of a small grocery-store owner in Baltimore. The family was poor, living in the slums. At thirteen, Posner dropped out of school and started working in his father's store. By the time he was twenty-one, he was a multimillionaire.

Posner claims he made his first million by the time he was eighteen, by putting together a chain of small grocery stores. Then, he says, he moved into real estate.

Victor Posner sold low-cost housing in the black slums of Baltimore. But, like many other developers at the time, he took advantage of the real estate laws. When he sold the houses, he didn't sell the ground under them. The buyer of the house had to pay a ground rent each year. (This is still legal in most places today, just less common.)

Keeping the land and charging ground rents was very profitable. A developer bought land and built houses on the land. The houses were sold at a price higher than the cost of both the land and the construction, so the developer now had a profit—but still owned the land. The land was then rented to the house owner.

The contracts for the ground rent could then be used as collateral for bank loans. The interest rate on the bank loans was less than the income from the ground rents, so the loans were essentially free—in fact, the developer was actually receiving income from his collateral over and above the cost of borrowing against it. Best of all, the collateral hadn't cost anything, since the sale of the house had cleared all costs and made a profit. Thus, the developer had gotten all his money back, made a profit, was receiving income from the ground rents, and had a chunk of borrowed money in hand from the bank *that wasn't costing anything.*

The borrowed money would be used to buy more houses and begin the cycle all over again. Best of all, the only taxes that were due were on the profit made on the sale of the house. The value of the ground rents—the collateral on which the bank was willing to lend money—was not taxable as a profit under the tax laws of the time. Of course, the developer had to pay taxes on the ground rents, but the loan interest was deductible and covered most of that.

A lot of people, including Posner, made a lot of money that way.

And Posner still owns most of that land. In the mid-seventies, those ground rents were bringing in close to $500,000 a year.

From the Baltimore slums, Posner moved into Florida real estate. He did well there too—and continues to do well. Today, Victor Posner's real estate holdings are worth at least $70 million and probably more.

Posner later adapted his Baltimore experience to Florida condominiums. Like many other builders in the sixties and seventies, when he sold condominium units he retained the ownership of recreational facilities such as the pools. Owners of the units must pay monthly fees to use the facilities in their own buildings—and the payment of those fees is a requirement of their maintenance contracts. Failure to pay can result in a lien being placed against the condo unit or even its contents.

Abuses such as this—perfectly legal at the time—led Florida to make changes in the laws governing condominiums. In the meantime, it was extremely lucrative for the developers, including Posner.

IN THE SIXTIES, Posner turned his energies to building a corporate empire, reportedly because he was "bored" with real estate. In 1965, Security Management Corp., his real-estate holding company, began buying stock in what is now DWG Corp. The company was then an ailing Detroit cigar and pipe-tobacco manufacturer. Posner made a tender offer for the company and was rebuffed. But management dissension soon gave him the opportunity he wanted and in June 1966 he gained control of DWG. Posner was off and running, using DWG as the vehicle to take over other companies.

Surprisingly, Posner doesn't even own a majority interest in DWG—his holdings total under 47 percent. But this has been his basic tactic in most of his takeovers. Posner usually doesn't go for outright ownership or even a majority stake. Instead, he seeks to become the largest single stockholder of companies that are not in a position to fight him because of poor financials or bad markets. He then exerts "managerial control," having himself elected chairman and chief executive and appointing his family to key positions. He treats the company as if he *did* own it outright. If outside directors protest, he ignores them. If they resign, he simply appoints more loyalists to the board. In some cases, Posner gained control with less than 25 percent of the stock.

Less than six months after gaining control of DWG, Posner made his first acquisition, Wilson Corp., a maker of shirts. Less than a year later, he bought 89 percent of National Propane, a bottled-gas distributor. One month later, in December 1967, he sold DWG's cigar business, leaving the company as a holding company for the other businesses.

Posner had begun his first phase of empire building.

AT THE SAME time as Posner went after DWG, he acquired control of two other companies. One was NVF Co., the world's largest manufacturer of vulcanized fiber. The other was Penn Engineering, which produced steelmaking equipment.

In neither case did Posner buy a controlling interest in the company. Posner and wholly owned SMC (Security Management Corp.) sought, as usual, only "management control" of the two companies. He owned less than 16 percent of Pennsylvania Engineering and about 32 percent of NVF.

The Street watched and waited to see what Posner would do with his companies. Posner was a new force in the market at a time when conglomerators were big news. Charles Bluhdorn was building Gulf + Western; James Ling was putting together LTV. Wall Street analysts followed the conglomerates carefully.

Posner, on the surface at least, seemed a typical conglomerate

builder. He was concentrating in one area, smokestack industries, mostly going after failing companies that were languishing
in the market. This was approved behavior in the terms of the
time; the buzzword on the Street was "synergy," a term borrowed from the drug industry. Synergism refers to the joint
action of drugs that when taken together are more effective than
if each had been taken separately. The wisdom on Wall Street
held that the same could be done with companies. Two failing
firms put together would be more effective than either one alone.
The firms didn't have to be in the same business: for instance,
cyclical companies with different cycles—when one was lagging,
the other would still be making a profit, and the whole company
would be healthy.

Synergy was largely to die as a concept in the debacle of the
seventies stock market when so many of the conglomerates came
apart at the seams. But in the sixties, stocks of conglomerates
were highfliers. Everyone watched to see what the magic of
synergy would do for Posner's budding empire.

The results were disappointing. Before DWG sold its cigar
business, its losses went from a pre-Posner $360,000 to a post-
Posner $4.8 million. Wilson went from a profit of $985,000 to a
loss of $725,000. NVF profits dropped from $1.6 million to
$344,000. Only Penn Engineering showed an increase, and part of
that was aided by two acquisitions Penn made: Northern Engineering Co. and Lectromelt. Together, Northern and Lectromelt
contributed more than two-thirds of the increased profit.

Over the next two years, Posner was to acquire "management
control" of small company after small company. In each case, he
would buy only enough to make him the largest shareholder.
Then he would elect himself to the board, vote himself a salary,
and go looking for something else. Companies he had acquired in
this fashion would then be used to buy other companies—using
the first company's money. Posner was thus gaining control of
businesses without putting up any money of his own. His captive
companies—in most of which he was a minority shareholder—
were buying the companies for him.

Analysts at the time were puzzled by what he was doing. The

companies he took over went frequently into the red. Where was he making any money?

The answer, it turned out, was in the relationships between the interlocked companies. By moving funds around between the companies, he could assure SMC a profit—with little risk—even if the other companies he controlled were in the red.

One example of such money movement, dug up by *Forbes* in 1969, concerned DWG and shows how SMC could be assured a profit *and* how Posner's aims could be achieved at the same time. Metropolitan Life had loaned money to DWG at 6-percent interest. After Posner took over DWG, Metropolitan refused to renew the loan. So SMC, Posner's own company, took over the loan— but raised the rate to 7 percent. SMC was now making above-market interest on a loan to a company it controlled.

DWG, in its turn, lent money to Penn Engineering—which was profitable and thus a good bet. But Penn was charged 10¼ percent on the loan—far higher than SMC was charging the financially less secure DWG. The profit on the loan, of course, would make SMC's loan to DWG much safer—Penn Engineering was, in effect, paying DWG money it could use to pay SMC and leaving DWG with cash as well.

And what did Penn Engineering do with the money? It made more acquisitions, bringing more companies under Posner's management.

The other way in which Posner was making money was in salaries. From the very beginning of his empire building, he made out well personally, regardless of how well or badly his companies were doing. Immediately after acquiring control of a new company, he would have himself elected chairman. His compensation was usually generous. His relatives and close business associates would be appointed to other highly paid positions.

The total of the compensation he received from all the various companies he ran soon added up to big numbers. By 1974, Posner was getting more than a million dollars a year in salaries alone— not counting stock options and other forms of compensation— from his captive companies. To put that figure in perspective, in 1974 the chairman of General Motors made just under $600,000, while the chairman of Exxon earned just over $600,000. The only corporate executive who made close to Posner's salary in 1974 was Harold Geneen, the chairman—and builder—of International Telephone and Telegraph, a company many, many times the size of Posner's empire all put together. Geneen made $813,000.

Posner was to continue to pay himself over a million dollars a year until the eighties. Then he started raising his own salary dramatically, reaching over $10 million in compensation in 1984 alone.

Wall Street's confusion as to how Posner could make money when so many of his companies were doing poorly cleared up as the amount of his salary became known. And companies began to dread that they would find out that Victor Posner was buying their stock.

LATE IN 1968, Posner made two tender offers. One was for Southeastern Public Services, which immediately began looking for a white knight (although they weren't called that then). The other was Sharon Steel, a large steel and coal producer with revenues of $220 million. NVF, which was making the tender offer, had revenues of $30 million. Jonah swallowing the whale was a lot less common in 1968 than it is today, and the market reacted with incredulity. Sharon, though, took it very seriously. It, too, sought a white knight.

Neither succeeded. Southeastern became a 63-percent-owned subsidiary of DWG. Sharon became an 86-percent-owned subsidiary of NVF.

Both deals came at the end of long proxy fights against managements determined to keep Posner out. But shark repellent was still in its infancy; the term had not yet even been invented. Posner bought both firms with what was then called "chinese paper," an early form of the leveraged buyout. By offering stockholders a package of debentures that added up to a premium over the market price, he was able to win control of both companies. The acquisition of Sharon Steel put Posner in the big time. Sharon was the fourteenth largest steel company in the United States.

By 1974, Posner's empire had revenues of $700 million, with net earnings of some $23 million. Despite the Street's distaste for his tactics, he was a force to be reckoned with.

POSNER MAY HAVE been a force in the market, but he was also a figure that continued to crop up in lawsuits and investigations. In 1971, for example, the SEC charged that Posner, along with two of his associates and three of his companies, had evolved a "fraudulent scheme" to use Sharon Steel's pension funds to channel money into other Posner companies.

The SEC suit charged that the activities began in June 1969, almost immediately after Posner gained control of Sharon. The suit claimed that the defendants had first sold off stocks and bonds in the pension funds, generating cash. They then had the funds buy stocks, bonds, and warrants in DWG, Southeastern Public Service, Wilson Brothers, and National Propane. In most cases, the SEC charged, the money was used to make more acquisitions—which benefited the Posner empire, but didn't do much for the Sharon Steel pension funds.

Posner ended up signing a consent degree, but he was also enjoined from ever having a fiduciary position on any pension plan of any Posner-controlled company.

One of the most interesting charges in the suit was that the Sharon Steel funds made loans to NVF and DWG. The money, the SEC said, was used to pay off NVF and DWG's debts—debts acquired in taking over Sharon Steel.

DWG and NVF had sold debentures to European investors on the condition, demanded by the buyers, that the two companies would buy them back on demand. In 1969, according to the SEC, some of those investors wanted their money back, and Posner used the Sharon Steel pension funds to buy the debentures. Thus, Posner was using Sharon's pension plans to pay off the costs of taking over Sharon.

Other suits attacked different areas of Posner's self-serving approach to his empire. In 1973, for instance, a suit on behalf of a minority shareholder of Sharon Steel, charging that Posner's salary was "excessive and exhorbitant," succeeded in forcing

Posner to reduce his salary from Sharon Steel to $225,000 from $300,000. Similar suits were filed by shareholders of other Posner companies.

The shareholder suits, though, had little real success. The problem was that, since all the Posner companies were independent corporations (which he just happened to control through his stock ownership), suits against Posner could only be brought company by company. Thus, although in 1973 his total compensation from all his companies was slightly over $1 million, no one could use that figure to show that he was excessively paid. Instead, as in the Sharon Steel suit, the shareholder could attack only that portion of the total that was generated by the company he held shares in.

The result was, at best, fleabites—and the fleabites were not only very costly to the suing shareholders, but also were defended by the companies paying the salaries. A Sharon Steel stockholder suing over Posner's compensation was faced with the knowledge that, as the defense was paid for by Sharon Steel, the stockholder's attempts to prevent Sharon paying money to Posner was costing Sharon money.

In 1977, the SEC again went after Posner, this time charging that he, his son Steven, and his daughter Gail had charged off some *$1.7 million* worth of personal expenses to Posner's companies. Posner settled with the SEC by paying the six companies involved $600,000, but it didn't end the controversy. The auditors of the companies asked for the remaining $1.1 million back. He eventually repaid all but about $100,000 of the $1.7 million.

Despite the harassment from the SEC and shareholders, Posner has never changed his tactics and continues to pay himself huge sums of money.

Another source of funds he has tapped over the years is his Miami Beach headquarters. Companies that are part of the Posner empire must rent space at the Victorian Plaza, which is owned by Posner's private real-estate company. In 1980, for example, NVF and its subsidiaries paid $1.7 million in rental fees for space at the headquarters and for the use of a company yacht and plane. The yacht and plane were, of course, at the chairman's

(Posner's) disposal. In 1983, the rental and use fees had jumped to $2.8 million.

Critics claim that this is a lot of money for a company to be spending for headquarters space on a not-particularly-fancy part of Collins Avenue, even if it is on the beach.

IN 1976, POSNER went after another big company: Foremost-McKesson, a San Francisco-based company that manufactures and distributes food, liquor, chemicals, and drugs. Foremost had sales of $2.6 billion; it was almost four times the size of all of Posner's empire combined.

Posner had been relatively quiet for a number of years; so the Foremost bid attracted a lot of attention. While he had picked up some smaller companies along the way (and made headlines with his SEC troubles), Posner had made no truly dramatic moves between 1969, when he took over Sharon, and the time he moved on Foremost. Many observers of the market had written off Posner as another sixties conglomerator who had lost his teeth as the stock market slumped in the seventies. They were soon disabused of the notion.

Foremost was vulnerable. Its stock price, which had been as high as 55½ in the mid sixties, had fallen to 15. Posner, who had purchased 9.9 percent of Foremost's stock through Sharon Steel, was offering a package of debentures for enough stock to increase his ownership to 80 percent. The deal was tempting to Foremost shareholders; among other things, the interest payments on the debentures would be twice the dividend on the equivalent amount of Foremost stock.

But Foremost fought back, taking full-page ads in newspapers, suing Posner—in fact, unleashing the full gamut of antitakeover techniques of the time. Within a couple of months, Foremost had spent over $500,000 on legal fees and $70,000 for newspaper ads in fighting Posner. Much was made of Posner's $1 million-plus combined salaries and the various SEC and stockholder suits. Foremost accused Posner of seeking to loot the company. Posner and his associates, Foremost said in a suit, "have engaged in a continuous and unified course of conduct to prey upon and defraud the shareholders of a ... series of corporations. ... At the guidance and direction of Victor Posner, they have taken over and looted at least eight corporations in as many years."

Posner fought back, pointing out that Foremost did not have entirely clean hands—Foremost had just signed a consent order with the SEC after the agency charged Foremost with $6 million in bribes to liquor wholesalers and retailers.

In the end, Foremost won, beating off Posner's attacks, although Posner held on to his minority interest in the company. The experience proved costly. Foremost charged in court that Sharon Steel had overstated its earnings in 1974 and 1975 though creative accounting, mostly in inventory and sales figures. Sharon was forced to restate its earnings. The restated earnings were down almost 50 percent from the earnings originally reported, from $14.6 million to $7.9 million in 1975.

Demonstrating the earnings errors allowed Foremost to persuade the court to grant an injunction preventing Posner from buying more shares. Although the injunction ran out in 1979, Posner stayed away from Foremost.

It was a black eye that would not help Posner's credibility in future takeover situations.

Another black eye that emerged from the same series of lawsuits was to sour Sharon's relationships with many longtime customers. In 1974, there were worldwide shortages of steel. Suits by Sharon's customers alleged that Sharon reneged on contracts to deliver steel at pre-shortage prices by claiming that it didn't have the steel to sell. The suits say that Sharon salesmen were told to refer callers to a company called Ohio Metal Processing, which had steel available—at a price higher than Sharon's contract prices.

Ohio Metal Processing, it has been claimed, was "an employee and a phone." In fact, Ohio Metal Processing was a newly created subsidiary of Sharon, set up, the suits said, to get full market price for Sharon's steel without alienating longtime customers.

Sharon denied the whole thing, claiming that Ohio Metal Processing was simply a warehouse operation that sold to other warehouse operations, not to Sharon customers.

The lawsuits by Sharon customers against Sharon for breach

of contract ran into the tens of millions of dollars. A lot of Sharon's customers went elsewhere as soon as the shortage cleared up.

This didn't help Posner's reputation any, either.

WHILE STILL PURSUING Foremost-McKesson, Posner made investments in three other companies: National Gypsum, UV Industries, and Burnup & Sims, Inc. Two of the three, Burnup & Sims and UV Industries, were to make headlines for years.

Burnup & Sims, which installs and services cables for telephone and cable TV companies, has generated news stories because, while it did not get away, neither did it succumb. Ten years later, Posner was still locked in a takeover battle with Burnup & Sims.

His ownership in Burnup & Sims has changed through the years as his takeover attempts have waxed and waned. Through the various companies he owns or controls, he had, by the middle of 1985, increased his holdings to 35 percent. The fight has swayed back and forth as first one side and then the other wins or loses in court. In 1984, Burnup & Sims's president and CEO, Nick A. Caporella, quit the company, claiming he couldn't work for Posner. The board of directors sympathized to the extent of granting Caporella a $4 million severance arrangement—a golden parachute. The board also persuaded him to stay on temporarily. Caporella (who, since he had already quit, was in a pretty invulnerable position) used the message from the president in the 1985 Burnup & Sims annual report to deplore the effects of Posner's attempt to take over the company. The raid, Caporella said, "robs it of its lifeblood. . . . Just as a spreading infection saps the human body of its vitality, there is also a disease of uncertainty. . . ."

The *Wall Street Journal* headlined its article about the annual report message "Boss Bites Owner."

When last heard from, Burnup & Sims and Posner were still exchanging lawsuits.

The third of Posner's 1976 targets, UV Industries, made not only news but also market history in its fight to avoid falling into Posner's clutches. UV made metal products and electric power equipment. Other subsidiaries were in coal mining and oil and gas exploration and production. For three years, from 1976 to 1979, Posner and UV slugged it out. In the end, it is hard to say whether anyone won or lost. One thing is certain, though; the shareholders of UV at the beginning of the raid—which included Posner, who had bought a large stake in the company—were clearly winners. The value of a share of UV stock multiplied as a result of the raid.

In the beginning, the raid was a fairly typical one. Posner accumulated a stock position in the company and began angling for control. UV used all its resources to fight back. But between 1976 and 1979, Posner acquired over 20 percent of UV Industries. UV eventually became convinced that it could not get rid of Posner. Preferring, as UV seemed to look at it, death to dishonor, the company's board finally announced a desperate measure. UV Industries became the first giant American corporation to voluntarily liquidate itself to avoid falling into the hands of a raider.

Many raiders have been charged with liquidating companies *after* they've taken them over, but few companies have gone as far as UV to avoid a raider's clutches. UV did not even merge with a white knight. It simply announced a plan to restructure itself as a self-liquidating trust, owned by its shareholders, which would then sell off all its divisions. The proceeds would be distributed as cash to the former shareholders.

Posner fought hard to prevent UV from forming the trust. In the end, he failed. UV restructured itself and announced it was selling its Federal Pacific Electric subsidiary for some $300 million. Further sales would follow over the years.

Posner had a large consolation prize, however. The sale of UV's assets was expected to net him about $135 million by the time the trust was wound up, and his shares in UV were worth considerably more than he had paid for them.

But he still wasn't satisfied. Even though UV was now a liquidating trust rather than a going concern, Posner continued to pursue it. On November 26, 1979, the trustees capitulated. All shares of the trust were sold to Sharon Steel for $517,754,000, with Sharon assuming all UV's liabilities.

Sharon paid for the purchase with a note and was forbidden to sell any UV assets until the note was satisfied. In September 1980, Sharon redeemed the note with $411 million in debentures, $82.6 million in cash, and another note for $23.9 million. UV belonged to Sharon Steel. Victor Posner had won.

Although part of UV was eventually to fall to Posner, the lengths UV was prepared to go in order to avoid him showed the depths to which his reputation had fallen. No company wanted to be part of Posner's empire.

OVER THE NEXT five years, Posner was to continue raiding company after company while the criticism of his methods mounted. By 1985, his empire included pieces of over thirty companies. In some cases, the interests were large enough to give Posner absolute control: Sharon Steel, 86 percent; APL Corp., 55 percent; Royal Crown Industries, 100 percent; Graniteville Co., 100 percent; Wilson Brothers, 54 percent. In other cases, he owned minority interests that nevertheless gave him control: Evans Products, 42.5 percent, Fischbach, 41.2 percent, Pennsylvania Engineering, 23.4 percent.

But Posner's empire cannot be divided up so simply. The 55 percent of APL is owned by Sharon Steel, which is, in turn, 86 percent owned. In some cases, Posner owns a majority interest in a company through another company in which he has a *minority* (but controlling) interest. National Propane is 100-percent owned by Southeastern Public Service, which in turn is 63-percent owned by DWG Corp.—which is controlled by a minority 46.8-percent interest held by Security Management Corporation, which is owned by Victor Posner.

Some chains of ownership are even more complicated. Chesapeake Insurance is 100-percent owned by Chesapeake Financial, which also owns Royal Crown. Chesapeake Financial is nearly 100-percent owned by other Posner companies—but the holdings are divided among Southeastern Public Service, Pennsylvania Engineering, National Propane, NVF, and Sharon Steel. Southeastern and National Propane own, together, about 60 percent of Chesapeake Financial—and Southeastern owns National Propane.

Keeping track of all this is a full-time job; Posner has been said to hold as many as thirty board meetings in one week. Outside board members of his companies have complained that they have waited hours or days in Miami Beach for board meetings to begin because Posner was tied up with other companies. On the other hand, Posner saves time by not holding stockholders' meetings. As of 1985, three of Posner's companies—DWG, Pennsylvania Engineering, and Wilson Brothers—had not held a stockholders' meeting in four years, despite the fact that they were all listed on the American Stock Exchange, which requires annual stock-holders' meetings.

This is part of the secret of Posner's success. Even when he or his companies are clearly breaking rules and regulations, the inertia of private and public regulatory bodies often results in the offenses going unpunished. Another factor to be considered is who is to be punished? The American Stock Exchange has only one real method of punishing a Posner firm for not holding annual meetings—it can delist the company so it is no longer traded on the exchange. The problem facing the exchange is this: the rule about annual meetings is meant to protect the minority or non-controlling shareholders. If delisting takes place, the blow will fall hardest on those very shareholders, for they will lose liquidity on their investments and find their stock harder to sell.

REGULAR READERS OF the financial columns might be pardoned if they take with a grain of salt reports that Victor Posner's empire is now in trouble. Consider the following headlines: "A Prime Target for the SEC," "Victor Posner: Living on Borrowed Time," "Victor Posner Isn't Sitting Pretty Now," "The Lucrative Agony of Victor Posner," "Victor Posner's Group Seems to Be Suffering from Financial Strains."

Anyone looking at that list could be pardoned if they thought that Posner was suddenly in trouble. But the truth of the matter is that almost since the beginning of his raiding activities, magazine and newspaper articles have been prophesying his imminent comeuppance. "A Prime Target for the SEC" was a *Business Week* article in 1971. Posner, however, survived—albeit after signing consent decrees. "Victor Posner: Living on Borrowed Time" appeared in *Forbes* six years later, in 1977. Again, the predictions of his demise were premature.

One reason for the continuing flow of negative publicity about Posner is Wall Street's distaste for his tactics and methods. Debates about Pickens or Icahn center on whether the participants think the raiders are helping or hurting the market, the economy, and the small shareholder. In Posner's case, the sides are much more polarized. His defenders claim he has bought up marginal or failing companies and, by centralizing control and cutting costs, saved them—and the jobs they represent—from going under. The only people hurt, they claim, are incompetent corporate management.

It is, basically, the same argument all the raiders use.

Posner's critics, however, go beyond the usual criticisms that raiders eat up scarce capital, divert managements' attention from operations, and ultimately are damaging to the economy. In Posner's case, critics claim Posner not only does nothing for the companies he takes over but also loots them for his own profit, ignoring the needs of the corporation, the minority shareholders, and in some cases flouting the law. Posner, they say, takes over companies only as a means of increasing the cash flow to himself and his family by any kind of manipulation he can think of.

The difference is one of degree. The Street is divided in its opinion of most raiders. In Posner's case, few outside of Posner's own circle are willing to defend his actions.

It is difficult, in hindsight, not to see an element of wishful thinking in the coverage of Posner's troubles provided by the financial press.

But wishful thinking isn't the only reason for so many premature predictions of disaster. Posner's empire is a tangled one, with interlocking ownerships among more than thirty companies, not all of which are publicly owned. Who owns what—and more importantly, who *owes* what to whom—is difficult to sort out. Posner has shown himself to be adept at transferring funds from one company to another, whether in the form of loans or security purchases or whatever. Just when an observer feels he has pinned down a problem in one corner of the empire, Posner shifts things around, rushing reinforcements to the endangered area from some other area less threatened. In many cases, it resembles the classic concept of borrowing from Peter to pay Paul—and then borrowing from John to pay Peter and from Paul to pay John.

What has kept it going is that many of Posner's companies, despite high salaries to him and his family and high costs charged against them, are still profitable. The profitable companies shore up the failing ones. One of Posner's firms, Universal Housing & Development Co., lost money for thirteen years but kept going on bank loans—many from Manufacturers Hanover, which has been one of Posner's prime sources of loans until recently—and loans from other Posner companies, primarily SMC.

POSNER FOUND ANOTHER source of dollars in the pension plans of some of his companies. While he can no longer make loans to his other companies using pension fund money—and he himself is not allowed to sit on the fund boards—several of his companies have made large amounts of money by terminating their pension plans.

It is perfectly legal. There is no requirement under the law that says a company must have a pension plan. The only requirement is that employees covered by a plan must be protected—but only so far as they are covered and vested.

Simply put, if a company is already committed to pay out $10 million in future benefits to employees, it is underfunded if it has less than $10 million in the fund and overfunded if it has more. Companies often overfund a plan to provide for the future—for instance, if the company knows that a substantial portion of the work force will soon be entitled to future payments by having met service or vesting requirements, it is easier and has less effect on the bottom line to store the money up gradually instead of having to make large payments all at once. Companies that are cyclical will also make bigger payments in good years so they can make smaller ones in bad years.

An underfunded plan must be gradually brought up to proper funding levels. An underfunded plan can't be terminated—but an overfunded one can. All the company has to do is buy annuities that guarantee the employees whatever payout has been vested. Whatever is left in the fund after purchase of the annuities goes back into the company coffers.

It works like this. A company has contracted to pay out $10 million, but some of that money isn't payable until years in the future, when employees retire. Annuities can be purchased at a substantial discount for those employees. For current retirees, annuities are bought that begin paying immediately. Then the plan is dissolved, and the company pockets the extra cash.

Of course, employees who weren't yet covered by the plan are out of luck, but that's the breaks of the game.

In 1984, DWG took over Graniteville Co. Graniteville had an overfunded pension plan. Immediately after the takeover, the Graniteville pension plan was terminated, annuities were purchased—and $36 million in excess was returned to the company treasury. DWG used the money to help pay off the cost of the leveraged buyout of Graniteville.

Around the same time, Pennsylvania Engineering, which had been a Posner company for many years, also terminated its pension plan. Pennsylvania's earnings have not been good recently. The $2.4 million surplus generated by terminating the pension plan was handy.

DESPITE CREATIVE FINANCING techniques, however, it does appear as if this time things really are catching up with Posner's empire. The last three headlines listed at the beginning of this section were all printed within weeks of one another in 1985. Increasingly, Posner's empire is showing signs of strain.

One of Posner's continuing problems has always been the loss of management when he takes over a company. In the past, he has made light of it, pointing out that he really doesn't want the management of a failing company to hang around. He wants new blood that hasn't made mistakes. That new blood has generally been his family. But no matter how talented his family members are—and some observers think that even twenty-three-year-old daughter Tracy has the ability to run companies—they lack experience. An executive who changes from one division of a company to another knows that he or she will face a learning curve, a period of familiarization, no matter how much raw talent and previous experience he or she has. Changing companies is worse. Changing industries is virtually impossible without subordinates and peers who can help supply the missing knowledge during the learning period.

As Posner's reputation has gotten worse, he has lost more and more experienced executives as they quit rather than work for him. At Royal Crown Industries, virtually the entire top management quit before, during, and immediately after the takeover. At Evans Products, the only senior executive who stayed on was the president, Monford A. Orloff. Regardless of the abilities of the departing personnel—and it should be remembered that a company's troubles do not always reflect an inability on the part of individual managers—the experience and knowledge lost of the industries involved was tremendous.

Relationships built up over the years with suppliers, for example, are disrupted or broken. At Evans, whose retail store chain was in bad trouble, nearing collapse, by early 1985, suppliers such as Stanley Works and Black & Decker Mfg. Co. cut off shipments, citing uncertainty about Evans's financial condition. The same might have happened with the original management in place— but suppliers are more willing to extend terms and credit to executives with whom they have built up a long-term relationship than to newcomers they don't know. Customers, too, like to deal with someone they know and trust—and someone who knows them. The loss of so many managers at one time cannot have helped the situation at either company. By early 1985, less than a year after Posner took over Royal Crown, the company had defaulted on the very loans it had taken out to finance the LBO. The year before, Evans Products had filed for protection under Chapter 11 of the Bankruptcy Code.

THE SIGNIFICANCE OF Evans's filing is greater than it appears. Many Posner companies have been in trouble before, but, like third-world nations who can't pay off their borrowings, they have owed so much to the banks that the banks have felt a need to loan more to keep them going—the alternative being a default that would cut sharply into bank earnings. Wall Street took Evans's filing as a sign that the banks had finally called a halt to the process. If so, a lot more bankruptcies could follow.

Sharon Steel, once the crown jewel of Posner's empire, has suffered along with the rest of the steel industry. In its September 1984 annual report, Sharon, the fourteenth largest steel industry in the United States, reported a net worth of $703,000. Its loan covenants require it to maintain a net worth of $275 million. In early 1985, Sharon missed its first payments on an issue of debentures.

The amounts of money paid to Posner and his family in salaries continues to rise as his empire falters. So do the rents charged to Posner's companies for space at the Victorian Plaza. Posner spokesmen claim the rising rents reflect more space used. Critics claim Posner is tranferring—legally—as much money out of his failing companies into his own hands as he can before the collapse comes.

Posner himself is, for the first time, in jeopardy from something other than the SEC. Posner is up on charges of criminal tax fraud. In 1975 and 1976, Posner donated land to Miami Christian College, deducting it as a charitable contribution. The federal government charges that Posner conspired with a Miami real estate appraiser, William Scharrer, to inflate the value of the land and evade $1.2 million in taxes. Scharrer, listed as Posner's codefendant, had already been tried and convicted. Posner hired superlawyer Edward Bennett Williams to defend him. In July 1986, he was found guilty. Appeals will, no doubt, drag on. Nevertheless, it is the first time Posner has been convicted, despite years of charges.

Yet Posner is still expanding. A month before Sharon missed the loan payments, and shortly after Evans filed for bankruptcy, another Posner company, Pennsylvania Engineering, was buying additional shares of Fischbach Corporation—the largest electrical contractor in the United States. Posner already owned a large chunk of Fischbach; the additional shares assured him of control. Part of the money came from the sale of an interest in Chicago Pneumatic Tool Co., but part came from the sale of Penn Engineering notes.

Fischbach wasn't alone. In October 1985, Posner bought additional stock in Salem Corp., a Pittsburgh-based maker of heavy equipment for the metal and coal industries, raising his stock holdings in the company from 25.6 percent to 27.4 percent. Since Birdsboro Corp. (of Birdsboro, Pennsylvania, a maker of rolling mill machinery and steel castings), another company controlled by Posner, owned an additional 23.8 percent of Salem, Posner's purchase gave him a majority holding.

Posner also spent much of 1985 embroiled in controversy with Pullman Co. and Peabody International Corp. Pullman (aircraft seating and galleys, food service systems, and truck trailers) and Peabody (pollution control equipment and supplies, fluid and material handling equipment, food service equipment, and automotive stamped-parts) had been exploring a merger. Posner was trying to prevent it and was seeking control of Peabody himself. The usual round of lawsuits and countersuits occupied a lot of print space throughout the year, especially when Pullman head Thomas M. Begel charged that Posner had offered him $10 million to scuttle the deal. Peabody finally resorted to what was called a "reverse poison pill" to head off Posner. In submitting the planned merger to Peabody shareholders, Peabody ruled that no votes would be accepted for or against the merger from Posner, any of his companies, Pullman (which had options to purchase nearly 18.5 percent of Peabody's stock), or any other holder of more than 20 percent of Peabody's shares. Thus, Peabody said, the merger plan would be decided by the small shareholders only. In the process, Posner was frozen out.

Though on the surface it appeared that Posner was conducting business as usual despite Sharon's and Evans's troubles and his own upcoming trial, behind the scenes the cracks continued to appear. After Posner bought the additional shares of Fischbach, assuring himself of control, Fischbach's performance-bond insurer, Chubb Corp., dropped the company. As a contractor, Fischbach is unable to operate if it cannot supply performance bonds on jobs it undertakes. In November 1986, Aetna Life & Casualty took over from Chubb.

But Aetna imposed conditions before it agreed to take on the bonding for Fischbach. The result was that, contrary to Posner's usual practice, nineteen of Fischbach's top executives were given employment contracts and Fischbach president Alfred Manville was given a free hand to run the company.

In addition, it appears that Aetna imposed other conditions as well. Posner hasn't taken any money out of the company or used Fischbach to make additional acquisitions. Posner had borrowed

—as usual—to buy Fischbach. Normally, he would have used Fischbach's assets to pay back that borrowing. With his empire leaking at the seams, he can ill afford to carry the Fischbach acquisition costs without taking money out of the company. The fact that he hasn't has persuaded some observers that Aetna is keeping a close eye on Fischbach's cash. In its January 27, 1986, issue, *Forbes* magazine, which has long followed—and criticized—Posner's activities, speculated that if Aetna continued to keep him away from Fischbach's assets, Posner may be forced to sell Fischbach to pay off the debt.

Regardless of the outcome, Aetna's moves are a further indication that the banks and insurance companies that have long supplied the wherewithal for Posner to operate have begun to pull back in their dealings with him. Add to this his conviction on tax charges, and Posner is not riding as high as he once did.

But regardless of the outcome of his appeals, Victor Posner will remain a very wealthy man. And despite the accumulating problems in the companies he owns or controls, Posner has pulled rabbits out of his hat before and kept his empire alive.

Much as corporate America—and the financial press—would like to do so, it is too soon to write Victor Posner off.

Critics have compared Posner to a vampire, sucking the lifeblood from companies. They should remember that vampires are notoriously hard to kill.

Afterword

ARE THE RAIDERS good or bad for the market? Do they hurt the small investor or help him? Are antitakeover rules long overdue or an unjustifiable entry of the government into a free market? Are charter changes to make takeovers more difficult a necessary tool to help management concentrate on its job or an infringement on corporate democracy?

The answer, unfortunately, is sometimes yes and sometimes no.

Regulatory bodies and House and Senate subcommittees have wrestled with those questions without any real success. Both sides can point to evidence supporting their points of view. Both sides can equally point out evidence that undermines their opponents' ideas. The answer seems to be that, in some cases, raiders and their raids are beneficial and, in other cases, they are not.

CERTAINLY NO ONE can look at the aftereffects of the Phillips Petroleum raid and say it was beneficial for the company. Phillips emerged from the raid so deep in debt that for years it will be selling off divisions in order to pay it off. In Phillips's case, the victory was truly Pyrric; had any of the raiders who tried to take over the company won, the devastation could have been no worse.

Disney, on the other hand, survived a raid and, seeking to avoid the problem in the future, did a major housecleaning that analysts felt was long overdue. Saul Steinberg's raid was probably the best thing to happen to a company that had allowed itself to become moribund.

Even successful raids that result in the liquidation of corporations can be beneficial. Irwin Jacobs has taken over company after company in fields related to his Minstar Corp., most of them firms that weren't doing very well. He has disposed of divisions he didn't want—giving them a chance to sink or swim in a different corporate environment—and merged the rest into Minstar. Minstar, today, is very successful. The divisions, sometimes failing, that he has merged into Minstar have done very well. He has taken marginal operations and made them efficient and profitable.

Diamond International is another case in point. Before Sir James Goldsmith arrived on the scene, Diamond was regarded as a forest products company sunk in lethargy and trapped in a bad market for its products. Goldsmith split up the company, sold off the various divisions to successful corporations, and kept the asset core for himself. Before he arrived, no one thought Diamond was worth a look. Now, some of Diamond's divisions are even operating successfully as independent companies.

It can be argued that even in successful takeovers and liquidations there is a human cost: the disruption of people's lives, the loss of jobs, the destruction of traditions. All this is true. It is also true that one of the reasons many American industries have fallen behind their foreign competition is a hidebound complacency that has often kept them from pruning and modernizing when they should have.

Even when the competition is domestic, the narrow views of an entrenched management can spell disaster. One analyst, commenting on the bankruptcy of Penn Central, stated that the company's management made the mistake of thinking they were in the railroad business. They weren't. Penn Central was in the *transportation* business. When trucking began to expand after World War II, Penn Central tried to compete head to head—and failed. Had management realized they were in the transportation business, they would probably have worked *with* the changes, rather than against them—and such things as piggyback and containerization would have happened a lot sooner. It didn't, and a giant corporation went belly up, with disruptions not only in the financial markets but also in people's lives.

The dislocations and human cost as entire industries shut down are far greater than the temporary ones that result from smaller-scale restructuring.

The problem is that determining which raids result in good and which in bad—even after the fact—is a difficult question. Carl Icahn's restructuring of ACF Industries resulted in layoffs and sales of divisions. Years later, critics and defenders are still arguing whether the results are good or bad.

In some cases the evidence is clear-cut, but they are few and far between. Even Victor Posner has his defenders, who say that while things may be bad in his empire, they would be worse if he hadn't come on the scene, a statement that is difficult to disprove.

When it comes to regulation designed to stop corporate take-overs, the old problem of not throwing the baby out with the bathwater arises. Many rules and much legislation affecting the securities markets and corporate takeovers are designed to pro-tect the individual investor. The question is, however, where does the individual investor's best interest lie?

Sir James Goldsmith, writing in the *Wall Street Journal* (Febru-ary 11, 1985), made just this point in dealing with antitakeover measures. "Corporate bureaucrats," he wrote, "begin to believe that the business that employs them has become an institution that is their property. Shareholders then become no more than an inconvenience. . . . If management refuses to explain its case to shareholders and to submit it to a free vote, then the conclusion is obvious. Management is acting for its own survival and is reneg-ing on its contract to protect the interests of those who have entrusted it with that responsibility."

Sir James is speaking, of course, on the subject of shareholder democracy. At least in theory, the company belongs to all its shareholders, and they have the right to sell it if they want to. If management tries to put in place measures to prevent the stockholders from voting for a takeover, whose interests are they protecting?

Raiders point out that there is one sure way to avoid a raid. Since raiders look for companies that are undervalued, corporate management, they say, only has to be sure that earnings and growth are steady and upward; the market will then fully value the stock, preventing takeovers. Undervalued stocks, the raiders say, are the result of management that has failed.

In a perfect world with a perfect market, perhaps. There can be many reasons for a stock's price to be low other than poor earnings. But the point should be taken that regulation, by its very nature, protects everyone—including some who shouldn't be protected.

There are a lot more Disneys out there that could use a shaking up. If raids are outlawed, who will do the shaking?

THE SAD FATE of Phillips Petroleum illustrates one charge against the raiders that does stick—the increased burden of corporate debt that their raids, successful or not, saddle companies with after the raid is over. Many analysts feel that the increased debt leaves companies vulnerable to downturns in earnings that would not have hurt them nearly as much before their debt service became crippling.

It is a valid point, but, once again, annoying as it is to those of us who like packages tied up neatly, it only applies sometimes. The LBO of Diamond International was paid off by the liquidation of the company, leaving both an asset core and the former divisions largely free of excessive debt. Had Pickens taken over Phillips, he probably would have done the same—and who is to say that Phillips wouldn't be in better shape today if it hadn't been so determined to avoid T. Boone Pickens?

And Phillips's and Diamond's stockholders aren't complaining. They made out very well on both deals.

LEAVING ASIDE FOR the moment the rights or wrongs of the

raiders' activities, why are they so successful so suddenly? What has happened in the last ten years to explain the multiplication of raids and takeovers?

There are two primary factors that have had a major impact on the market in recent years and have contributed to the sudden rise in takeovers and takeover attempts. Both have had far-reaching effects and neither was anticipated by the corporate managements affected.

The first factor was a change in the way institutional investors regard their holdings. Institutions—pension plans, mutual funds, insurance companies, etc.—had always been regarded by corporate managements as friendly investors. Not only did it look good to investors and lenders that the management had attracted the faith and money of large—presumably knowledgeable—institutions, but management also regarded institutions as friendly in the event of a takeover threat or proxy fight. Institutions, unlike individual investors, were interested in the long haul, while the conventional wisdom regarded the individual as after a quick profit. In the event of a proxy fight or takeover threat, institutions could be counted upon to side with management. After all, the institutions had bought into the company in the first place because they liked what management was doing. The institution was more interested in the slow, long-term growth in value of their holdings than in picking up a quick profit of a few dollars. Individual investors, though, might be swayed by the promise of a premium over market price. It was safer to have a lot of stock in institutional hands.

Institutional fund managers also got to know the senior managers and were much more likely to side with them in a fight than with an outsider they didn't know. All in all, institutions were good to have in large numbers on the shareholder lists.

All that changed in the seventies. The sixties had been good years for institutional money managers. It was easy to make money in the market for institutions and individuals alike. The seventies were a rude awakening for everyone.

The seventies market, mostly moribund when it wasn't going down, wreaked havoc among institutional money managers. Institutions might have been willing to wait for long-term profits, but first there had to *be* long-term profits, and in the seventies there were few institutions consistently making profits. The pressure on institutional money managers to produce was intense. One result was a reexamination of long-held concepts. One that fell by the wayside was the idea that it was always best to side with corporate management. The quick profit of 10 percent, 15 percent, or more looked better all the time.

The institutions discovered something individuals had known for years: there's no such thing as loyalty to a stock.

Suddenly, corporate managements found that those friendly institutional investors were just as quick to dump stock as any fickle individual. In fact, in some contests, management found that an appeal to loyalty or faith in the future worked better with individual investors than it did with the institutions.

The same institutions who once stood shoulder to shoulder to keep Steinberg away from Chemical Bank were now eager to sell to the raiders.

The other factor that decreased the number of friendly investors involved with a corporation's stock was the increase in the influence exerted by the arbitrageurs in a takeover situation.

There have been arbitrageurs for as long as there have been financial markets, and risk arbitrageurs have always been involved with tender offers and takeover situations. It was the risk arbitrageurs who helped make the market liquid and gave investors a way to sell stock at a price near a tender price without waiting for its conclusion. But, while an arbitrageur is a classic case of an investor who has no interest in the corporation beyond a quick profit, their influence in takeover situations has, until recently, been small.

One man is largely responsible for the change in that situation: Ivan Frederick Boesky.

Ivan F. Boesky is of Russian descent. His father left Russia at the age of twelve and later went into the restaurant business in Detroit, Michigan. Ivan Boesky seems to have been something of an overachiever. Before he was thirty, he had been an English teacher in Iran, a lawyer, a tax accountant, and a Wall Street securities analyst. He got interested in risk arbitrage, and within ten years, in 1975, he had established his own privately owned firm, Ivan F. Boesky Corporation. His personal fortune is estimated at over $150 million.

Boesky changed the rules of the game of risk arbitrage simply by the scale on which he operates. He has often taken positions in companies so large that he has broken the 5-percent barrier and been obliged to file with the SEC. Positions the size Boesky takes are significant in a proxy fight or takeover battle. A 5 percent—or larger—position can be enough to tip the tide of battle decisively one way or the other.

And, as an arbitrageur, Boesky has no interest beyond selling to the highest bidder as quickly as he can. Arbitrage firms, including Boesky's, generally leverage their capital by borrowing. Interest payments eat into profits. The quick turnaround is the name of the game.

The arbitrageur has no interest at all in sticking with corporate management—unless they offer more than anyone else.

Boesky's large investments have brought in some enormous profits. As his company is private and doesn't report earnings, no one outside the firm knows the bottom line for sure, but Street estimates say he made $50 million on Texaco's takeover of Getty, $65 million on the Chevron-Gulf deal (both Pickens's raids), and perhaps $150 million on the attempted takeover of CBS by, among others, Ted Turner—and these are only three of the hundreds of major deals he had been involved with. But he doesn't always win; his losses are in the same league with his gains. When Pickens allowed himself to be bought off by Phillips Petroleum, Boesky is thought to have lost between $40 million and $70 million. Boesky, along with the rest of the Street, had expected a bidding war.

Time magazine once called arbitrageurs pilot fish, referring to the fish that follow sharks to gather morsels of food the sharks overlook. With the changes Boesky has made in the scale of the risk arbitrageur's investments, however, the arb is no longer seeking mere morsels. He has become a player in his own right—and one who sometimes holds the decisive hand.

Boesky may be about to make more changes in the market. In March of 1986, Boesky announced that he was raising an unprecedented $1 billion, some five times the capital he had available in the past. $250 million of the money is being raised from equity investments in limited partnerships. The remaining $750 million is to come from high-yield bonds—junk bonds. The bonds would pay, in addition to interest, a portion of any profits from the new firm, Ivan F. Boesky & Company L.P., the successor to Ivan F. Boesky Corporation.

The sheer amount of money being raised is staggering. Speculation on the Street centers on what he is going to do with it. With the frequency of corporate takeovers lessening, the opportunities to invest that much seems small, unless Boesky plans to take the enormous risk of concentrating most of it in one or two investments.

But there is one other interesting speculation—one that must make jittery corporate executives worry even more. Some observers are speculating that Boesky might create deals himself. By buying a large-enough chunk of a corporation, he would, without saying so, signal to any interested raider that his stock was for sale—and that the corporation was a candidate for a raid.

Instead of waiting for someone else to start a raid, Boesky would be in the situation of initiating it himself. He, rather than a raider, would be putting the company in play.

THERE ARE A lot more raiders—and a lot more raids—today than five or ten years ago. The changes in the market—the rise of the arbs and the change in the ways institutions view their holdings—have laid the groundwork for raids, making it easier to take over a company. This merely explains why more raids today are successful, though. It doesn't explain why there are so many more raids in the first place.

There are two other pieces of the puzzle that explain the multiplication of raids in the late seventies and early eighties. One is the market itself. The ideal target for a raider is an undervalued company. The market shakeout of the seventies, as inflation rose and the economy faltered under repeated shocks, cut the bottom out from under many otherwise healthy companies. In a market moving sideways or down, many companies were selling for below their breakup value. Simply enough, the low market prices meant there were lots of companies that were ripe targets for raiders.

But market value alone does not make a raid. A raider still has to have the money to take over the company. Here the fourth factor of the raiders' market comes into play.

The late seventies and early eighties may go down in history as the age of the leveraged buyout. It is the increasing ability of investors, corporate managements, and raiders to make LBOs that has been the final stepping-stone to the dramatic changes going on in corporate ownership.

The LBO owes much of its current success to the ease with which money can be raised using high-yield, lower than investment grade, securities—junk bonds. And modern junk-bond financing can be traced to one firm—in fact, to one man at that firm: Michael R. Milken of Drexel Burnham Lambert Inc.

Milken operates out of Drexel offices at the corner of Wilshire Boulevard and Rodeo Drive in Beverly Hills, far from Drexel's corporate headquarters in New York. Milken's office has become the center of the junk-bond world.

Milken became interested in junk bonds while still in business school. He discovered an interesting fact: low-rated bonds defaulted only slightly more often than investment-grade bonds. Since low-rated bonds paid far higher interest rates than investment-grade ones, if their default rates were only slightly less, the risk-reward ratio was heavily skewed in favor of lower-rated bonds.

After college, Milken became a bond trader. He put his research to work and soon became the acknowledged expert on junk bonds. Slowly, he convinced an elite group of wealthy investors that he had discovered a new way to make money.

In the course of developing customers to buy junk bonds, Milken got to know people like Saul Steinberg and the Belzbergs when their firms sold low-rated bonds through Drexel. By the late seventies, it all came together. Milken, through persuasion and investment savvy, had virtually created a market for junk bonds. He, and Drexel, had also established a relationship with many raiders who were looking for ways to raise money. A profitable partnership was born. Drexel catapulted into the top rank of investment banking firms, and Michael Milken became a millionaire.

It was not as if Milken and Drexel had created something

entirely new. An early form of the junk-bond LBO had been common practice in the sixties. Then, the standard form of conglomerate takeover was to issue what was called "chinese paper" backed by the corporation being taken over. But Milken had developed the product and the market into a method of raising enormous amounts of money very quickly. And, of course, the success of the early investors who bought junk bonds bred a market for more. Nothing succeeds like success.

And all the pieces were in place for the raiding explosion that has rocked corporate America. All that needed to be added was the incredible drive—self-confidence, chutzpah, brass—of the raiders themselves.

And, being self-starters, they added it.

They also help out each other—for the best of motives, making money. Most raider syndicates are private, and the names of the partners are not made public. In the few cases where it has become known who was investing in whose syndicate, many of the same names crop up. The Belzbergs were, apparently, investors in Pickens's raid on Phillips. Saul Steinberg has been rumored to be an investor in syndicates put together by both Carl Icahn and Irwin Jacobs.

It is not surprising that this would be the case. The raiders generally have large amounts of capital available, either their own or borrowed money, that can be committed to deals they find attractive. That alone would single them out for attention by other raiders looking for funds. They also have the temperament to invest in takeover raids: while the average investor might balk at risking the huge amounts of money involved, the raiders do this every day.

Many of the raiders also share another common bond: they are clients of Drexel Burnham. Through Milken and other Drexel partners, they have gotten to know one another. And, when a raider asks Drexel to raise funds, it is only logical that Drexel would first turn to its other clients and give them first crack at the participations. So raider supports raider—and, as profits are made, the amount of money available for the next syndicate becomes ever larger.

THE ACTIVE INVOLVEMENT of Drexel and other houses in the affairs of the raiders has raised questions about their role in raids. It is not that the houses, including Drexel, are doing anything new. Investment bankers have always raised money for clients and acted as advisors in takeover and merger situations. What have changed are the stakes.

When Pickens took a run at Unocal, Drexel picked up a $15 million fee for doing the financing and for offering advice. Although the fee is large, it is not out of line with other fees earned by other investment banks for similar services, especially given the sheer size of the Unocal deal. What is interesting is that if Pickens makes a profit on his Unocal stock, Drexel would earn an additional $15 million. And, had Pickens won and taken over Unocal, Drexel would have collected $67.5 million.

This is not unusual today. Many, if not most, of the large investment banking firms have been involved with contingency deals of this kind. Some who have acted only as advisors in takeover battles have had multimillion-dollar fees contingent on whether their side won.

The problem with this kind of fee is that it raises a large question about the relationship of the investment banker-advisor to the deal. If Drexel can earn $67 million if Pickens wins but only $15 million if he loses, doesn't that make Drexel a partner in the deal?

Investment bankers aren't supposed to be participants in the deals they structure for others. The issue raises some regulatory questions that have yet to be answered.

THE SUCCESS OF the raiders has inevitably brought them into the arena of legislatures and courts. The result has been a spate of rule-making and court decisions that have, at least for now, changed the rules of the game.

In March 1986, the Federal Reserve Board changed the margin rules governing junk bonds, making it harder to use them. The Delaware Supreme Court—extremely important in the corporate world because so many companies are incorporated in Delaware and thus fall under its jurisdiction—recently made two rulings that hit raiders hard. In one, it ruled that Household International Corporation was within its rights to institute a poison pill. In the other ruling, the court ruled that Unocal could exclude T. Boone Pickens from a tender offer on the grounds that he was a known raider. It was a blow to a basic tenet of shareholder democracy—that a corporation had to treat all its shareholders alike, a concept that had also been used in attacking the payment of greenmail.

But not all the cases have gone against the raiders. Revlon lost its bid to avoid takeover by Pantry Pride when the court limited its right to "lock up" assets to favor one bidder over another—a variation on selling the crown jewels. The SEC is considering rule changes to negate future use of the court decision in the Unocal case. Even the Fed's anti-junk-bond decision was made on a 3-2 vote, and provisions of the ruling had been weakened before passage in the face of pre-issue opposition.

Perhaps most chilling was the decision against Texaco in the suit Pennzoil brought over Texaco's purchase of Getty. Pennzoil thought it had a merger agreement with Getty. When Texaco came up with a better offer, Getty backed off and accepted Texaco's bid. Pennzoil sued Texaco—and won a $10.53 billion judgment. If it holds up on appeal, the ruling will make companies think twice about overbidding in a situation where a merger or takeover is near.

But the biggest change in the raiding environment has been the dramatic increase in stock prices since the end of the last recession. In a rising market, fewer companies are good targets for raiding because fewer are undervalued. In addition, the old saw that a rising tide lifts all boats applies to the market as well. As stock prices rise in general, even struggling companies benefit and it becomes more expensive to take over even those that remain undervalued—not only does the price of purchase rise, but the gap between market value and breakup value also tends to narrow. Even with lower interest rates, the possibility of making a profit becomes slimmer.

WITH THE TAKEOVER game getting tougher, with new decisions in court cases, restrictive legislation, and more effective shark repellent coming into being every day, what's left for the raiders? Where do they go from here?

Carl Icahn, for one, objects strongly to the changes, especially legislative and regulatory ones. "What the American shareholder is today," he says, "is an oppressed majority. We have no rights. We have no chance. When somebody like myself comes along, he has to live through lawsuits. He has to live through the issuance of stock [diluting his position]. And I say Why make it even harder? Why get rid of the dissident? Management today has no answerability, no answerability whatsoever. There is no such thing as corporate democracy. There is no answerability."

But despite his objections, he is not deterred. The new environment, he says, "is going to keep a lot of people from entering the game. The same thing would happen if you suddenly changed all the rules of tennis—shrank the court, raised the net, and made players hit every third shot left-handed. A lot of people would quit, but the top twenty players would continue to play."

For the raiders, the game isn't over yet—poker, tennis, chess—or takeovers.

Glossary

ANTITRUST Laws to protect against unlawful combinations, monopolies, and unfair business practices. These laws are especially applicable in merger situations when competitors merge, reducing competition.

ANTITRUST CONSENT DECREE A consent degree settling an antitrust suit, often by the acquiring company agreeing to sell or spin off certain assets.

ARBITRAGE Buying and selling identical securities in order to make a profit on price discrepancies. Arbitrage can involve stocks, bonds, a combination thereof, currency, or any other regularly traded commodity.

ARBITRAGEUR Someone who engages in arbitrage.

BANK HOLDING COMPANY A company that owns all the stock in a bank. Citibank formed the first bank holding company (Citicorp). The holding company can engage in businesses and operations that the bank itself is legally forbidden under federal and state banking laws.

BOOK VALUE The value of a corporation determined by subtracting liabilities from assets. Since assets are often carried at cost minus depreciation, the book value of a corporation may understate actual value. Book value may be greater or less than market value.

BUYBACK   Term used to describe the purchase of stock in a corporation by the corporation, diminishing the number of shares outstanding.

CALL   An option giving the owner the right to purchase a fixed number of shares of stock at a stated price for a given period of time.

CAPITAL ALLOCATION   Where money is invested or spent.

CHINESE PAPER   An early form of Junk Bonds. Chinese paper was generally low-rated debt securities of a corporation used to finance acquisitions.

CONCEPT STOCK   Especially a creature of the sixties stock market boom, concept stocks were stocks of companies that may not have had earnings but appeared to have growth potential due to a new idea or invention that looked good even though not yet proven.

CONSENT DECREE   An agreement signed by a party to a suit, especially an SEC suit, in which the signatory, while not admitting guilt, agrees not to perform the acts stipulated in the suit. Sometimes described as saying "I didn't do it and I won't do it again."

CONSENTS   Similar to a proxy, a consent gives someone the right to vote a shareholder's stock for or against an issue. Unlike proxies, however, consents do not require a shareholder meeting.

CONTRARIAN INVESTMENT   Investment that goes against the grain of the common wisdom on the street. A contrarian investor would tend to sell when everyone else was predicting a boom and vice versa.

CONVERTIBLE BONDS, CONVERTIBLE DEBENTURES Debt securities issued by a company that, under certain circumstances, can be converted into other securities, especially stock.

CONVERTIBLE STOCK   Equity securities issued by a company that, under certain circumstances, can be converted into other securities, such as bonds or other classes of stock.

CROWN JEWELS   The most valuable divisions or assets of a company.

DEBT-TO-EQUITY RATIO   The ratio of debt—what a company owes—to equity—the value of the company after liabilities have been subtracted. A high debt-to-equity ratio is often taken as a sign of too much debt; a low one of an asset-rich company.

DIVESTITURE   Disposing of assets or divisions to satisfy regulatory authority. Frequently undertaken to settle antitrust accusations.

DIVIDEND A payment to shareholders out of the profits of the corporation.

DIVIDEND, LIQUIDATING A payment to shareholders of money from the sale of the assets of the corporation. Specifically, the term applies when a corporation is liquidating itself—i.e., selling off all its assets and going out of business.

GOLDEN HANDSHAKE Substantial compensation package given to corporate executive when leaving a company.

GOLDEN PARACHUTE Package given to corporate executives guaranteeing substantial compensation in the event of a takeover.

GREENMAIL The practice of buying a substantial portion of a corporation's stock and threatening a takeover or proxy fight solely in order to persuade the threatened company to buy back the stock at a profit to the greenmailer.

HEDGING Buying or selling options or commodity futures in order to minimize the risk of loss if prices turn in an adverse direction.

HIGH-YIELD BOND A bond paying a higher than usual rate of return, generally because it is of lower quality.

HOLDING COMPANY A corporation formed strictly for the purpose of owning other corporations. Frequently, the only assets of the holding company will be the stock in the other companies.

INVESTMENT BANKER Not a banker at all, an investment banker acts as a corporate adviser in mergers and acquisitions, arranges financing, and arranges and distributes security offerings. Investment banking was separated from regular banking during the radical reform of the financial markets that followed the stock market crash of 1929 and the subsequent bank failures.

JUNK BOND A low quality, subordinated bond or debenture, typically paying a very high yield.

JUNK BOND FINANCING The issuance of large amounts of junk bonds. The typical method of paying for a leveraged buyout or corporate takeover.

LEVERAGED BUYOUT The method of taking over a company (or of a company taking itself private) by issuing securities backed by the target corporation's assets to finance the purchase.

LIQUIDATING DIVIDEND see Dividend, Liquidating.

LIQUIDATION Selling off assets. When a corporation is liquidated, all its assets are sold and any cash remaining after payment of creditors is distributed to shareholders.

LOSSMAKER The opposite of a profit maker. A product, company, or division that consistently loses money.

LOW-GRADE BOND   A bond whose rating from the major ratings services is less than Investment Grade (investment grade bonds generally carry ratings of Baa or higher from Moody's, for example, and similar ratings from Standard & Poor's).

MONEY CENTER BANK   Generally refers to the large New York City and similar large banks that are the major movers in both corporate and international lending.

MONEY MARKET   The market for bank instruments such as Banker's Acceptances and Certificates of Deposit. Along with the markets in treasury securities, it is movements in the money market that first signals changes in interest rates.

OPTIONS   Contracts that give the buyer the right to buy or sell a security or commodity at a specified price for a designated length of time.

OPTION TRADING   The buying and selling of options. Since the establishment of the Chicago Board Options Exchange and similar exchanges and the standardization of option contract expiration dates and terms, most option trading takes place on the various options exchanges.

PAC-MAN DEFENSE   A takeover defense in which the target company attempts to turn the tables and take over the company that initiated the hostile takeover.

POISON PILL   A provision of a corporate charter or of shareholder rights that comes into effect in the event of a takeover and that will be detrimental to the acquiring company.

POISON PILL DEFENSE   The setting up of a poison pill as a deterrent to a takeover.

POSITION (as in taking a position)   Acquiring a large block of stock in a company.

PROXY   A legal document (actually a power of attorney) giving someone the right to vote someone else's stock. Proxies may be specific, giving the right to vote in favor of or against certain proposals, or general, giving the right to vote for or against anything that may be proposed.

PROXY FIGHT   Term given to the competitive solicitation of proxies by opposing forces in a corporate fight with each side trying to gain enough proxies so as to swing the vote in its favor.

PRUDENT TRUSTEE RULE, PRUDENT MAN RULE Guidelines for persons having a fiduciary responsibility. Basically, the concept can be expressed as "would a reasonably prudent man, having the same information, have acted in this fashion?"

PUT   An option giving the owner the right to sell a fixed number of shares of stock at a stated price for a given period of time.

RAIDER   Term applied to individuals or companies who practice hostile takeovers.

RISK ARBITRAGE The specialized area of arbitrage that deals in the securities of companies involved in takeovers, mergers, or liquidations.

ROYALTY TRUST A form of partnership that issues limited partnership certificates similar in form to stock. Since a royalty trust is a partnership, however, earnings of the trust are not taxed as corporate profits. The distributions from a royalty trust are taxed only once, on the recipient's tax return, thus avoiding the double taxation (once on the corporation's profits and once on the individual's tax return) of dividends. Royalty trusts specifically derive their income from royalties, generally from extractive assets (oil, coal, etc.).

SCORCHED-EARTH DEFENSE A defensive technique against a hostile takeover in which the defending corporation sells off its most desirable assets, encumbers itself with liabilities, or otherwise renders itself unattractive as a takeover candidate by leaving nothing but "scorched earth" behind. Named for the classic Russian defense against an invader.

SHARK REPELLENT Any defense or combination of defenses put into place to make it more difficult for a hostile suitor to gain control of a corporation.

SPIN OFF The disposal of assets of a corporation by creating a new company owning the assets to be disposed of and then distributing the stock in the new company to the shareholders of the old one.

STANDSTILL AGREEMENT An agreement signed by two parties in a takeover fight in which each agrees not to acquire any more stock for a specified period of time. Some standstill agreements basically provide a breathing space, but others are clear victories for one side or the other, since they impede the opponent's acquisition of stock while still allowing the defender to erect barriers to acquisition.

SYNERGY, SYNERGISM Term borrowed from chemistry. It was popular especially in the sixties and referred to the concept that unrelated lines of business might, when combined, multiply a corporation's strengths and minimize weaknesses (eg. by combining two cyclical businesses in one corporation the hope would be that when one was lagging the other would be booming).

TAKEOVER The action in which one company acquires another.

TARGET COMPANY The object of a takeover.

TENDER OFFER A public solicitation in which cash, securities, or a combination thereof are offered for shares in a company. Tenders may be friendly or hostile or even buybacks. Tender offers are governed by securities regulations and are for a specified period of time.

UNDERVALUED ASSET   Generally an asset that is carried on the books of a corporation at less than its current value.

WARRANTS   Securities that give the holder the right to acquire other securities (stock, bonds, etc.) at a specified price for either a defined or indefinite length of time. Warrants and options have similarities but, in general, warrants are exchangeable for longer periods of time.

WHITE KNIGHT   A merger partner brought in on a friendly basis in order to thwart a hostile takeover.

WHITE SQUIRE   A friendly company induced to take a large position in a threatened company's stock to prevent acquisition by a hostile suitor. A true white squire does not take over the target company.

WHITE SQUIRE DEFENSE   An anti-takeover move in which a target company seeks out a white squire.

WRITTEN CONSENTS   see Consents

Index